A Plain & Easy Introduction to the Harpsichord

A Plain & Easy Introduction to the Harpsichord

Ruth Nurmi

University of New Mexico Press

Albuquerque

To Martin
who saw heaven within the mountain

The way to study the past is not to confine oneself to mere knowledge of history but, through application of this knowledge, to give actuality to the past.—*I Ching*, Hexagram 26

Preface

When I made the transition from piano to harpsichord a number of years ago, I was fortunate in having fine teachers. Even so, there was a great deal of information about the music and about the instrument itself that I had to learn the hard way; there just isn't time in lessons to deal with it. What I have tried to do in this book is to make as much of this information as possible available in one place.

The book has another purpose as well: to provide an introduction to playing the harpsichord for the person who already has keyboard facility. Competent harpsichord teachers are increasing in number as this marvelously expressive instrument is revived as a standard keyboard instrument. All too often, however, it is played by performers of other keyboard instruments without sufficient awareness of the rather different technique it requires. While I hope my discussion of harpsichord technique and the exercises that accompany it will be of some value for anyone seriously studying the instrument, I have written the chapter on technique primarily for the person who has access to a harpsichord but not to a teacher.

In addition to giving an introduction to harpsichord technique, I have discussed registration, continuo playing, and special notational problems that the harpsichord player encounters because most of the music for it assumes knowledge of conventions no longer in use. I have given as much information on editions of music as I thought appropriate in an introductory book. And I have tried to give some practical information that I wish had been available to me on buying an instrument and keeping it in working condition, as well as on tuning, a necessity for any harpsichordist. Some of this information was gained by bitter experience, but I have also benefited greatly from help given by Earl Russell and my husband Martin.

I would like to express my appreciation to the Kent State University Research Committee for a typing grant and to Martha Bixler, Robert Palmieri, and James Waters for reading parts of the manuscript. I am grateful to my teachers Arthur Loesser, Irene Bostwick, and Egbert Ennulat for their help and encouragement and to Howard Allen for his continuing interest and down-to-earth advice on this project. And I owe a very great and special debt to Sylvia Marlowe—who, however, is no more responsible than any teacher for the use a student makes of what he has learned—and to Martin, who was always there.

Acknowledgments

Acknowledgments are due to the following publishers for permission to reproduce the works indicated; the fingering and articulation marks in these works are mine.

Bärenreiter Verlag: J.-P. Rameau's "Gavotte," Variation no. 3, and "Le Tambourin"; Handel's Sonata in F major for Violin and Harpsichord.

G. Henle Verlag: J. S. Bach's Inventions; French Suites nos. 4 and 5; Prelude no. 5 from *The Well-Tempered Clavier,* Book II; *Six Little Preludes;* and Fugue in C major.

G. Schirmer: F. Couperin's "Les Baricades Mistérieuses.

Harvard University Press: "My Lady Carey's Dompe."

W. W. Norton: C. P. E. Bach's *Essay on the True Art of Playing Keyboard Instruments.*

Contents

1

THE INSTRUMENT

MODERN HARPSICHORDS

The harpsichord can no more be considered an historical instrument than the violin or cello, except that little music was written for it between 1800 and 1900. During this period the piano almost entirely replaced it as the standard keyboard instrument, but that trend had more to do with a development in taste than with some absolute inadequacy of the harpsichord. The rediscovery of J. S. Bach has led naturally to the rediscovery of the harpsichord, and our century learned, largely through the pioneer efforts of Wanda Landowska, that, although the piano had replaced the harpsichord for a time, it had by no means superseded it. Today a great deal of serious music is being written for the harpsichord, much of it stimulated or commissioned by Sylvia Marlowe, who was also one of the first to play jazz on it. The harpsichord is also widely used now by popular groups and for TV commercials and background music in TV dramas, especially, for some reason, when the action involves skulduggery.

As the piano gained ascendency at the end of the eighteenth century, some large harpsichords were converted into pianos by changing the action. It is a curious fact that the harpsichords that, through the records of Landowska, did most to repopularize the harpsichord showed a reversal of this process. Landowska's instruments, built by the piano firm of Pleyel in Paris, were rather like modern pianos with a harpsichord action, having heavy frames and thick woodwork. The early Pleyel instruments were very heavy with eight-foot registers (those at notated pitch) that had a weak bass.

No doubt it was because of this that Landowska persuaded Pleyel to install the sixteen-foot register (an octave below notated pitch) which the firm, erroneously, gives her credit for inventing in a legend inscribed on their instruments. The modern Pleyels have a better eight-foot bass than the earlier ones.

Until around the 1950s, the sound that most people associated with the harpsichord was that of modern ones like the Pleyel, with the sixteen-foot register liberally used. On recordings, which most people played with the volume, treble, and bass turned up, the harpsichord sounded very impressive indeed. Audiences for recorded music are more sophisticated today, but some people are still disappointed when the live harpsichord doesn't overwhelm them with the rumbling cascades of tone they are accustomed to hearing from woofers and tweeters. Yet these recordings of the modern instrument, souped up by hi-fi enthusiasts, served a purpose in presenting the harpsichord in terms on which it could compete with any instrument ever invented, even though the presentation falsified it. They at least aroused interest.

Much earlier, in the 1890s, Arnold Dolmetsch had made instruments along the lines of those existing before the development of the piano of today, which is a massive iron structure with twenty tons of pressure in its strings. But it wasn't until the middle of the twentieth century in America that harpsichords built according to historical principles, with light construction and soundboards, gained in popularity; these came about notably through the work of Frank Hubbard and William Dowd, who carefully studied existing historical instruments. Various other makers in England and Germany—such as Martin Skowroneck of Bremen, who made exact copies of historical instruments—were engaged in a similar enterprise. The success of these instruments did not come about just because they were like historical ones; they had an interesting sound, a lot of it, and a rich bass without a sixteen-foot register.

Somewhere between the stout instruments of Pleyel and Neupert (a German firm) and the lighter ones of Hubbard and Dowd lie those of John Challis, built since the thirties.[1] Challis's instruments have good volume and are extremely reliable because of excellent workmanship. They are modern instruments, and in recent years Challis has used metal (aluminum or aluminum alloy) frames and soundboards on some instruments, with the result that they seem to stay in tune indefinitely. Many harpsichord makers in America learned their craft from him, as he had earlier learned his from Dolmetsch.

Concert-sized harpsichords range in character today between instruments with massive frames, open on the bottom like pianos and equipped with sixteen-foot registers, to those with light construction, closed on the bottom and equipped with two sets of eight-foot registers (at notated pitch) and one set of four-foot registers (an octave above notated pitch). In between there is enormous variety, often showing a tendency in their "improvements," as Ralph Kirkpatrick has observed, to "reinvent the modern piano."[2] Although some makers pattern their instruments very closely after specific historical ones, using wooden jacks and slides—and even raven feathers for quills—most makers of harpsichords that are based on historical principles improve the actions by using modern materials like Delrin for jacks and quills and punched metal for slides. They also provide convenient screw adjustments for voicing that were unknown in earlier times. Most makers of harpsichords of the modern type use wooden frames, although the timbers are often so heavy that it seems to me they might as well be replaced by metal members.

The modern "production" type of instrument (a model produced in large quantities), in addition to having a sixteen-foot register, frequently has its registers in concert models arranged in the so-called Bach disposition, in which the sixteen-foot register and one eight-foot are played by the lower manual and the four-foot and the other eight-foot are played by the upper. To be sure, a few harpsichords with sixteen-foot registers were made in Germany in Bach's time, but Raymond Russell and Frank Hubbard have shown rather conclusively that the Bach disposition was the result of a later modification to install a sixteen-foot register on an instrument owned by Bach.[3] Some players who get used to the odd distribution of registers in this disposition seem to like it, but it requires excessive use of the coupler to get some often-used combinations (the coupler joins the upper manual to the lower so that both manuals sound when keys on the lower manual are depressed).

Since the basis for the Bach disposition's historicity is pretty much gone, there is no reason to perpetuate it for historical reasons. It does distribute the weight of jacks more evenly between the two registers than does the more conventional historical arrangement that has only one eight-foot register on the upper manual, but most of this advantage is lost in the frequent need to use the coupler. The traditional disposition of a historical "double" harpsichord (with two manuals) has an eight-foot and a four-foot register on the lower manual and a more nasal eight-foot register on the upper (plucking a little closer to the nut, or end of the string); it also has a provision for coupling the upper to the lower manual. If a sixteen-foot register is added, it is made to be played on the lower manual.

Another difference between the historical and modern type of harpsichord is in scale and plucking point. Scale has to do with string length and plucking point with how far from the end the string is plucked.[4] On the whole, modern instruments are designed to have an even tone throughout the register because they pluck the string farther from the end than historical ones; historical instruments, on the other hand, have a tone that varies considerably in character from bass to treble, giving the effect of several different sonorities on one register. For this reason polyphonic music is easier to hear on an historical instrument than on a modern one when the voices lie in different parts of the register.

The Sixteen-foot Register

Although very few historical instruments had sixteen-foot registers, there is no reason why a harpsichord shouldn't have one if its player likes its effects. It can produce a very impressive subterranean rumble and a delightful organ-like quality when played in combination with only the four-foot stop. But a good instrument can have a perfectly adequate bass without it, and unless the sixteen-foot register has its own separate soundboard, as it did on the Hass instruments in eighteenth-century Germany, it adversely affects the basic eight-foot registers. It stiffens the vibrating system by adding a thick bridge and another set of heavy strings, altering the soundboard's "drumskin" resonance, which gives the harpsichord bass in the eight-foot registers much of its characteristic sound. On most instruments, if a sixteen-foot register is installed on a common soundboard with the eight-foot registers, the player will probably want to use it to compensate for losses in the quality of the eight-foot registers. To some extent, therefore, the sixteen-foot register on a common soundboard with other registers becomes a cure for faults of which it is itself the cause. Where a sixteen-foot register is an option, the cost runs about a thousand dollars, and of course it adds an extra set of strings to be tuned. William Dowd used to have the sixteen-foot register available as an option but has dropped it.

Pedals

One feature of today's harpsichords that excites a certain curiosity is the presence or absence of a pedal mechanism. There may be as many as ten pedals. Most full-sized concert harpsichords being made today (historical instruments are slightly less than eight feet long and modern ones are up to ten feet long) can be obtained with pedals to engage and disengage the registers. There is of course no damper pedal. Most makers of historical instruments now strongly prefer hand stops and install pedals reluctantly if at all because they are expensive, require adjustment, and did not appear on historical instruments until late in the eighteenth century and not in all countries even then.[5]

In Germany, for instance, hand stops were considered an entirely adequate means of changing the registers throughout the baroque era, and pedals were never introduced. There are few, if any, Flemish instruments that were equipped with pedals. Although many of them had two and even three manuals, pedals appeared only late in the eighteenth century. Italian instruments were even simpler; they also had no pedals and in addition were limited to one manual, except for instruments that were fitted with an elaborate arrangement of keys devised for nonenharmonic tuning.

In fact, pedals appeared only in France and England, where after 1750 musicians began to think that a wider range of dynamics was necessary for adequate musical expression in shaping the musical phrase. The development of the piano came partly in response to this desire for greater dynamic variation than was normally possible on the harpsichord. Consequently, there were numerous attempts in both of these countries, particularly in France where the tone of the harpsichord was greatly admired, to "improve" the harpsichord mechanically so that it could compete with the piano— namely so that it, too, could play loud and soft.

In France a frantic profusion of efforts toward this end included knee levers (1759) and pedals (1769) that advanced the quills by successive degrees under the strings to make crescendos and decrescendos. Neither the knee nor the foot levers accomplished this purpose, as common sense should have predicted, because the quills got hung up on the strings in the advanced position. Late eighteenth-century harpsichord makers in England tried another way to get crescendos and decrescendos: They installed a pedal to operate a Venetian swell, a tightly fitting cover over the soundboard which consisted of rotating slats—like a Venetian blind lying horizontally—that opened and closed to increase or decrease the amount of sound. This device was also doomed to be unsatisfactory because when the slats were more or less closed they not only diminished the sound but gave it a muffled, choked quality; and when they were completely open they achieved nothing more than the ordinary harpsichord with no swell at all. It is interesting that an entire century earlier, in the 17th century, a pedal device had been introduced in England. It was neglected and subsequently abandoned because no one at that time felt the need for changes of dynamics within the phrase.[6]

The pedals on today's harpsichords, both modern and historical ones, are used only to engage and disengage the registers, not to provide crescendos. However, some performers do engage in occasional tricky footwork to try to get these effects, putting down pedals that engage additional stops on several top notes of a scale passage, for instance, or even putting down a pedal for one climactic note. This kind of stunt is not stylistic for eighteenth-century music, although it may be done with justice as well as effectiveness in contemporary harpsichord music.

Most of today's concert performers do use harpsichords with pedals, although a growing number use instruments with hand stops only. Pedals do add considerable convenience, freeing the hands entirely for playing the notes, and since a harpsichordist has nothing else to do with his feet anyway, he might as well use them to work the pedals, if he does so knowledgably and intelligently. Pedals make possible additional tonal contrast where appropriate, and, if tastefully used, do no violence to the music.

BUYING A HARPSICHORD

There is less standardization of the harpsichord than of any other musical instrument except the organ, and buying one—or, more often, commissioning one to be built—is much more complicated than buying or ordering a piano. Almost all makers say their instruments are consistent with "historical principles," but the amount of consistency varies widely. Since there is so much variation among instruments, you should be able to try several possibilities before making a decision. This is often difficult to do, except in large cities, but much preferable to getting one sight unseen. Although I much prefer the historical type of instrument, several leading performers use modern instruments, so any flat statement that any one instrument is preferable to another is hazardous. Moreover, makers continue to make new contributions to the art.

A few general comments, however, are possible for the readers to whom this book is addressed. The standard harpsichord keyboard needed to play the repertoire is five octaves, from FF to f′′′. A few sonatas by Scarlatti call for g′′′, and some makers will put on the extra two notes if requested; but you can get by without them. A five-octave range, however, requires a long instrument (about eight feet) for a good bass. Smaller instruments, for the home, often have a range of four and a half octaves, with the missing notes coming off the bass end. Many of the instruments with a narrowed range have two manuals, and some of them even have a sixteen-foot register.

Finished Instruments

A full-sized concert instrument with two manuals, at least two eight-foot registers, and a four-foot register usually costs about five thousand dollars—or more, depending on case and other features. Sometimes they are available used; but there is no real decrease in cost if the instrument comes through the maker because he will have done considerable reconditioning or even rebuilding before selling it. Unless you are rich or deeply, unshakably committed to the harpsichord as your instrument, it is probably not wise to buy immediately an instrument suitable for concert work. The amateur who wants to play for his own enjoyment or play concerted music with friends can get along very well with a one-manual instrument with a few modest features. Although an additional eight-foot or four-foot stop adds variety, one eight-foot register is all that is needed for a great deal of music; and it is best to stick to this basic register for some time while learning the technique of the instrument. The works of Scarlatti were written for an instrument with one manual and two eight-foot stops; and a large amount of the Bach repertoire, such as the Inventions, Sinfonias, and *Well-Tempered Clavier,* can be played on one manual. A fine one-manual instrument of the historical type, patterned after the extemely light Italian harpsichords or the Flemish ones, costs less than two thousand dollars. Such an instrument has a full keyboard and is excellent for continuo or other ensemble playing and quite adequate for occasional solo work. An instrument like this would seem to me preferable to having a shorter two-manual one, with or without a sixteen-foot register, because within its limits it is a genuine type of harpsichord and not a "baby grand" version of a larger one.

Kits

In America the most widely used harpsichord is no doubt the one built from a kit sold by Wallace Zuckermann, who now reports that he sells about four thousand a year. At any harpsichord concert in America, there seems to be at least one person in the audience who has built one of these instruments. They are about four and a half feet long; have one eight-foot register and a buff, with room to add another eight-foot register if desired; and have a range down to AA. The original Zuckermann kit was very inexpensive and not too difficult to put together for a person with some skill in woodworking since it was adapted to kit construction by the use of a straight bentside. This kit has now been replaced by the newer, improved Zuckermann kits, which are more historically oriented and, necessarily, a little more expensive. Zuckermann's long experience as a repairman as well as a kit supplier has given him a no-nonsense approach to harpsichords that is reflected in his down-to-earth, even entertaining instructions for building the instrument and is realized in the finished instrument. The harpsichord revival in this country owes much to the Zuckermann kit. A complete description of his new kits may be obtained from Zuckermann Harpsichords, 160 Sixth Avenue, New York, N.Y. 10012.

Much more elaborate and expensive kits for one- or two-manual instruments that are suitable for concert work if well built are available from the scholarly builder Frank Hubbard. You can buy a basic kit with keyboard, soundboard, bentside, and so on with elaborate instructions or at additional cost you can buy one with some parts, such as the case, already assembled. The price of the basic kit is about seven hundred and fifty dollars for a one-manual instrument and nine hundred and fifty for the two-manual. These instruments have a full keyboard. Before assembling a kit as expensive as these, it would be well to have some experience in wood-working or to know someone who could bail you out of trouble. Some other makers offer kits as well. Information on kit manufacturers is available in Zuckermann's book, *The Modern Harpsichord* (New York: October House, 1969, $15).[7]

Electronic Harpsichords and Amplification

An electronic harpischord made by the Allen Organ Company is also on the market. One of its advantages is that it stays in tune as well as an electronic organ and also stays in adjustment. But for most purposes it is not a substitute for a real harpsichord. It is like a specialized electronic organ designed to simulate the sound of the harpsichord, as its touch simulates the tracker touch of an organ. In large ensembles it could be used to add a bit of color, but alone or with a small group it sounds like what it is, an electronic harpsichord, ingeniously designed but nonetheless an imitation.

An electronically amplified harpsichord, like that formerly made by the Cannon Guild with microphones and amplifiers built in, is not the same thing as a harpsichord that generates its tone electronically. Electro-acoustic harpsichords are made by the Baldwin Piano Company and are called "combo" harpsichords. This instrument really works like an electric guitar, with the sound being picked up magnetically directly from the strings, not from the soundboard. While it might be useful to supply some sonority for popular music, it can hardly be taken seriously as a harpsichord.

It is possible to *reinforce* the tone of any harpsichord slightly without essentially altering its tone in a large ensemble such as a symphony orchestra, and sometimes it is wise to do this when playing a continuo part so that other members of the ensemble like singers in recitatives can hear the continuo. A microphone hung over the soundboard and about twelve inches above it where the curve of the side is sharpest works quite well. If the amplification is not too great, the microphone reinforces the harpsichord naturally without noticeably amplifying neighboring instruments. But amplification that gets so loud that most of the sound is coming out of the loudspeaker makes the instrument too much like an electric guitar.

Quill Material

One decision that has to be made when ordering a harpsichord, from makers who offer a choice, is the quill material. Leather and Delrin are most common. Leather, being softer than Delrin, damps the string very slightly on the pluck, suppressing the upper partials, or overtones, a little. Leather has the advantage that, for a stop with a softer tone, half hitches work better with it than with Delrin. A hitch is a device that holds the knee lever or pedal locked in the "on" position with the plectra under the strings ready to play; a half hitch locks the lever or pedal halfway so the plectra do not extend so far beneath the strings, thus taking a smaller bite and producing a softer tone. Half hitches, then, are used as a soft stop.

Delrin is a remarkable material in that it is so unsusceptible to fatigue from constant flexing and so strong that it can be scraped very thin without breaking. Other makers use softer plastics, which in action behave more like leather than quill, but I have not seen any soft plastics that have the durability of leather or Delrin. Perhaps some of them would work well enough if the instrument is not voiced too loud.

Other Practical Considerations

Earlier I mentioned the desirability of being able to try out an instrument of the kind you are thinking of buying. If you cannot try it out and are not pretty sure the instrument you are ordering is one you would like to keep, it is a very good idea to have clearly understood return privileges. Selling harpsichords privately is a great nuisance at best and may be costly; returning the instrument because you don't like it may be impossible and in any event would cost you freight. So you probably would be better off in the long run to go to some trouble to give the instrument a fair trial before concluding any transaction.

Earlier I also suggested that a first instrument should probably not be a large, elaborate one suitable for concert performances unless you are sure to need it for that purpose. If you get an adequate but simpler instrument, such as a one-manual Flemish model, many makers will take it back later at full allowance on a larger one—so a return privilege is included in the original purchase. Since one-manual instruments of this type can be bought with two eight-foot registers and a four-foot register (called "2 x 8'; 1 x 4'" in the language of harpsichord specifications) that provide a lot of variety, you may never find it necessary to "trade up."

If you will be using your harpsichord for performing, one extremely important consideration is its portability. A Zuckermann kit harpsichord is easily moved. A one-manual Italian instrument about eight feet long can easily be carried by two men, because the wood is only about a quarter of an inch thick and it is very lightly braced inside. It may weigh as little as seventy pounds and can be easily transported in a station wagon. At the other extreme are the huge production instruments, nine or even ten feet long and framed with thick timbers; they can weigh about four hundred pounds. Moving one of these is really a job for professionals. An historical concert double harpsichord weighs about half as much or less and can be handled by two or three reasonably vigorous amateur movers even in the worst circumstances (going down a curved staircase, for instance); it can also be carried in a station wagon. The portability of the historical instruments, especially those without a pedal mechanism, which is easily damaged, is a strong argument for them, because the owner of a harpsichord will probably find that he will want to use it or have it used in a variety of places even if he is not a professional.

So far my discussion has wholly concerned harpsichords that are wing-shaped and have strings running away from the keyboard. However, for use in the home or in a small church, a spinet might be appropriate. A spinet has a shape that varies from a modified triangle, sometimes with one of the sides bent, to various polygons, and it is strung transversely. The jacks pluck the strings through holes in the soundboard, and there is only one set of strings. The compass of a spinet can run a full five octaves, and the sound even in the bass can be quite good, being usually more "rounded" than that of the ordinary harpsichord because of a relatively different plucking point. Some makers of harpsichords also offer spinets at something less than half the cost of a large one-manual harpsichord.

Another type of harpsichord, built in a rectangular case, is the virginal (or "virginals," as it was historically named), and in general the remarks about the spinet apply to it although its compass is shorter. These are primarily instruments for the home. Some harpsichord makers also build clavichords and reproductions of early pianos, but these instruments are not relevant to this book.

Some harpsichords, characteristically the imported production harpsichords, are usually available for immediate delivery through dealers; these are made up in standard models with names such as "The Couperin" and "The Vivaldi," with "The Bach" usually being reserved for the largest, most massive instrument. Others are built to order in more or less standardized models but with a good deal of latitude in features such as pedals, quill material, disposition, and case style and finish. Orders are placed directly with the maker. Unfortunately, getting a concert instrument from a well-known maker on order is often a matter of waiting two years or even more after a deposit has been made. Such makers can usually provide a modest instrument more quickly.

Wolfgang Joachim Zuckermann (better known as Wallace Zuckermann, the manufacturer of the popular kits) surveys over a hundred modern builders in his *The Modern Harpsichord*.[8] Not too many years ago most people would have had to strain to name more than a half dozen. These builders—one would have to say *manufacturers* in talking of the large producers in Germany, such as Neupert—produce a bewildering variety of instruments, from exact copies of particular historical instruments to modern instruments that come close to being plucking pianos. Zuckermann, writing from the point of view of a modest builder, restorer, and technician who has now turned critic, can write objectively because he is not in competition with anyone except suppliers of kits for simple instruments. He gives a sensible account of what a harpsichord should be, which in general is what the historical harpsichords were. He then reviews the work of the modern makers with a trenchancy that occasionally borders on acidity; but he gives an enormous amount of detailed and technical information.

Anyone who is seriously contemplating the acquisition of a harpsichord (by either building a kit or buying one) would do well to consult Zuckermann's book. Zuckermann, however, is very hard on what he calls the "production harpsichords." Anyone who likes the organ-like characteristics of harpsichord tone that are produced by the sixteen-foot stop, especially with the four-foot stop, should try these instruments out for himself and compare them with instruments of the historical type, like those by Hubbard and Dowd. Dowd's are quite widely available. He should satisfy himself, playing long enough to allow a good exposure to tonal characteristics and touch in different kinds of music and with different registers singly and in combination. The sixteen-foot register may seem impressive—as it should to justify its extra cost and inconvenience—but a harpsichord stands or falls on its basic eight-foot registers. The sixteen-foot register adds an extra resource to the instrument, for tonal variety, but it loses its effectiveness when overused. The bread and butter stops are the eight-foot registers, which should be pleasant and interesting to listen to by themselves; they should have a sonorous full bass and a crisp reedy tenor and they should be playable with the light, quick touch that belongs to the harpsichord. Any instrument that needs the sixteen-foot register to avoid tonal monotony is not going to prove satisfactory in the long run.

The interest in baroque music that we have seen in recent years, and especially in the last decade, has lasted long enough to reestablish the harpsichord as an instrument in its own right, and rescue it from being considered just a quaint variation or predecessor of the piano. The time will soon come when a touring harpsichordist will be able to depend on finding an instrument wherever he is engaged to play—although opinions about instruments run strong, and some performers will probably still insist on playing their own.

2

TECHNIQUE

FROM THE PIANO TO THE HARPSICHORD

Tone Production

The keyboard is so familiar a sight in our piano-oriented musical culture that it tends to be regarded as the dominant feature of any instrument of which it happens to be a part. It is, of course, a very obvious feature because it is the visible part of the action, but the visual similarity among keyboard instruments should not obscure the fact that a keyboard does not itself produce musical tones but is merely a collection of levers, conveniently operable by the fingers, that actuates the mechanical means of tone production. These means may be a hammer that strikes a string as in the piano, air which passes under pressure past or through a pipe as in the organ, or a plectrum which plucks a string as in the harpsichord.

These three keyboard instruments, then, do have a keyboard in common, but there the resemblance ends, for the piano tone is produced by percussive action, the organ tone by blowing, and the harpsichord tone by plucking. And while keyboard facility alone will enable a player to produce some kind of musical sounds on any of these three instruments, he will not be able to produce music in the real sense of the word unless his playing takes into account the technical means needed to produce tones, whether by beating, blowing, or plucking.

The harpsichord may be considered a very large lute or guitar with an attached keyboard to activate the plucking of the strings. When you push the key down, the jack, which sits on the other end of the key lever, moves up

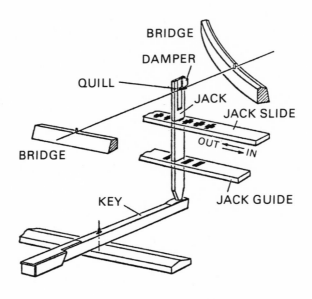

BRIDGE

DAMPER

QUILL

JACK

JACK SLIDE

OUT — IN

BRIDGE

KEY

JACK GUIDE

Figure 1.   The harpsichord's action.

about a quarter of an inch, carrying the quill with it (see Fig. 1). As the quill moves up, it comes into contact with the string, bending slightly as it pushes the string up and a little to one side until the string is displaced as far as possible by a quill of that length; then the string very suddenly snaps off the quill and vibrates freely. As the finger releases the key, the bottom of the quill comes in contact with the string and the tongue in which the quill is set pivots away from the string allowing the quill to go down past the string without plucking it. Just before the jack returns to its position of rest, a felt damper on the jack body stops the vibration of the string. If the damper is working properly, the string's vibration will stop almost instantaneously. The amount of force required to produce this stroke is very small.

I will not attempt to discuss the mechanics of action on the piano or organ, for that is not the purpose of this book, but a few general comparisons between piano and harpsichord action will, I hope, illuminate my detailed discussion of harpsichord technique. Piano action is a friction device, an indirect action through a series of levers that actuates a hammer. The stroke on the piano key grabs the hammer mechanism, sends the felt head of the hammer flying against the string and then disengages part of the mechanism. Each key on a grand piano has over seventy parts.

Harpsichord action, on the other hand, is a direct one in which the force pressing down the key is directly transmitted to the plectrum that plucks the string; there are only half a dozen parts in the harpsichord key mechanism. On the harpsichord the only part of the tone-producing mechanism that is disengaged after setting the string into vibration is the tiny plectrum. The rest of the mechanism continues to be directly connected with the key, and because of this a strong blow on the key merely causes the mechanism to bounce between the cushions that limit its movement (the key bed and jack rail), producing a great clatter of mechanical noise.

The amount of dead weight needed to produce a barely audible tone on the piano in its middle range is between two and three ounces. The same amount of dead weight, or a little less, is needed to produce a tone on the harpsichord in its middle range. But the piano tone thus produced is not very usable, whereas the harpsichord tone is not much softer than it is with a normal stroke.

The difference between the amount of live weight (force) needed to produce usable tones on piano and harpsichord, however, is another matter. On the piano, tones that are usable at all, even at the soft end of the dynamic range, are produced only by the exertion of some force, and louder tones require proportionately more. And since tones of thunderous dimension can be obtained on the piano, the maximum amount of force needed to play the instrument is very great indeed. On the harpsichord, however, there is only a small difference in the amount of force needed to produce a pluck that makes the softest tone and that which violently displaces the string to make a tone of maximum possible loudness. This is because the volume of tone on the harpsichord is the result of the displacement of the string by a push from the plectrum and is determined more by the size and stiffness of the plectrum than by the amount of force used by the player.

Within limits you can produce a greater amount of tone by beating the harpsichord, but by doing so, the proportional increase in mechanical noise (thumping and rattling) greatly exceeds the increase in amount of tone. In addition, another thing happens from a fierce blow. If you beat the harpsichord, you alter the geometrical shape of the string from the triangle of the string attached at both ends and stretched by the plectrum to a string that is so suddenly wrenched from its point of rest that it actually sags between the plectrum and its two ends like a clothesline—and it produces a quite different sound.[1] A player can sometimes use this altered tone for expressive effects, as in massed chords in Scarlatti, and it is often a requirement in contemporary music, but this sound is a variation of the characteristic harpsichord sound.

Because of the great amount of force needed to produce adequate sound on the piano, finger strength is inadequate to do the job by itself, and arm weight must be added in order to equalize the strength of the fingers in the softer passages and to aid in the production of all tones of moderate or great loudness. On the harpsichord, with its much narrower dynamic range, tones of even maximum possible loudness can be produced by the fingers alone. The main difference, therefore, between piano technique and harpsichord technique is that in piano technique arm weight and force cannot help but get involved most of the time, while harpsichord technique is basically finger technique. (Some modern harpsichords do, to be sure, require the use of arm weight when several registers are sounded together, and especially when the coupler is engaged.)

There is a corresponding difference in touch on the two instruments. Although there is a great variety of piano touches, much of the time the piano stroke is a percussive one in which the key is actually struck from above to make the note sound. The harpsichord stroke, on the other hand, is essentially a push rather than a blow, in which the force applied to the key from the key surface is transmitted directly through the plectrum to the string, which is pushed from its position of rest as it is plucked. The essential difference in the two strokes, then, is that between a percussive and a nonpercussive touch.

Otto Ortmann speaks of percussive and nonpercussive touch on the piano in his *Physiological Mechanics of Piano Technique*. He defines percussive touch as that in which the finger passes through a part of its descent before it meets the key-resistance, and nonpercussive touch as that in which the key-resistance is present from the beginning of the finger's movement.[2] In applying Ortmann's definition of the nonpercussive touch to the harpsichord, I would make the qualification that only a part of the total resistance, that supplied by the inertia of the harpsichord key itself, is met at the beginning of the finger movement, but that it is the greater part (about an ounce and a half). The remainder of the resistance, that supplied by the quill as it passes the string (about an ounce), is met after the key—and the finger with it—begins to descend a very small fraction of a second later. If you push the key down slowly and gently, you will feel the exact point at which the quill comes into contact with the string, and you will find that you must increase the force at this point in order to get the quill past the string. This does not radically alter the fact, however, that the harpsichord touch is basically nonpercussive, because the finger is in contact with the key at the beginning of the stroke, which it cannot be much of the time on the piano.

The finger stroke which depresses the harpsichord key must, then, be a quick push, made with sufficient energy to get the quill past the string without delay and must be followed by immediate relaxation in the finger (and by stopping its descent), so that the key does not continue with the same speed and force to the bottom of the key bed. The mechanical reasons for a quick attack are (1) to get a good displacement of the string, (2) to control the timing of the individual sounds when using a single register, and (3) when two or more registers are used, to make them sound as if the strings are being plucked simultaneously. The mechanical reason for immediate relaxation is to avoid the excess mechanical noise that results from banging the key down.

Once the key is down, the finger in its relaxed state must remain flexibly in contact with it, so that the weight of the finger will control the key, holding it down and preventing it and the jack from bouncing around. This potential out-of-control bouncing is one reason for the impracticability of pianoforte staccato on the harpsichord, except for intentionally percussive effects. This practice is contrary to piano technique, where there is no need for the continuity of finger contact with the key because there is none between key and hammer.

The proper finger stroke is easier to achieve if you are comfortably situated at the harpsichord; and, since the readers of this book will long ago have learned how to be comfortable while playing their respective instruments, little need be said about seating position here. The way a performer sits at the instrument sometimes seems of more consequence than it probably is when one observes the concert pianist carefully adjusting his bench just before he begins to play—an act probably of more use in adjusting to his audience than to his instrument. Harpsichordists don't go through this ritual because their chairs usually don't adjust.

Eighteenth-century writers are sometimes distractingly thorough in their description of how the player should sit, Couperin among them. He tells his readers to seat themselves so that the center of the body is at the center of the harpsichord and nine thumb-lengths away from it, to turn slightly to the right but to avoid pressing the knees too closely together, to keep the feet side by side but with the right foot well out, and as a final admonition he cautions them not to beat time with head, body, or feet or to grimace when playing. His remark that the player's "under-surface of the elbows, wrists and fingers should all be on one level"[3] is his most practical bit of advice, because it incidentally describes what he regards as the desirable hand position as well. Rameau, on the other hand, tells the player that his elbows should be higher than the keyboard, although the hand position he describes turns out to be the same as Couperin's.[4] Actually, the player of a two-manual instrument will of necessity follow both Couperin's and Rameau's suggestions on elbows anyway, for if the elbows are on the level with the upper manual, they will of course be about two inches higher than the lower manual.

Rameau and Couperin both tell their readers that the slightly arched hand, with fingers curved so that the fingertips rest on or reasonably near the ends of the keys in a natural, comfortable position is the best hand for harpsichord playing. The usefulness of their advice, which was based on empirical evidence as well as common sense, is given elaborate scientific support by Ortmann.[5] His reasons for endorsing the arched hand and curved fingers is that, while the wrist and each of the finger joints have a wide latitude of movement, they move most easily and smoothly and with the greatest control near the middle range of that latitude; and, therefore, the hand position that holds the fingers so that each joint can move approximately in its middle range is the most usable position for this purpose. It does make good sense to use the fingers in the middle range of their movement wherever possible, and it is also easier for the player to maintain constant contact with the key if the hand is curved.

Various hand positions have been adopted with good results, however, and the reader who has found one of his own which is comfortable will probably not want to change it any more than he would want to change his speech patterns. For that matter, the term "hand position" is actually an abstraction, for while mention of it suggests plaster-cast rigidity, the hand never stays put but moves from a lovely arch here to a spider-like extension there as it pursues and attacks the keys.

Nevertheless, for physical reasons, an arched hand with curved fingers allows the fastest finger stroke and gives the fingers their greatest independence. Since the harpsichord key must be put down rapidly in order for the quill to pluck the string, speed is essential. The curved position also allows the great finger independence needed to produce the articulation, which is the principle means of expression in harpsichord playing. Consequently, the curved finger stroke is the most usable stroke for the harpsichord player most of the time.

Finger movement should originate entirely from the hand-knuckle, the point where the finger joins the hand, the other finger joints serving only to shape the finger. (Rameau refers to this joint as the "root" of the finger.) At the moment the finger stroke is made, the player's attention should be entirely on the hand-knuckle and not at all on the finger tip as the source of energy—or on the key as a target. If he will imagine a strong physical sensation of the source of power being localized in the hand-knuckle, he will find it quite natural to produce a forceful stroke at will.

An important point that both Rameau and Couperin make is that beginners at the harpsichord should play on a lightly quilled instrument if possible, so that the force needed to get the quill past the string will be little enough that the player needs only finger force to produce tones. Their advice was directed mainly to the tender student with undeveloped fingers, but it is just as useful for the hardened piano player, for he will unconsciously tend to use more power than he needs. If stiff quills give him an excuse, he will be very apt to play the piano on the harpsichord by hitting the harpsichord key as hard as he hits the piano key. In order to make the touch on his harpsichord as light as possible, the player should regulate the register so that the quills are taking the smallest bite which will produce adequate sounds, and of course he should play on only one register at the beginning. Part of the time he is playing he can disengage the register, which will give him only the key-resistance to overcome. Then, if his stroke is too heavy, it will very quickly show up, because the mechanical thumping will be harder to ignore for lack of any string sound.

Theory of Touch

A good touch on any keyboard instrument is much easier to recognize than it is to describe or explain. There are difficulties in talking accurately about touch on the piano, as has often been demonstrated since Sir James Jeans pressed the piano key with his umbrella, and even the *Harvard Dictionary* is unequal to the task, admitting that the word "touch" is used in piano teaching "somewhat vaguely" to mean "the method of producing different tone qualities, from soft and lyrical to harsh and percussive."[6]

One can define a good harpsichord touch, as it pertains to production of tone quality, as one which plucks the string solidly without producing a lot of mechanical noise. Because a given quality of tone on the harpsichord is a necessary but not sufficient condition for adequate expression on that instrument, however, this definition is only partial. It is, in fact, only half of the story—the first half. Thus far the discussion of the technical means of tone production on the piano and the harpsichord has been limited to just that—the production, or more specifically, the beginning, of tones. But the player of a keyboard instrument can control not only the beginning, but the ending, of tones, and any discussion of keyboard technique must take this fact into consideration.

Here there is a fundamental difference between the piano and the harpsichord. The expressive powers of the piano depend on its great dynamic range and the infinite variety of intensities, which is to say "tone qualities,"[7] that can be obtained within this range. The pianist's main concern then is to attend to the variety of ways in which he can set the string in motion to begin each tone. The duration and termination of tones are to a great extent out of his control when the damper pedal is used, because the use of the damper pedal affects all of the strings simultaneously.

The harpsichord, in contrast with the piano, has such a narrow dynamic range that the harpsichordist cannot rely heavily on variations in tonal intensity as the chief musical resource of his instrument. Therefore, the beginning of tones is not his main concern. Because the tones are always individually rather than collectively damped, however, he can exert precise control over the duration and termination of each note. The harpsichordist's art thus lies in the subtle manipulation of tonal endings; this is the art of articulation. I use the word "articulation" here in the same sense Ralph Kirkpatrick does, as "a subsidiary of phrasing . . . the mere detaching or connecting of notes."[8]

FINGER STROKES

The basic finger stroke has two parts: the attack and the release. The manner of attack controls the quality of the tone, and the timing of the release controls its duration. In addition, the speed of the release determines the rate of damping, or cessation, of the tone. The attack must always be swift, but the release may be fast or slow. Although the attack and the release are often one continuous motion, they will be separated here for learning purposes.

Attack

We will begin with the attack. Place your right hand lightly on the keys in the natural curved-finger position, with each of the five fingers touching the key surfaces. It will be helpful if you will use your left hand at this point to support the right elbow, so that there is no tension in the arm at all. Now imagine that energy is stored up in the hand-knuckle of the index finger. Then with a quick exertion of force from this joint, press the finger down swiftly, moving the key, concentrating all your attention on the sensation of movement in the hand-knuckle as you do it. Do not try to be aware of any feeling in either of the other finger joints or in the fingertip or the feeling in the hand-knuckle will lack intensity accordingly. Harpsichord technique is primarily dependent on the ability of the hand-knuckle to deliver the energy for swift, light finger strokes, and consequently it is of the utmost importance that you be able to isolate this sensation. It may help you to feel this sensation even more intensely if you take your hand off of the keyboard and move the fingers in the same way but back toward the palm of your hand instead of against the key.

As soon as your finger has delivered this force to the key, producing a sound, relax the hand-knuckle immediately and completely. It may be that you will relax it so completely that the finger will even bounce up a little, and if it does, don't worry about it; most of the time it will probably not bounce. Now do the same thing with the third, fourth, and fifth fingers, and finally the thumb. The thumb works a little differently than the other fingers, of course, but the sensation will be the same, and that is the important thing here. The attack, which consists of the exertion from the hand-knuckle, followed by its immediate relaxation, is now completed. At this point, only the weight of your finger is holding the key down. No additional force is being applied.

Release

Because the string must be plucked quickly in order to produce the desirable kind of tone quality, there is only one kind of attack stroke which is feasible in harpsichord playing. The string may be damped at any rate of speed, on the other hand, and therefore the key may be released quickly or slowly. When the key is let up, the jack returns to its position of rest, bringing the damper to rest on the string. If this happens quickly, the vibration of the string is stopped almost instantaneously, bringing with it a sudden, almost audible, silence; if it happens more slowly, the vibration dies down a little more gradually. If the jack comes down very slowly, as it does when there is weight on the fingertip as the key is being released, there is a measurable time lag between the point at which the plectrum passes the string and that at which the damper reaches it. Since the plectrum has a slight damping action as it passes the string, the period of time over which the string is being damped in a very slow release is lengthened even further. Both the instant stoppage of tone and its gradual tapering off are needed for expressive playing, and therefore the player must be able to release the keys at different rates of speed.

There are two basic types of releases which control the rate of damping of the string. I will call the first type the instant release and the second the gradual release. The instant release allows instantaneous damping of the string. Because of the speed with which it is made, it is done with the simplest kind of finger movement, a sudden, precisely timed lifting of the finger off of the key as it retraces the same arc by which it came. Like the attack stroke, it consists of exertion followed immediately by relaxation in the hand-knuckle. This release is used more often than the gradual release, because it is the quickest and simplest way to let the key up. The following diagram shows the path the fingertip makes in comparison with its path in the attack.

Figure 2.   Attack and instant release.

Now we will try the instant release on the harpsichord. Place your right hand on the keys in playing position. Again, imagine the source of energy as being localized in the hand-knuckle and lift the index finger up as far as it will go. Then let the finger relax completely so that it will fall by its own weight back onto the key. It is very important that the finger return to the key surface for two reasons: (1) Precise timing of the tones depends on the fingers all moving an equal distance before the string is plucked; therefore, they should all make their attack strokes from the key surface; (2) Accuracy is greatly insured by the fingers' constant contact with the keys.

The finger is now ready for its next stroke. Do the same thing with each of the other fingers. In actual playing you will not need to lift your fingers so high above the keys, but you should do so in these preparatory movements and in the exercises which follow to develop flexibility and control as well as the finger independence which is so important in harpsichord playing. You will find that this release requires more effort than the attack because, in bringing the fingers up and back as far as I have specified, you are pulling the muscles to the extreme point of their range whereas the attack stroke uses only the middle part of the range.

Because it stops the tone instantly and precisely, the instant release is an essential part of legato playing, and it is the only kind of release possible in all fast passages, whether legato or articulated. Used in single melodic lines or at exposed points in thicker textures, it has a percussively accentual effect, the result of the sudden intrusion of silence into sound. In textures of two or more parts, it contributes much to the clarity and rhythmic vitality of individual lines, as well as their separation, because it draws the listener's attention to tonal beginnings.

Gradual Release

The second type of release, the gradual release, produces a gradual damping of the tone. It is used less often than the instant release, because it takes a little more time. Whereas the instant release is always made in the same way, the gradual release may be made with one of three different kinds of finger movement: (1) the lifting motion used in making the instant release done more slowly, (2) a rolling motion, in which the wrist is rotated slightly as weight passes from fingertip to fingertip, and (3) an elliptical motion, in which the fingertip moves in toward the palm of the hand as it comes off of the key. The lifting motion is ordinarily used on the release of a single note where the position of the hand doesn't permit the elliptical movement. The rolling motion is useful in releasing two or more notes in one continuous gradual release. The elliptical motion should always be used in the release of single exposed notes in passages where the other fingers are free.

Now to try the three motions on the harpsichord. For the first kind of gradual release, make the same lifting motion as in the instant release but more slowly and deliberately.

For the second kind make the rolling motion by rolling the weight of the hand from one fingertip to another, letting the last key up slowly as you push the finger off the key. The desired sensation here is that of pressure on the fingertip. Make this motion on adjacent keys and on intervals of various sizes up to an octave, using the most appropriate fingerings for each interval.

For the third kind make the elliptical motion by moving the finger into the palm of the hand, completing an elliptical motion of which the attack stroke forms the first half. The following diagram shows the path the fingertip makes in the attack followed by the elliptical release movement.

Figure 3. Attack and elliptical release.

A little practice in making this movement will be helpful in acquiring the proper control over it. Place your right hand on the keys in playing position. Prepare for the release by depressing the key with your index finger. Now press on the fingertip as you move it along the surface of the key toward you. Then lift the finger as it nears the edge of the key, allowing the key to come up. Continue the elliptical motion with the finger until it returns to the surface of the key, ready for its next attack. The desired sensation in this motion is also that of pressure on the fingertip rather than exertion in the hand-knuckle.

In the elliptical motion the finger is in contact with the key over a longer period of time than in the other two releasing motions and thus exerts more control over the lowering of the damper onto the string. This release may be made at various rates of speed, depending on the amount of weight the player puts on the finger and the rate at which he lightens it, but it cannot be made as fast as the instant release.

The gradual release is an important part of harpsichord technique because it is responsible for much of the expressiveness possible on the instrument. It is the graceful way to finish notes when their terminations are plainly audible, as in solo passages or the ends of phrases. In addition, it draws attention to longer notes within the phrase, prolonging their audible length and intensifying them, so that single tones can dominate even relatively thick textures. It is not a part of the legato touch, nor is it used in fast passages.

The elliptical motion used in the gradual release has another application when it is used by two or three alternating fingers, and that is in the scratching motion so useful on fast repeated notes. For, while one finger alone cannot recover itself quickly enough for fast repetition of notes using this stroke, two or three fingers working together (particularly the thumb, index and middle fingers) can play repeated notes at maximum speed in this way, one depressing the key while the other is moving into playing position. For an example of this see Scarlatti's Sonata in D minor, K. 141, L. 422.

EXERCISES

Now that you have tried out the attack and the various release strokes, the next step is to practice them systematically. The next part of this chapter will be devoted to a set of exercises to develop finger technique on the harpsichord. Exercises 1–4 pertain to the basic finger stroke used to play individual notes, while Exercises 5–12 apply specifically to the three basic touches which are the means of combining notes: detached or articulated touch, legato, and legatissimo.

I have fingered these exercises so that they begin with the strongest fingers, proceed to the weaker fingers and end up with the thumb. Whenever possible I have used nonadjacent finger combinations for ease of movement and absence of tension. All of the exercises are written in the five-finger position; I have avoided using passages which require the passing under of the thumb, because this confuses the application of the mechanics of the finger stroke by adding another motion. You can apply these mechanics to scales later on without any difficulty.

The exercises are written in the middle range of the instrument and should be played there by each hand at first, thus avoiding the slightly heavier touch in the bass until you are used to making your strokes in the quickest, lightest manner possible; a little later you should play the exercises in all ranges of the instrument. Play the exercises with only one hand at a time, for you cannot direct your conscious attention intensely enough to two fingers simultaneously. If you become tired, switch to the other hand immediately.

Set your metronome at ♩ = 60 for the first three exercises. Use the metronome here only to set the tempo and to check it from time to time; do not play the exercises to it, for this will take your attention away from the physical sensation you are trying to feel and direct it to listening to the insistent ticks instead. If you don't have a metronome available, you can set the tempo with reasonable accuracy by slowly counting "thousand one, thousand two," and so on. However, do not continue to count as you play.

Each exercise is very short (about half a minute at ♩ = 60); but if you follow the directions and concentrate intensely as you play the notes, you will accomplish a great deal in only five or ten minutes of daily technical practice. Do not attempt to do all of the exercises in any one sitting, however. It is much better to spend two or three minutes at a time, alternating technical practice with actual playing, so that the technique will more quickly become automatic.

Perhaps the exercises will seem tedious and too simple to be of any real use; perhaps the movements I direct you to make in playing them may seem too small and inconsequential to be taken seriously. My answer to such reservations is, first, that I have purposely made the note patterns in the exercises as simple as possible because the objective is not to be able to play the exercises but to concentrate completely on imagining and developing the kinesthetic sensations that are absolutely essential for an adequate harpsichord technique. Second, it is true that, compared to the larger and more powerful hand, wrist, and arm movements that are a part of piano technique, the finger movements a harpsichord player uses seem tiny. The scale *is* smaller. And the motions are not difficult to do—consciously. But you must make them automatic; you must make them a part of you, so that they can serve you, leaving your mind free to think only of musical considerations when you are playing. This is the goal that I hope these exercises will help you attain.

Exercise 1 is for the attack stroke, Exercise 2 for the instant release, Exercise 3 combines the two, and Exercise 4 combines the attack with the elliptical motion used in making the gradual release.

Exercise 1: Attack

In Exercise 1, a half note is allowed for each stroke, so that you can make the stroke to the count of "one" and feel the relaxation in the hand-knuckle at the count of "two." I have allotted enough time in the exercise so that you can consciously transfer your attention from the sensation of exertion on "one" to the relaxation on "two." Later on the exertion-relaxation will be automatic and continuous and then you can speed up the tempo successfully.

Since you are practicing only the attack stroke in Exercise 1, do not concern yourself with the position of the key after you have relaxed the hand-knuckle, whether it remains partially or fully depressed, and do not attempt to let the key up deliberately. Your attention should be only on getting the key down with the proper muscular action.

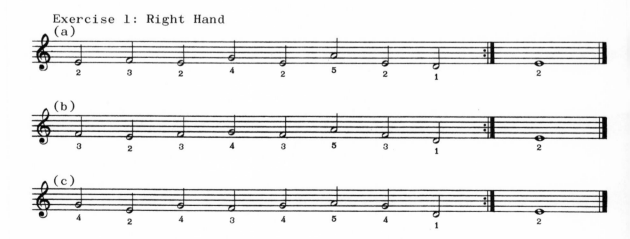

Exercise 1: Right Hand

Exercise 1: Left Hand

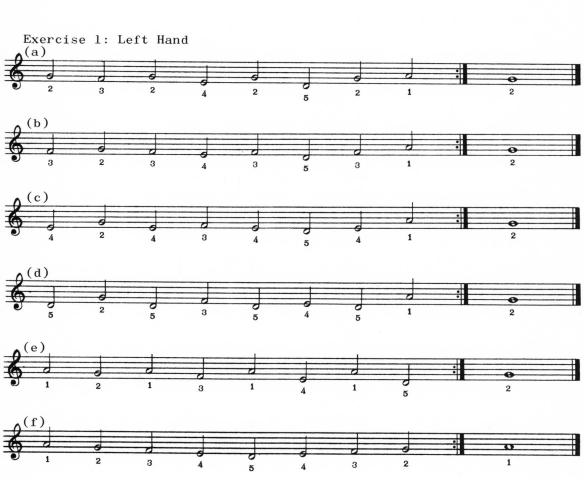

Exercise 2: Instant Release

You may practice Exercise 2, that for the instant release, at the harpsichord if you wish, using the order of notes from Exercise 1, but it can be done just as well on any flat surface, because it does not require the moving of keys. On the count of "one," lift the finger up and let it fall back to the surface immediately, as I have described in detail above. Use the count of "two" to concentrate on the feeling of relaxation in the hand-knuckle. Move the fingers in the same order as you did in Exercise 1, alternating hands from time to time so as to avoid tension or fatigue.

a.	2	3	2	4	2	5	2	1, etc.
b.	3	2	3	4	3	5	3	1, etc.
c.	4	2	4	3	4	5	4	1, etc.
d.	5	2	5	3	5	4	5	1, etc.
e.	1	2	1	3	1	4	1	5, etc.
f.	1	2	3	4	5	4	3	2, etc.

Exercise 3: Combining the Attack and Instant Release

Exercise 3 is a combination of Exercises 1 and 2 and should be done at the harpsichord. In this exercise each attack and release of a note receives four counts. Play the half notes as you did in Exercise 1, making the sound on "one" and feeling the relaxation in the hand-knuckle on "two." Release the note as you did in Exercise 2, lifting the finger up at the count of "three" and feeling the relaxation in the hand-knuckle at the count of "four."

Use the finger patterns from the first two exercises. I have notated the first pattern; the others are analogous.

Exercise 3: Right Hand

Exercise 4: Combining the Attack and Gradual Release,
Using the Elliptical Motion

The purpose of this exercise is to enable the player to acquire control over the elliptical motion in the gradual release of the key. Practice it only at slow metronome markings (♩ = 40–60). Make the attack stroke on the count of "one" and the release slowly on the count of "two." Use most of the count of "two" to let the key up, pressing down on the key on the count of "two" and gradually releasing that pressure as you move the finger slowly back to starting position.

Exercise 4: Right Hand

ARTICULATION

The art of articulation is the chief expressive resource of the harpsichordist, because what happens to each tone after it has been sounded is more important to the shaping of a phrase than the actual sounding of the tones themselves—this includes its duration in relation to the tone which follows and how it is terminated, i.e., the rate at which it is damped.

There are three basic touches which supply all the possible relative durations of consecutive tones on the harpsichord. They may be referred to as (1) the detached touch, in which one tone ends before the next one begins; (2) the legato touch, in which one tone ends as the next one begins; and (3) the legatissimo touch, in which one note overlaps the next. And there are two means of terminating the individual tones: (1) instantly and (2) gradually.

The legato touch is the basis for the study of articulation, or tonal duration, on the harpsichord, because it is nonemphatic and nonexpressive; it presents the notes clearly but blandly and impartially. It is also an indispensable tool; the player must have absolute control over it to master the refinements of the other two touches. While legato presents the notes—the raw material, if you like—the detached and legatissimo touches enable the player to organize those notes so that they express what he thinks the composer meant them to express.

The detached touch provides accent and emphasis; it establishes beats and can even delineate the pulse within the beat; it focuses attention on points of interest; it adds sparkle and brilliance. In short, it makes the music dance.

Legatissimo, on the other hand, makes the music sing. It softens and rounds angular contours; it simulates crescendos and diminuendos; it molds and shapes the melodic line. Together, the touches, used deftly, tastefully, and imaginatively, provide almost unlimited possibilities for a variety of nuance and expression on the harpsichord.

Articulation Symbols

One practical problem for all harpsichord players is how to indicate such articulations in the score. You will soon realize that there are so many articulations, and the effects are often so small, that you simply cannot remember them all without writing them down in some detail. Besides, you will want to change your ideas as you work out a piece, and a written record is necessary even as a basis for making changes.

I have found it helpful to use a few simple symbols of my own devising to mark kinds of articulation directly in the score, pencilling them in lightly so that they can be easily erased and replaced with other markings if desired. Here is a short explanation of these signs.

1. *Detached Touch.* The signs for the instant release are the vertical line (|) and the diagonal slash (\ ) . The signs for the gradual release are the curved lines (⌠, ⟍) and (⌊, ⟍) . The vertical line should be long enough to avoid confusion with fingering marks, and it should be carefully written, so that it can be placed exactly on the beat or subdivision of the beat.

The diagonal slash drawn through the head of a note indicates that the note should be released as soon as it is played. This sign is also very useful on tied notes, where it is easier to see than the vertical sign.

The gradual release signs serve both for single notes released gradually and for continuous gradual releases of two or more notes. The length of the sign can vary, depending on the number of notes it includes. The signs are the same for all three motions used in making the gradual release.

The gradual release frequently takes longer than one subdivision of a beat, and since the sign itself takes up more than that amount of space in the score, we can only be concerned with exact placement of the vertical part of the sign, which indicates the point at which the release is begun. The amount of time taken for the release is determined empirically by the player and is not shown by the length of the curved part of the line. In a continuous gradual release of double notes or chords, the direction of the curvature indicates the direction of the release: ⌠ for a release toward the treble, and ⌡ for one toward the bass.

2. *Legato Touch.* No marking is needed. Since all but legato notes are marked, you can assume a legato touch unless something else is indicated.

3. *Legatissimo Touch.* The sign for legatissimo is ⌐¬ . It may be used alone or combined with other signs. If legatissimo notes are followed by a legato note, the sign is used by itself; if followed by an instant release, the sign is written ⌐⊣ ; and if followed by a gradual release: ⌊⌠ or ⌐⌡ .

Detached Touch

We will begin with the detached touch, since it involves only one finger at a time, whereas the other two touches involve two fingers. In the detached touch one note is released before the next one is sounded, and the silences between the notes give emphasis to individual notes and lend shape to the phrase. On the harpsichord these silences are often more important than the notes themselves, and the more precisely a player is able to control their length, the greater the subtlety and expressive range of his playing.

The exercises which now follow are designed to give you practice in making silences of all possible lengths, from those that are so short they are barely audible to those that are so long as to use up most of the value of the note. In Exercises 5–7, I have notated the silences as rests of three different lengths: In Exercise 5, the note and the rest each receive half the beat; in Exercise 6, the note receives three-fourths of the beat and the rest one-fourth; and in Exercise 7, the note receives one-fourth of the beat and the rest three-fourths. At moderate to fast speeds the examples would approximate portato, nonlegato, and staccato touches, respectively.

We will begin with the exercise that is easiest to do, that in which the notes and the rests are of equal length, and proceed to those in which the rests are shorter or longer than the notes. We will use the same finger patterns that we used in the exercises for the basic finger stroke. Use the instant release in the next three exercises. None of the gradual releases are fast enough to work well here.

A metronome is indispensable to do these exercises with precision. Begin the exercise with your metronome set at ♩ = 40, and as soon as you feel comfortable at that tempo, move the metronome up to the next marking. As your fingers become more flexible, you can expect to get the speed up around ♩ = 138, while still retaining perfect control of your movements, although there is some tendency for tension to develop at the faster speeds. Play the exercise with one hand at a time and alternate the hands at intervals of a minute or so. Exercises 5–7 use the first of the finger patterns in Exercise 1. Follow it with the other finger patterns in the same exercise.

In Exercise 5 the tones are notated as eighth notes and the silences as eighth rests. Count two to each quarter note, depressing the key to the count of "one" and releasing it to the count of "two."

Exercise 5: Right Hand

In Exercise 6 the tones are notated as dotted eighth notes and the silences as sixteenth rests. Count four to each quarter note, playing the note on "one" and releasing it exactly at "four." Again, set your metronome at ♩ = 40 to begin with, gradually turning it up until it becomes impossible to make the strokes precisely.

Exercise 6: Right Hand

In Exercise 7 the tones are notated as sixteenths, and the silences as dotted eighth rests. Again, count four to the beat, playing the note on "one" and releasing it exactly at "two." Use the metronome in the same way as before.

Exercise 7: Right Hand

You will be able to make your releases with more precision, especially as the speed increases, if you count out loud, accenting the count on which the *release* occurs.

When you can do the preceding exercises at all the indicated tempi, you will be able to make silences of any length which it is possible to hear. For didactic purposes I have notated the silences with tedious exactness here. However, these are just exercises; you will not, of course, find such literal indications in the music. Prior to the twentieth century, composers did not write down their intentions as thoroughly as they do today, so the performer has to use his imagination in interpreting the notes. For instance, a row of quarter notes might be played: ♪ ♪ ♪ or ♪. ♪. ♪. . Or a passage in eighth notes might be played: ♪ ♪ ♪ or ♪. ♪. ♪. , even though there may be no indication in the score that this is the case. It is safe to assume, however, that while a note may justifiably be shortened as much as half of its value, if the composer had wanted it to be shorter still, he would have written the next shorter note value. Therefore, do not translate ♩ into ♪ .

Legato Touch

The concept of legato playing on the piano, in practice at least, tolerates various degrees of legato, from a "light" or "dry" legato, in which the notes never encroach on each other and some even stop short of actual connection, to a more "singing" legato, in which some of the tones overlap slightly, particularly in crescendo passages where the increasing intensity from one note or group of notes to another blots out the slight blurring which would otherwise result. Furthermore, although one sounds more transparent than the other, both kinds of legato playing are convincing as legato; and each serves a definite stylistic purpose, the "light" kind of legato for Mozart sonatas and the more lush kind for Chopin or Brahms.

On the harpsichord, however, the concept of legato can be thought of in absolute terms and can be described as the precise connection of tones, so that the cessation of one tone coincides exactly with the initiation of the next. Any interruption of the tones, however slight, is clearly recognizable to an alert ear as detached playing, and any overlapping falls into the category of legatissimo. And legatissimo is a category that must be treated with respect on the harpsichord. When consecutive tones are played at about equal intensity, as they are on the harpsichord, frequent or haphazard overlapping that is permissible and even desirable on the piano can produce a muddy and rhythmically unstable effect.

Technically speaking, legato playing on the harpsichord requires the scissors-like movement of two fingers, one making the attack and the other the instant release, so that the first tone sounds right up to the point where the second tone begins, but not an instant longer. (The gradual release motions cannot be used here, because they are too slow and cause overlapping of tones.) Your technique for both the attack and the instant release strokes should by now be quite automatic when you do each stroke separately. In the legato touch, however, you must combine the strokes, simultaneously making the attack with one finger as you do the instant release with the other. The attack stroke will be easy to do, because you hear a tone as you depress the key, but the release may seem rather abstract at first, because you will be moving one finger as you hear a sound produced by another.

Before you play the exercise, practice on the keys with two fingers at a time. Begin with the second and third fingers. Depress the key on which the second finger is resting. Now let that key up with the instant release motion and at the same instant depress the key on which the third finger rests. (Be sure that you let the second finger drop back to the key surface after lifting it, so that it can make its next attack stroke from key level.) Now make the instant release motion with the third finger while you make the attack stroke with the second. Continue, alternating the two fingers, until you are making the strokes with ease. Let the attack strokes play themselves, as it were, and concentrate only on the physical sensation of the release. Do *not* try to feel both strokes at once, or you will feel neither very keenly. The exercise for legato playing is as much mental as physical, for you must get used to the distraction of hearing one tone while concentrating on the sensation of releasing another.

Now practice Exercise 8. Play it slowly (♩ = 40, or more slowly if you wish) and make no effort to increase your speed until each pair of fingers has learned to work automatically. Do not play with the metronome, because it is distracting. It is also unnecessary, because we are working only for the simultaneity of the attack and release strokes, not for the relative timing of the notes. When you are able to play the exercise comfortably at ♩ = 40, move the metronome up by degrees until the tempo is so fast that you no longer have time to lift the fingers high in making the release. In actual playing a more modified scissors action will do and you will not have to lift the fingers so high. But you should do so now, in order to attain precision and control of your movements and to develop finger independence.
Use all the finger patterns in Exercise 1.

When I present this exercise to my students, they invariably ask, "Do I really do all of this in actual playing? Can I ever lift my fingers so high quickly enough to do it in fast passages?" And I assure them, "No, indeed

you don't have to do all of that in playing music. There isn't time in fast passages to lift your fingers so high; you will perhaps not lift them at all." But in practicing these exercises you must make the exaggerated motions described here, because it makes you feel the muscle action and exercises the muscles thoroughly. You are doing the same thing the athlete does when he runs nine miles every morning so that he can run one mile in the race with ease and have a great deal of energy left to spare.

Legatissimo Touch

Legatissimo is perhaps the most difficult of the touches to use convincingly. It should be the most sparingly used of the three, because excessive overlapping of harpsichord tones makes the music hard to hear. Used tastefully and in moderation, it adds warmth and grace to otherwise angular or wooden passages. Used to excess, it can quickly become cloying or mannered or make the music lurch.

Legatissimo touch can involve two or more fingers at a time. Either the instant or the gradual release can be a part of it, and, accordingly, exercises for both kinds of releases follow.

Legatissimo with the Instant Release

One problem with legatissimo playing is that it tends to invite sloppiness more readily than the other touches do, partly because the tonal endings do not stand out clearly as they do in the detached touch. The following set of exercises is designed to counteract that tendency by affording you practice in maximum finger independence and control through the use of the instant release with legatissimo playing. In addition, it is excellent ear training.

In Exercise 9, count two to each quarter note, making the attack strokes on "one" and the releases on "two." In Exercise 10, count four to the quarter note, making the attacks on "one" and the releases on "four." In Exercise 11, count four to the quarter note, making the attacks on "one" and the releases on "two." Count aloud in all of these three exercises, accenting the count on

Exercise 9: (♩=40–72)

Count: 1   2   1   2   1   2   1   2   etc.

Exercise 10: (♩=40–72)

Count: 1 2 3 4 1 2 3 4   1 2 3 4   1 2 3 4   1 2 3 4   1   etc.

Exercise 11: (♩=40–72)

Count: 1 2 3 4 1   2   3   4   1   2   3   4   1   2   3   4   1   etc.

which the *release* occurs. Begin slowly and gradually move the metronome up, but do not exceed the speed at which your hand can remain relaxed. The first of the finger patterns from Exercise 1 is notated below. Follow it with the others from the same exercise.

    In Exercise 12, count aloud two of each quarter note, with the attacks on "one" and the releases on "two." The rhythmic pattern in this exercise will tend to offset any tension which may develop as a result of the delayed action of the releases. Alternate it with Exercises 9–11.

Exercise 12: (♩=60–138)

Count: 1 2 1   2   1   2 1 2   1 2 1   2   etc.

LEGATISSIMO WITH THE GRADUAL RELEASE

    The gradual release with legatissimo produces a smooth, singing sound. In order to manage this, the player makes the release of two or more consecutive notes as if it were one continuous gradual release. The sensation is one of weight being passed from one fingertip to another as the wrist rotates slightly. The last finger to come off of the keys presses down on the key before releasing it either by rolling the weight off of the key or by bringing the finger toward the palm of the hand as in the elliptical gradual release motion.

The following examples are illustrations of the application of legatissimo in linear playing. Play them for an appreciation of some of the effects possible with harpsichord legatissimo. In the first example release all of the held notes on the rest in one continuous motion, as just described, beginning with the finger that played first and rotating the wrist so that the notes are released in the order in which they were played. Listen for a continuous sound.

In the next example, release the held notes in the same way, taking the release time off of the last held note, so that you play the following note on time.

The speed at which the release is made will depend on the tempo, of course. The main consideration is that you must arrive at the following note in time, no matter what the tempo.

In actual legatissimo playing it is up to you to decide whether the instant release or the gradual release are more appropriate or expressive. In fast tempi, or on short notes in slower tempi, you may have time only for the instant release. In all other cases, however, it can be a matter of choice, and then you should allow your ear to decide. A few guidelines might be of help at the outset, however.

1. When a note follows two or more legatissimo notes, it is difficult to make it sound through clearly. Use the instant release on all held notes as the following one is being sounded to focus attention on that following note. This is a particularly useful device when stepwise passages follow leaps, as in the

following example from J. S. Bach's Invention no. 2, measures 1 and 2. The markings used to indicate touch in these examples are explained on pp. 30–31.

2. The gradual release is apt to be most useful when legatissimo notes are followed immediately by rests or by detached notes as in Invention no. 9, measures 1 and 2.

3. Legatissimo is useful at the four principal cadences in Invention no. 11. It has a broadening effect in approaching the cadences in measures 6 and 18:

and helps to recover the tempo after the cadences in measures 11 and 16:

Double Notes and Chords

Thus far we have been concerned with the playing of single notes. These technical devices can now be applied to the playing of double notes and chords. The main problem in playing a melodic succession of double notes on the harpsichord is that of clarity. Because you cannot play one of the lines louder than the other, as you can on the piano, the passage will sound indistinct unless you emphasize the melody line in some other way. The solution is simple: make the melody notes last slightly longer than the others.

Play the following short octave passage slowly and with the suggested fingering. You will note the lack of continuity in the bass, even though you may be trying to make the passage as legato as you can without finger substitution.

Now play it again, releasing each octave, thumb first, with the continuous gradual release you learned to use in releasing linear legatissimo notes. Note the continuity this lends to the bass line. This is due to the fact that the lower notes last slightly longer than the upper ones. Now try a similar octave passage in the right hand, releasing the upper note last. You will note here that the treble line will have the kind of continuity the bass did in the previous passage.

You will get a more percussive effect, and still retain a legato-sounding line, if you release the harmony note instantly, as in the following example. Release the lower note here instantly on the count of "one," and the upper note gradually on the count of "two."

Count: 1 2   1 2   1 2   etc.

You can use the same principle in playing thirds, sixths, octaves, and, in fact, all double notes. Just bear in mind that the outer voices—the soprano in the right hand and the bass in the left—will come through more clearly than the inner voices. If you want an intense, drone-like sound, particularly effective on repeated octaves, release *both* notes gradually and simultaneously, letting the keys up only far enough for the plectra to clear the string, and then swiftly bang them down again. You will have a chance to apply these devices in the music at the end of the chapter.

Played well, chords supply harmonic background, accent, and texture in harpsichord music. Played badly, those notes become indistinct blobs or ugly lumps of sound. The basic problem in chord playing, as in playing double notes, is that of clarity. The main difference is one of tone production: double notes are usually sounded together, whereas very often the notes of a chord are not. They may be played solid, or they may be arpeggiated. If the usual arpeggiation line appears before the notes, the chord should of course be arpeggiated; but if it does not, which is more often the case, it is up to the player to decide how it should be played.

What the player does with the chord should depend on what effect he wants. If he wants a heavy accent, the percussive sound of a solid chord supplies it. If he wants a full sonority plus a strong feeling of the beat, a quickly rolled chord ending with an accent on the last note will do it. If he wants a smooth swell of sound to set a soft mood while defining the tonality, the proper choice is a chord rolled more slowly, with an accent on the first note and a slight acceleration into the last note.

Wherever he arpeggiates, however slightly, the player must know where the beats are and fit the individual notes of the chord into them rhythmically. The tempo often forces a choice on him or at least narrows the possibilities. For instance, there is little he can do in a relatively fast tempo except play solid chords or arpeggiate them only slightly. But, in any case, he should never allow sloppy arpeggiation to obscure the beat or destroy the rhythm.

Once the chord is played, whether arpeggiated or not, it is important that the sound be terminated appropriately, or the chord will leave an unsatisfactory impression. There are two basic ways in which to terminate the sound. You may release the notes all at once, or one by one in a continuous gradual release. If the notes are released all together, silence rushes in with its peculiar jarring effect. If the notes are released evenly, one by one, the effect is that of a smooth gradual dying out of the tone.

If the chord is a full one played by both hands, the least obtrusive way of terminating it is to make the continuous gradual release in both hands at once, beginning with the thumbs and ending with the fifth fingers, so that the outermost tones of the chord are heard together for a brief instant at the end. A left-hand chord played in the bass should usually be released downward, so that the lowest tone leaves the final impression. Likewise, a treble chord played by the right hand should usually be released upward.

It is neither possible nor desirable to chart out in advance all of the possibilities here. It is much better that you take these few hints and discover the refinements for yourself. The best thing to do is to listen to recordings and decide what sounds most convincing. And you should experiment, listening critically to yourself, asking yourself what effect you want and trying various ways of producing it. What is appropriate in one context will be out of place in another, and the only way to learn to do the right thing in the right place is to experiment and listen. A solid chord that gives the needed vitality in a Scarlatti sonata will sound blunt and ungainly in a Bach sarabande. Or a lush, drawn-out arpeggio that provides the proper degree of expectancy for the opening of a Rameau prelude will get the Italian Concerto off to a limp start.

SPECIAL TECHNICAL PROBLEMS

We have discussed two facts about the harpsichord that the player must deal with effectively to realize the instrument's expressive potential. They are (1) that the sole means of sustaining tones is with the fingers and (2) that, because of the limited string displacement, the dynamic range of the instrument is very narrow within any given registration. Of the problems raised by the harpsichord's peculiarities, that of clarity is probably the most crucial, the most difficult, and the most fascinating to deal with. In the list below I would like to suggest some ways in which these problems may be handled. Some of them are tricks that produce illusions. Experience will suggest others.

The special techniques listed apply the basic technique set forth earlier in this chapter. In using a mixture of the three touches, it might be well to keep in mind that, while legato is the foundation of a good harpsichord technique, unalleviated legato is like unpunctuated prose: It leaves the job of organization completely to the listener. Therefore, détaché and legatissimo are necessary aids to musical organization—détaché for separating and legatissimo for binding. Détaché selects and emphasizes important notes; legatissimo groups them, subordinating some to others by softening their effect.

1. *To give the illusion of connecting notes that cannot be connected with the fingers.* The gradual release is a good connective trick and can be used for continuity between notes whether they lie under the fingers or are at opposite ends of the keyboard. Double notes or chords released gradually, melody note last, can give the illusion of legato playing.

2. *To make crescendos.* Arpeggiating a chord and holding down all the notes as they are sounded gives the effect of a crescendo into the last note. In a scale passage, holding several notes into the last one produces a slight swell into the last note and a slight accent on it as the others are released.

3. *To make tidy phrase endings.* Holding the penultimate note into the last one and releasing both notes gradually as in double notes or chords produces a smoother, more finished ending.

4. *Use of legatissimo.* A little goes a long way. It should be used sparingly or muddiness will result, and the point at which the notes are released should be marked in the score, for that note will stand out more clearly than its neighbors.

5. *Voice leading in a polyphonic texture.* Because the soprano is the easiest voice to hear, the bass next easiest, and the middle voices most difficult, articulation must be most emphatic or broad in the middle voices.

6. *Voice leading in two-part texture.* A note or a whole passage played détaché in one hand will stand out most clearly if it is "covered" by legato (or legatissimo) in the other. If two notes are terminated simultaneously, the releases should be staggered to avoid a break in the line. If a percussive ending is desired, both notes should be cut off at the same instant.

7. *To make a melody sound out clearly against an accompanying figure.* The thicker the accompanying figure, the more emphatically the melody must be articulated in order to sound above it—or through it.

8. *To bring out harmony notes in a lute-like figuration.* Legato and legatissimo are an effective combination for clarity that does not impede the flowing movement. When two or more consecutive legatissimo notes are released as another note is played, that note comes out more strongly, and the one immediately preceding it almost as much so. Note this example from J. S. Bach's Allemande, French Suite no. 4 (BWV 815).

SUGGESTIONS FOR STUDY

The last section of this chapter is devoted to the study of a few selected pieces of music from harpsichord literature, with suggestions on articulation. As you study these pieces, please regard the articulative indications as possibilities rather than as unalterable recipes for playing the music. Use them as a starting point, then go ahead on your own as soon as possible and work out other pieces of your own choosing.

Six Little Preludes—J. S. Bach (BWV 933–38)

PRELUDE NO. 1 IN C MAJOR

Play all chords, as well as double notes, solid. Release them with the continuous gradual release, upper note last, for the melody rides on them.

Play the mordents so that the final note coincides with the first bass sixteenth note, accenting its entrance. Make the bass notes in measure 1 and other similar measures legato.

Play the half trill in measure 11 so that the last note coincides with the first bass sixteenth note.

Release all of the quarter notes exactly on the following beat.

Make gradual releases on the first of every pair of eighth notes for an agogic accent (measures 5–6 and 13–14). Make instant releases on the other eighths.

Playing this piece according to the instructions above brings out its solidity and unpretentiousness. Try other ideas to see how they affect the piece: faster mordents, detached sixteenth notes in such measures as the first one, different groupings of the bass notes in measures 5–6, and so on.

PRELUDE NO. 2 IN C MINOR

This is a good piece to start with, because virtually all of the right hand notes can be played legato, leaving you free to listen to the left.

The articulations in the bass realize some of the harmonic implications and determine the rhythmic pulse of this charming piece. To keep the rhythm steady, release the quarter bass notes exactly on the attack of the eighth notes in the right hand.

Take care to release the quarter notes in measures 2 and 4 on the third beat and not an instant before or you will lose the feeling of that beat.

Watch measures 14 and 15; there is a tendency to shorten the notes here, which causes rushing.

Gradual releases in measures 16–18 give weight to the line of rising quarter notes in the right hand.

The use of legatissimo at the cadences in measures 20, 32, and 40 has a slightly broadening effect without interrupting the movement.

PRELUDE NO. 3 IN D MINOR

Detach the first sixteenth note in measures 1 and 2 with the instant release. This accents the downbeat and also delineates the pulse by allowing the second sixteenth note to be heard clearly. You need not repeat the procedure in the answer in measures 3 and 4 because in measure 3 the articulation in the right hand accomplishes the same thing and in measure 4 the trill would drown out any bass articulations anyway.

Follow the gradual and instant release marks on the eighth notes carefully for small but unmistakable rhythmic effects.

In measure 22, treat the dot as a rest for a clean beginning of the ornament in the next measure. I have written out a suggested realization.

This piece is similar in character to the fourth Invention, also in D minor.

BWV 935

PRELUDE NO. 4 IN D MAJOR

In measures 3, 4, and 6, both voices in the right hand will come through clearly if you make the gradual releases as indicated, thumb note last. Since the dissonant thumb notes are heard an instant after the slurred notes are gone, the two notes remain distinct from each other.

In measure 5, there is a mechanical problem. The B in the left hand *must* be released, although we do not want it to sound detached. If the slurred D in the right hand is detached too, as corresponding notes in the other measures have been, the effect will be too lumpy. The solution is to cheat a little by holding the D while you release the C#. It will sound enough like the other measures to pass unnoticed if you do it with confidence. Sometimes tricks like this are necessary.

In a three-voiced texture, more extreme means are frequently necessary to make the middle voice sound through than are necessary with either of the outer voices. In measure 23, for instance, the D must be played very short if the imitation is to come through clearly; it is not enough to release it halfway through the beat as you did with the A in measure 21.

The effect of a simultaneous release in all three voices is so arresting that it should be used sparingly. It occurs in this piece only at the two final cadences (see measures 19 and 47).

In measures 33 and 34, the use of the thumb for all of the quarter notes in the middle voice insures adequate separation for audible voice leading.

PRELUDE NO. 5 IN E MAJOR

The sixteenth notes in this piece are basically legato; the eighths are basically detached. Against this background, slurring a few pairs of eighth notes (as in measures 3, 5, and 6) adds harmonic interest and initiates a rhythmic idea that becomes intensified in the sequence in measures 17–18 leading to the climax of the piece.

Legatissimo emphasizes the brief pedal point in measure 9 and realizes the melodic implications in measures 17 and 18.

BWV 937

PRELUDE NO. 6 IN E MINOR

This prelude is a study in accent. Using ornaments, Bach shifts the accent from first to second to third beats, against a regular four-measure phrase structure throughout. The proper use of articulation is necessary to make the accents as vivid as possible.

In measures 1–8 regular movement is required with a strong feeling of one, at ♩. = 50. Mordents accent the downbeat. Play them so that the third note coincides with the first sixteenth note.

In measures 9, 12, 14, and 16 accent is on the second beat. In measures 22, 24, 25, and 27 accent is on the third beat. In measures 42 and 44, after an eight-measure section in regular movement, there is a return to accents on the second beat.

Fugue in C major—J. S. Bach (BWV 953)

There are two main problems in playing fugues on the harpsichord. The first is that the subject, and the countersubject as well, must be articulated so that they are immediately recognizable whenever they appear. This is easy, since they usually have some obvious features anyway. The second problem is clarity; the voices must be constantly made distinguishable from one another, so that the ear can follow their progress without undue effort. This is a little more difficult to do, because the solutions are less obvious. And it is more difficult on the harpsichord than on the piano because dynamic accents cannot be used as effectively.

The subject of this fugue is a scale embedded in sixteenth-note figuration. The scale is heard even if we don't articulate any of the notes, but detaching the scale notes, as I have done in the first two measures, makes them easier to hear and also adds rhythmic vitality. There are eight statements of the subject in this fugue, and seven of them are articulated so that the scale notes are made explicit. One statement (measures 17–18) is played legato, which intensifies the effect of the suspensions that accompany it. The articulations in the other seven statements are varied according to the requirements of each situation: in two statements the subject itself is articulated; in the other five statements the articulations appear in the other voices but suffice for the subject as well.

The motif that Bach uses as a countersubject in this little fugue is the counterpoint to the final notes of the answer in measure 4. It is primarily a rhythmic figure and is articulated accordingly in its three somewhat extended appearances. Its entrance in measures 6–8 is straightforward (slurs followed by legato); it bounces a little more in measures 10–12, and still more in measures 29–32, intensified by expanded melodic intervals.

Articulation for clarity in a fugue must occur exactly on beats, or on subdivisions of beats. If they occur elsewhere they cause rhythmic sloppiness and can also be misleading. Since this fugue moves in sixteenth notes, there are four possible points in every beat on which to detach notes.

In measures 3–8 the eighth notes are held their full length and are released on the rest, on the third subdivision of the beat. This lends stability to the movement and actually appears to articulate the subject.

In measures 9–12 if you play the eighth notes detached, as I do here, they should be released exactly on the second and fourth subdivisions of the beat, again for rhythmic stability.

In measures 14–17 the texture is thinner here, but the eighth notes should again be released exactly on the third subdivision of the beat, for steadiness. It is rather difficult to do here because the left hand plays two voices, but it will be easier if you accent the sixteenth note that is played as the eighth note is released. The aural effect of the accent is so small as to be practically inaudible; it therefore doesn't interfere with the rhythmic pattern, but the kinesthetic sensation is vivid and helps the problem of coordination in the left hand considerably.

In measures 19–22 treat the tied sixteenth notes on the first and third beats as rests, as well as the tied-over eighth note on the fourth beat of measure 19. Letting in a little air here will call attention to the note immediately following and clarify the voice leading. All or part of such tied notes should be treated as rests wherever it is necessary to keep the lines clear. Be careful with such notes of longer duration than an eighth, however, that you don't get holes in the music. If it *sounds* like a rest, your articulation is too long.

In measure 21 using the fourth finger on both the C# and the C forces an articulation on the fourth subdivision of the first beat. This falls into the classification of articulations that simulate a legato. If you used a legato fingering here, the C would actually not be quite clear. In passages such as this, where the effect you want is that of legato quarter notes against legato sixteenths, the quarter notes should be released on either the third or fourth subdivision of the beat or they will not sound through the greater volume of tone underneath them. An extended example of this principle can be found in the third variation of Rameau's Gavotte, where most of the melody notes must be articulated in this way so as not to be drowned out by the counterpoint underneath them:

Fugue in C major—J. S. Bach

Prelude no. 1 (BWV 846): Arpeggiated figures

Exclusive use of legato and legatissimo will make this piece very "pretty"—and rather dull. Judicious use of détaché and dynamic accent will add interest by emphasizing the pulse, and more emphatic détaché in measures like 5 and 7, followed by legatissimo in measures 6 and 8, will produce small crescendos and decrescendos.

Prelude no. 2 (BWV 847): Perpetuo moto figures

Détaché playing of the sixteenths in each hand on the first and third beats supplies accents which the ear needs in this homogeneous texture to keep easy track of the beat. Most of the other sixteenths can be legato, with light détaché in places for harmonic interest and lightening of the texture.

Prelude no. 4 (BWV 849): Dotted notes

Since the motif ♩. ♪ ♩ is ubiquitous here, it must be clearly heard, though unobtrusive, with the dot treated like a rest. In measures like the eleventh, where the motif is doubled, you will leave a hole unless you observe the rest in only one voice and play the other legato. The tied-over eighths in measures 6, 7, and so on should be treated like rests.

Prelude no. 7 (BWV 852): Tied-over notes

The tied-over sixteenths in measures like 2, 3, and 4 should be treated as rests. Bach has supplied continuity here in an inner voice with the tied-over eighth notes; they should, unlike the eighth notes, be held their full duration and not released until the eighth rest.

Prelude no. 8 (BWV 853): Disjunct intervals

The notes of the rising motif ♪ ♩. ♪ are most easily heard and have a rising inflection if each one is accented and played détaché, with the shortest possible rest before the following note. The inversion as a falling motif, however, seems to descrescendo, and is usually clear enough when played legato and in some cases can even be played legatissimo.

Prelude no. 15 (BWV 860): Arpeggiated figures

The opening arpeggiated figures should be played legato with a sharp, accented détaché on the first and thirteenth sixteenth notes in the right hand to give it sparkle and impetus. In measures 11 and 12, a left hand legatissimo on the ascending part of the arpeggios anchors the bass and produces short surges. An effective treatment of the climax is to use a legato right hand against a partly détaché left hand in measures 16 and

17 (♫ ♪) leading to legatissimo right hand figures (for crescendo) in measure 18.

Prelude no. 21 (BWV 865): Broken chord figures and rapid scales

The only way to keep this piece clear—and steady—is to play legato right hand thirty-second notes against left hand eighths that are released exactly halfway through. Legatissimo helps stabilize the harmony of the rapid scale passage in measure 9; hold the A and C into the D in the left hand and the D, B♭, A, and G into the F in the right hand. Use legatissimo again on the last eight notes in measure 18.

Brandenburg Concerto no. 5 (BWV 1050), cadenza—J. S. Bach

For the cadenza in the first movement, measures 195–213, you need full use of articulative techniques to realize the powerful impact of these climactic measures. I have suggested some possibilities in the following example. The effect can be produced by means of articulation alone on one 8′ set of strings; the addition of other registration at certain points will intensify it. The marks that I have added in the score indicate most of the suggestions for articulation, but, in the opening measures of the pedal point (201–2), I have also added some extra stems on the pedal notes in an attempt to notate more clearly and exactly what might be played. There are very few notes marked legatissimo here other than the low As, but they are very effective. The continuation of the pedal A from measure 203 grows in intensity as the articulation on the first and third beats goes from legatissimo (203–4) to legato (205) to unaccented, gradually released détaché (206), and finally to accented détaché (209), hovering without further accent in measures 212–13 before moving to the B in the deceptive cadence in measure 214.

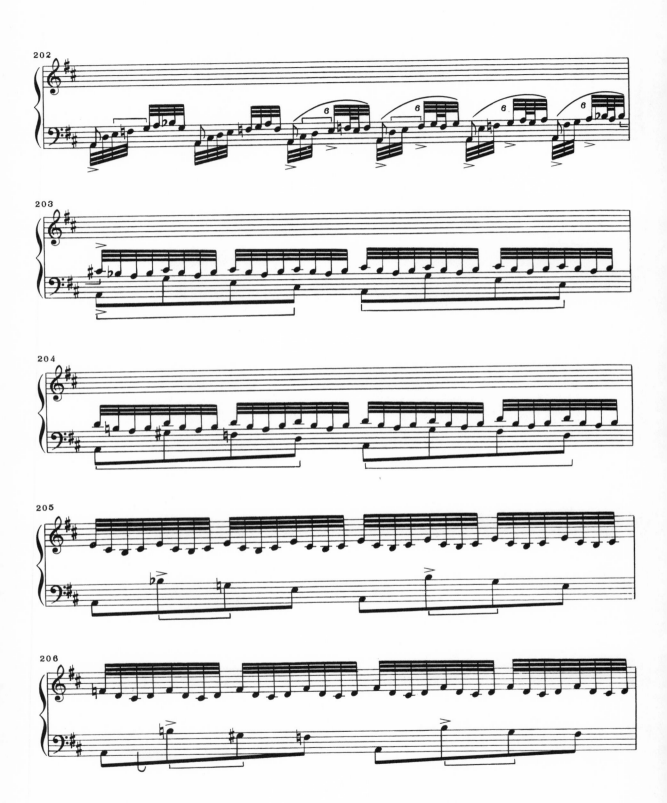

"My Lady Carey's Dompe"—Anon. c. 1525

The bass is typical of many English virginal pieces. The alternation between tonic and dominant harmonies makes inevitable accents on the first beat of every odd-numbered bar, resulting from the release of both bass note and its octave. No attempt should be made to connect notes from one harmony to the other. The first beats of the even-numbered measures get a lesser accent, because the previous thumb note is held until the bass note is repeated. I have marked the first six bars; the rest of the bass is the same with a few exceptions: In measures 14 and 22, the thumb note is held, where it would ordinarily be released, because the melody note requires articulation and double articulations would make a hole in the music. There are also several places like that in measure 15, where the melody note duplicates the bass note, necessitating an articulation for mechanical reasons if you are playing on one manual.

You should make your articulations in the melody by ear to some extent, because how well it sounds over the bass will depend on the balance of tone between treble and bass on your harpsichord. The bass on the virginal was very light, and if you are playing the piece on an instrument with a heavier bass, you will have to articulate a little more broadly. If you are playing the piece on two manuals, you can register accordingly.

Most of the markings in the score are self-explanatory, but a few points might bear some comment. Articulate only the B♭ in measure 10 while you hold the G for a smoother downbeat in the next measure. In the corresponding spot in measure 22, however, release both G and E, because a more emphatic downbeat is better there.

In measures 37–38 release the first of every group of four notes to give vitality to the sequential movement.

In measure 45 I like a very short D in the right hand, rather than the half note. I think such minor changes are justifiable in very early music, before notation became more thoroughly and painstakingly worked out.

"Les Baricades Mistérieuses"—François Couperin

This beautiful piece is difficult to play and you must expend care and patience in learning it to make the lute-like figuration sound as Couperin intended it to. A superficial glance at the score might suggest a lot of finger substitution, but there is actually very little, and I have marked the little that is necessary. Instead, precisely timed releases and extensive use of the legatissimo technique you practiced in Exercise 9 are the answer to the phrasing and voice leading most of the time.

It is necessary to practice the piece slowly and, allowing the duration of one eighth note for each release, lift the fingers high on each release with exaggerated, even jerky movements, so that you feel the muscular action keenly. Then when you play the piece at speed (Couperin's marking is "vivement") you will be able to retain adequate control over your finger movements even though they must be fluid and continuous.

Notes may be released for any one of three reasons in this piece: to repeat notes, to phrase, or to clarify the voice leading. Therefore, a knowledge of the phrase structure, as well as of the harmonic scheme, is essential.

The harmonic scheme is simple and symmetrical. The piece modulates from the B♭ tonic in the rondeaux to the key of the dominant in the first couplet, and, after touching on the key of the supertonic in the second couplet, modulates to the key of the subdominant in the third couplet. The phrase structure is more complex, with couplets, phrases and phrase groups of varying lengths alternating with the regular eight-measure phrase structure of the rondeaux. Both the harmonic structure and the phrase structure are most clearly shown in tabular form:

Rondeau	8 measures (4 + 4)	$B^{\flat}$
First couplet	12 measures (4 + 4 + 4)	$B^{\flat}$—F—$B^{\flat}$
Rondeau	8 measures (4 + 4)	$B^{\flat}$
Second couplet	6 measures (2 + 2 + 2)	$B^{\flat}$—c—$B^{\flat}$
Rondeau	8 measures (4 + 4)	$B^{\flat}$
Third couplet	22 measures (4½ + 10½ [2½ + 2 + 2 + 2 + 2] +4 + 3)	
Rondeau	8 measures (4 + 4)	

I have marked the releases in laborious detail because such detailed visual reminders are necessary in the learning stages. Everything that is not marked is to be played legato. I have suggested a few fingerings in cases where they are not entirely self-evident, especially where substitution is needed for legato fingering. On the third beat of measure 35, hold the right-hand chord until the left hand has sounded the bass note. Use the thumbs on most of the notes in the inner voices in both hands, because such articulation makes the voice leading much clearer than the most elaborate legato fingering would do.

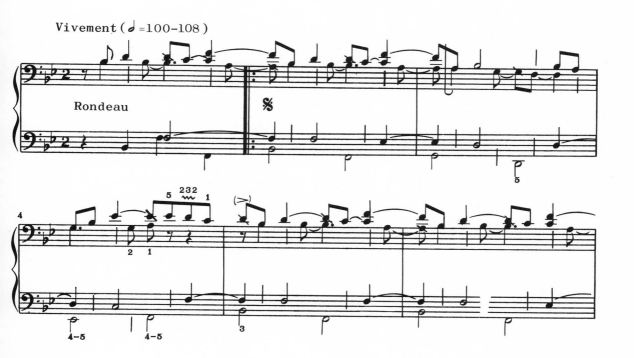

1er Couplet

"Le Tambourin"—Jean-Philippe Rameau

Much can be learned about harpsichord playing by studying this familiar piece. Although the notes are so simple that almost every young piano student has been exposed to the piece (usually without the ornaments), it must be played with considerable care and knowledge of the harpsichordist's craft or its marvelous vitality will be lost. The form is the usual one for the rondeau alternated with couplets or reprises as in "Les Baricades"; but here there is no final return to the rondeau and the tonality is E minor throughout.

The left hand is an excellent example of what can be done with a few notes. It is essential that you retain the drone effect of the low bass E in spite of the numerous rests of some length; you can do this by releasing the chords exactly on the second beat and downward with the gradual release (done quickly, of course). In spots like that in measure 3, the thumb note must be released before the second beat so that it can play the F#, but the two lower notes can be held their full length and released *on* the beat.

Most of the chords are played solid, but they are occasionally arpeggiated quickly for emphasis, and in measures 21–25 they are beaten. There is no time to worry about how they are released; just get off of them quickly. In measures 26–28, release the chords as marked, letting the keys up only far enough to allow the quills to pluck the strings again. Final chords such as that in measure 8 and the last chord in the piece cannot be played as written unless you have a very large hand. My suggestion is to take the G an octave higher in the right hand and add an E in the thumb of the left. Roll only the left hand notes. I have added a long mordent to the right hand E on the final chord.

In the rondeau, two-measure phrase groups predominantly composed of slurs are alternated with phrase groups which are primarily legato. Keep the slurs crisp. There is no need, even in slow practice, to separate the attack and the release on the detached notes, for the two are continuous.

Although it can be played at a more moderate tempo, this piece really sparkles at a tempo of $\quarternote$ = 132. At this tempo, however, the trills must be limited to three notes beginning on the main note rather than on the usual upper note. Exceptions are the trills in measures 16, 29 and 44, which can begin on the upper note and last a little longer.

The first two right-hand notes in measure 23 should sound slurred, even though they are an eleventh apart. If you do a little sleight of hand and accent the B, releasing it quickly while you hold the left hand E as long as possible, you will get a simulated slur.

In passages of repeated patterns like those in measures 25–28 and 40–42, you will find it effective to use dynamic accents followed by sharp releases on the first beats in measures 26, 28, 40, and 42.

The final four measures of the piece can be repeated as a *Petite Reprise,* played softly as an echo effect.

Sonata in D major, K. 492, L. 14—Domenico Scarlatti

If you play this piece at all fast (my tempo is about ♩.=100), the eighth-note trills cannot be played as four-note stopped half trills without distorting the rhythm. In passages like that in measure 3, I would play the first trill like an acciaccatura and the second one as a triplet beginning on the main note.

In measures 10, 13, and 15, the absence of the third on the fifth beats of the measures strongly suggests slurs on beats 4–5, instead of articulations on every eighth note as in the beginning.

In measures 20–25, if you are playing at a moderately fast tempo, the short appoggiaturas can only be played together with the eighth notes they precede, as acciaccaturas. Play the little notes in measures 17 and 31 in the same way. Scarlatti writes appoggiaturas in various ways (♪ ♪ ♪ ♪ ♩ ♩) and often links them to the main note by a slur.[9] Playing the chords with as little space between them as possible emphasizes the fact that Scarlatti is dwelling on the key of the dominant.

You can achieve an arresting effect in measures 26–28 by holding the eighth notes in the right hand their full length. The left-hand figure is phrased upward throughout, with an articulation on its last note.

In measures 36–42 to get the scales to surge into the following beats, treat the tied-over sixteenth notes in the right hand as rests (just as you do the rests in the left hand), and detach the final note of the scale for clarity. Don't worry about doubling the speed of the notes as the notation appears to dictate; just accelerate each scale into the following beat.

The brief state of suspended animation in measures 54–58 is heightened by the slurring of the right-hand notes. The slurring may be continued throughout the long sequence which follows in measures 58–70. Play this section quietly, articulating as unobtrusively as possible and adding no accent. Scarlatti has provided accent enough with the rests.

3

FINGERING

Fingering, of course, is really an aspect of technique, but I would like to treat this important matter separately. What I propose to do is 1) to give the reader some information on sixteenth- through eighteenth-century fingerings for a first-hand understanding of how baroque music would have been played by baroque musicians, and 2) to show the reader what is distinctive about harpsichord fingering, so that he can make the necessary adjustment while retaining as much of his piano fingering as may be useful to him.

It has sometimes been suggested, by those interested in archeologically exact re-creations of early music, that harpsichord players should return to old fingerings. This seems to me rather misguided, and almost impossible anyway for anyone trained in the piano keyboard technique that developed mostly during the nineteenth century. To be sure, musical considerations of early music were reflected in the older systems of fingering and no doubt conventions of fingering had an effect on the kind of music written for keyboard instruments. But these musical considerations can be grasped by a modern performer through his ears and mind without attempting to replace his modern fingering technique with one based on the early principles. As an aid to understanding some features of earlier keyboard music, it is useful to try some of the old fingerings, and to help make this possible I shall include some few notes on these fingerings in a brief historical sketch. But the main emphasis in playing music for the harpsichord should be on the music. Whatever fingering works to sound the right notes at the right time and for the right duration is good fingering.

THE DEVELOPMENT OF KEYBOARD FINGERING

The fingering technique for eighteenth century harpsichord playing was the product of a long development from inauspicious beginnings. To see this technique in perspective, it might be useful to review its historical development briefly. The earliest keyboard fingering was, I suspect, akin to the amateur typist's hunt-and-peck system and certainly no better. Even as late as 1702, Saint-Lambert, in *Les Principes du Clavecin,* gives the player carte blanche: "There is nothing more free than the art of fingering. Everybody just looks out for his convenience and the best way."[1] No doubt this laissez-faire policy was able to reign partly because of the rather obvious correlation between keys and fingers, peculiar to keyboard instruments. A musical person with no keyboard training at all can quickly learn to get about in a fairly facile way on a keyboard with no assistance except that of his ears, because all he has to do is to put his hands on the keys in a natural position and press his fingers down.

This natural position, or something very close to it, was the earliest hand position used. The hand was virtually flat, the thumb being allowed to hang down in front of the keyboard much of the time, and hence the middle three fingers (which also happen to be the longest) got the most use in passage work. The thumb was often used, of course, on the initial note, and the fifth finger on the terminal or turning note of a passage. All five fingers were apparently on the keys only when they were playing double notes and chords, and a crossing technique of the second, third, and fourth fingers, sometimes with and sometimes without the addition of the thumb, sufficed most of the time. This seems awkward by modern standards, and would have been impossible except in short groups of articulated notes.

The flat hand position and all it implies seems very inefficient to us today, because we are used to the arched hand and, on the piano at least, supporting, steel fingers. And we are apt to give this flat hand technique much less than its proper due without investigating its positive aspects. The flat hand, first of all, was adequate for instruments that did not require brute strength. Furthermore, since it is a natural, comfortable position, the flat hand tends to remain relaxed. Lateral motion of the wrist is more readily possible with the flat than with the arched hand, making the crossing of the middle fingers an easy matter. Trilling with weak finger combinations such as 4-3 and 5-4 is also easier in this position. Some of the most mystifying of the old fingerings are considerably illuminated if we play them with the flat hand. I would suggest trying the pieces in the *Fitzwilliam Virginal Book* and *My Ladye Nevells Booke of Virginal Music* containing the original fingerings, which are listed in Appendix A.

These casual fingering practices were also made possible by the vertical nature of much of the early music, as well as by the fact that modulation was limited before tempered tuning. C. P. E. Bach's remarks help to put the situation in perspective:

> Our forefathers were more concerned with harmony than melody and played in several parts most of the time. We shall soon learn that in this style the position of each finger is immediately apparent since most passages can be expressed in only one way and are variable to only a limited degree. Consequently, they are not so treacherous as melodic passages with their far more capricious fingering. Furthermore, in earlier times the keyboard was tuned differently and not all twenty-four keys were available as they are now. Consequently, the variety of passages was not great.[2]

These remarks about the excessive concern with harmony as opposed to melody might seem a little overstated, but it certainly seems to indicate that the earliest fingering practices grew out of chord-playing experience. And even with the playing of melodies, the melodies were very much attached to a chordal foundation, as even a superficial perusal of the *Fitzwilliam Virginal Book* will show; "figurations" is a more accurate term than "melodies," for they move within a triadic framework rather than sing.

The early player was not particularly concerned about legato, because the long seamless passage had not yet come into vogue. Instead, he articulated his passages in short groups of notes, often in two's and three's, breaking up longer phrases into pieces of irregular size and length, depending on the notes he wished to emphasize. The highly articulated nature of the early keyboard music was an inevitable consequence of the only kind of fingering technique yet devised, and, although the results were musical much of the time, the choice between predominantly détaché playing and the common modern legato was simply not open to early musicians. A little later, when longer, smoother passages seemed desirable, these long passages were often divided between the two hands, largely avoiding the difficulties encountered when one hand is solely responsible for them.

Moreover, early fingering, far from assuming the fingers to be all equally strong, capitalized on the theory of "good" and "bad" fingers. Though the various theorists couldn't agree on which were which, the "good" fingers (meaning the stronger ones) were given the accented notes, while the "bad" (weaker) fingers played the unaccented notes.[3] Actually, as it turned out, the fingers that got the greatest use were the middle three, and, although the third was regarded by both the Germans and the Italians as "bad," it got the most use of all. Surely, theory and practice were widely divergent in this case.

Diruta remarked, in *Il Transilvano* in 1597, that because the third finger "must play all the bad notes, and again all the bad notes which skip," it seems to be "the hardest worked, since nothing usual is done without it."[4] But this observation didn't stop him from regarding the finger as "bad."

The next stage in the development of fingering, if we may describe such an empirical process by that term, was that in which the thumb was brought up onto the keyboard and remained there along with the other fingers. Once the thumb had a permanent place on the keys, the hand could be considered a single unit, a tool which could be contracted and expanded, allowing greater ease, smoothness, and flexibility in playing. Evidence of this practice is exemplified in such pieces as the "El. Kiderminster" on page 81 of the first volume of the *Fitzwilliam Virginal Book.*

The next and perhaps most crucial step was to pass the fingers over the thumb in a kind of pole-vaulting motion that recognized the fact of the opposing thumb and established the thumb as a pivot. At this point smooth *ascending* scale passages in the left hand and *descending* ones in the right became possible over the entire compass of the whole keyboard. In Spain, Fray Tomas already advocated this technique as early as 1597, as did Alessandro Scarlatti and others somewhat later, and the possibilities it opened up for facile and legato passage work and arpeggio playing must have made themselves felt rather quickly. It made possible the cross-hand technique of the Neopolitan School, which greatly influenced Domenico Scarlatti's writing and which J. S. Bach used in his C minor Fantasy and exploited to great lengths in the Goldberg Variations.

The last stage, and apparently the most difficult step of all, was that in which the thumb was passed *under* the fingers. One observation is customarily ignored in accounts on fingering of the period: while the passing of the fingers *over* the thumb occurred very early in fingering history, the action that is, practically speaking at least, its opposite, the passing of the thumb *under* the fingers, was not used until much later. An investigation of fingering indications in music of the time will show that this motion is not used by Alessandro Scarlatti in his toccatas or by Couperin in his *L'art de toucher le clavecin* (1717). And even C. P. E. Bach in his *Essay,* as late as 1753, gives not one but three separate fingerings for the ascending scale of C major for each hand, with the suggestion that:

> None of them is impracticable, although those in which the third finger of the right hand crosses the fourth, the second of the left hand crosses the thumb, and the thumbs strike f are perhaps more usual than the other.[5]

In other words, the old crossing of the middle fingers in the middle of the scale still held its own with the passing under of the thumb, even at the very end of the baroque period.

It is true that mankind is reluctant to replace traditional forms and practices even when better ones have been found, but I think there is another factor operating here. Keyboard players of the time would not have been able to explain it, but they knew it in their bones from their empirical, trial-and-error approach: A double action of the thumb is required for the thumb to pass under the hand, whereas only a single motion is needed for the hand to pass over the thumb. Otto Ortmann explains this phenomenon in *The Physiological Mechanics of Piano Technique.* He applied it to piano technique, but the movements are exactly the same on the harpsichord.[6]

This double action of the thumb was difficult to learn, especially for rapid tempi, and this difficulty is reflected in the dearth of baroque passages for sweeping scales and arpeggios where the right hand ascends and the left hand descends. It is interesting, for instance, that in Bach's C minor Fantasy, a piece written in 1736 and containing advanced techniques for the time, *all* the arpeggios descend in the right hand and ascend in the left; not one of them requires the passing of the thumb under the hand. And even in the Goldberg Variations, certainly the most virtuoso work of the late baroque, there are very few fast passages that call for this motion.

C. P. E. Bach suggests that in passages where the thumb *must* pass under the hand, the note following the thumb note be taken by the same finger that preceded the thumb, so as to avoid the "awkward shift" caused by having to pass the thumb under two or more fingers. He goes on to explain that this will work, however, only in passages where a single note follows the thumb in the same direction. "Should two tones follow, the fingers are to be played in their usual order."[7] Scarlatti seems to have written a few arpeggios where the thumb passes under, but his sonatas abound with those in which the hand passes over the thumb.

Early Fingering Devices

There are a few fingering devices, developed early in keyboard history, that serve specialized purposes. I have not tried to include them in the foregoing sketch, but would like to enumerate them below, because they are still applicable today. They are:

1. *Sliding a finger from an accidental to a natural.* This is often the simplest way of enabling the hand to cover six notes moving in one direction or to avoid finger substitution, and it is indispensable in polyphonic passages when

the other fingers may be occupied. Since the sliding finger cannot help but play the natural key a little more heavily than usual, this resulting heaviness may be used for subtle dynamic effects such as small swells or accents.

2. *Change of fingers on a repeated note.* Fray Tomas advocated this practice early (1597), advising the use of 2 3 2 3 in the right hand, and 1 2 1 2 or 2 3 2 3[8] in the left. The device was picked up by the English virginalists as an aid to phrasing and articulation, and Couperin used it in a most refined way for very delicate articulation, such as that in the "port de voix," the French lutenists' term for "appoggiatura."[9]

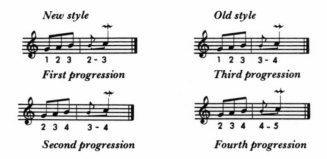

It makes possible very short and hence barely audible silences between notes, due to the fact that while one finger is letting the key up, the other finger can move into place to push it down again immediately. If the note is repeated with the same finger, the result is a longer silence between the notes.

A later extension of the same principle occurs in the broken chord figures in Variations 5 and 6 of Rameau's "Gavotte." Still another application of the same basic principle is the fast alternation of two or three fingers on the same note, a scratching motion which makes playable the mandolin-like repeated note passages, so common in Scarlatti sonatas.

3. *Repeating the same finger on consecutive notes.* Used by the English virginalists to aid articulations between short phrase groups. (See "El. Kiderminster," measures 18–19, *Fitzwilliam Virginal Book,* vol. 1.) It still serves the same purpose, though it is a fairly crude device.

4. *Finger substitution (change of fingers on a held note).* This was an early organ practice where legato was absolutely essential due to the uniform dynamic level of organ tone and the rather slow moving polyphonic style. The practice is so habitual with organists that a conscious effort is needed to avoid its overuse in harpsichord playing. Although substitution is a legitimate part of harpsichord technique, it is needed much less frequently than on the organ, because the notes move at a faster rate. Also, even longer notes on the harpsichord often need to be set apart by small silences, for clarity and

definition, especially in polyphony. The tendency shown by some modern players to make everything legato results not in continuity but in muddy voice leading and dynamic flatness. Perhaps they have been misled by what seems to me an overemphasis on substitution in eighteenth-century writings, probably a didactic overemphasis attempting to convince students who didn't want to bother with this rather troublesome extra motion.

The reader will want to know more about the subject, and he should play some early musical examples with their original fingerings. An hour spent at the keyboard in this way will do much to demonstrate to him the stylistic effects of early articulation, as well as to help him establish realistic tempi for the early pieces. I have listed a few readily available sources in Appendix A.

Fingering from a Modern Perspective

As we have noted, a player who comes to the harpsichord from the piano brings with him a conception of fingering based on nineteenth- and twentieth-century piano technique. There is nothing wrong with this approach. He can use a good deal of piano fingering on the harpsichord as long as he is not bound by these conceptions simply because both instruments have keyboards. The classification of keyboard fingering practice into three main categories (normal, expanded or contracted, and passing fingering) is as useful on the harpsichord as on the piano. Normal fingering, with the hand in the closed, five-finger position, suffices for passages limited to a five-note range. Expanded and contracted fingering is required for a slightly wider range or for passages involving frequent changes of direction and relocation of the thumb. And passing fingering enables the hand to negotiate the entire compass of the keyboard through the use of the thumb as pivot.

These categories are useful in describing a common ground for fingering practice, but they could apply just as well to a cardboard keyboard as to either a piano or harpsichord one. For differences between piano and harpsichord fingering, we must look at a few basic facts about the instruments themselves. The most important single factor is, of course, the piano's percussive action, which accounts for its wide range of dynamic variation, versus the harpsichord's plucking action, which, because it is activated by the keyboard, allows for a very limited range of dynamic variation. The guitar, or the harp, for instance, are capable of more dynamic variety on a single set of strings than the harpsichord because the fingers pluck the strings directly and can vary the displacement of the string to a greater extent.

The percussive principle on which piano tone production is based, plus its necessarily heavier action, makes the modern system of piano fingering a complex science developed to serve a musical-athletic art. It depends on mechanical requirements needed to produce great masses of sound, speed, continuity throughout the keyboard, and, of course, a flawless legato. Arm weight is needed to equalize the strength of the fingers, because inequality of finger strength would otherwise show up in unequal dynamics. On the other hand, the harpsichordist's art relies for the most part on his fingers alone. Instead of great physical power, he needs flexibility and precision for the fine, precisely timed finger movements needed to initiate and release tones on an instrument capable of only subtle degrees of dynamic variation.

The second most important factor is the means of damping tone on the two instruments. The piano has a supplementary damping device, the damper pedal, that may be used independently of the fingers; the harpsichord has only one means of damping, the individual dampers, which are dependent on fingers alone. The damper pedal may enable the pianist to hold down notes that his finger can't reach (the harpsichordist doesn't need to do that anyway); but, unless he foregoes the use of the pedal, he lacks the control over releasing each tone that the harpsichordist has. It is this control that makes the art of articulation possible on the harpsichord and that in turn enables the player to compensate for the limiting effects of the instrument's narrow dynamic range.

FINGERING AND ARTICULATION

Articulation, the harpsichordist's key to expression, is a refined art with complex requirements that can be met only by a refined fingering technique. Because the fingers are wholly responsible for the many small and precisely timed movements necessary for the termination of notes, fingering practices on the harpsichord differ in some ways from those on the piano, where the task is conceived somewhat differently.

The relationship of fingering and articulation has been noted previously in connection with certain early fingering techniques, such as crossing the middle fingers and changing fingers on a repeated note, but it seems to me that this relationship is much more generally applicable than has usually been emphasized. Legato fingering that is practical for a given passage, for instance, may be impossible for the same passage played détaché, because détaché notes require more facility and control than legato notes of the same value. The fingers have to move twice as quickly to play détaché notes as legato notes, since in détaché the release must be completed before the next note is sounded rather than along with it or afterward. Therefore, the actual speed of finger movements needed for a passage of détaché eighth notes is the same or greater than that for a passage of legato sixteenths.

Moreover, the actual duration of notes is of equal importance in this interrelationship. Notes that are negotiable with a given fingering at a particular tempo may be impossible with the same fingers at a faster tempo. It seems reasonable to say, therefore, that fingering, articulation, and tempo are *all* interdependent, and that fingerings will vary for the different combinations of articulation and duration.

This interdependence will be more clearly demonstrable if some, admittedly arbitrary, categories are set up as a means of classifying specific musical examples according to the degree of facility and control needed to play notes of varying articulations and lengths. Since the détaché notes require more effort than legato or legatissimo notes and short notes require more than longer ones, it follows that short détaché notes require the greatest control and long legatissimo notes the least. Therefore, for the purposes of this classification, we might combine the three articulations with notes of short, moderate, and long duration, making a total of nine categories requiring progressively lesser degrees of control. The categories may be described as: 1) short détaché notes, 2) moderately long détaché notes, 3) long détaché notes, 4) short legato notes, 5) moderately long legato notes, 6) long legato notes, 7) short legatissimo notes, 8) moderately long legatissimo notes, and 9) long legatissimo notes.

Fingerings also vary in practicality and difficulty with respect to the type of movement and the speed at which they must be made. The most facile and controlled movements, and those which can be made at the greatest speed, are those vertical finger movements made from a normal hand position with the hand nearly flat and the fingers close together and parallel to the keys (as they will naturally be if the hand is loosely placed on the keys). And the movements affording a lesser degree of control (unless the notes are connected) and taking more time are the non-vertical finger movements made with a greatly expanded hand position. Arm movements made to shift the hand position on the keyboard naturally take the most time, although the control with which they are made depends on the hand position.

Choice of fingering consequently depends on the demands for each type of articulation at each particular tempo. The desired objective is to make the fingering suit the mechanical and musical needs of each passage—the smallest, most economical movements for the fastest or most difficult passages or individual notes and larger or more time-consuming movements where the demands for efficiency are relaxed. Actually, alternation of tiny, precise, and extremely controlled movements with those that are larger and freer helps a great deal to maintain the relaxation necessary for a combination of endurance with perpetual control.

In order to make this discussion as explicit as possible and to allow the reader a chance for practical experimentation on his own, I have extracted specific illustrations of these categories from Bach's Two-Part Inventions. The particular articulations and tempi are my own and may differ from those of other players, but they will, at any rate, serve to illustrate the point. They may also be modified or altered altogether. The following categories assume the tempi I have suggested at the beginning of each invention.

Following is a list showing suggested articulation and duration of various kinds of notes in the Inventions. The indication that sixteenth notes in a particular Invention exemplify, let us say, the détaché, short category refers only to the sixteenths that are selected to be played détaché (they are indicated in the music reproduced in this book). The other sixteenths in that piece will probably be played legato and therefore fall into another category of articulation.

1. *Détaché: short notes*
   Invention no. 5: sixteenth notes
   Invention no. 6: thirty-second notes
   Invention no. 14: thirty-second notes
   Invention no. 15: sixteenth notes
   It is the sixteenth notes in the subjects of Inventions 5 and 15 that are played détaché. Most of the remaining sixteenths are played legato, a much easier task.

2. *Détaché: moderately long notes*
   Invention no. 4: eighth notes
   Invention no. 5: eighth notes
   Invention no. 7: eighth notes (These are more difficult because of the numerous mordents and trills on the eighth notes.)
   Invention no. 8: eighth notes
   Invention no. 10: eighth notes (The eighths are triplets.)
   Invention no. 13: eighth notes

3. *Détaché: long notes*
   Invention no. 1: eighth notes
   Invention no. 2: eighth notes
   Invention no. 9: eighth notes

4. *Legato: short notes*
   Invention no. 3: sixteenth notes
   Invention no. 4: sixteenth notes
   Invention no. 8: sixteenth notes
   Invention no. 12: sixteenth notes

5. *Legato: moderately long notes*
   Invention no. 1: sixteenth notes
   Invention no. 2: sixteenth notes
   Invention no. 6: sixteenth notes
   Invention no. 7: sixteenth notes
   Invention no. 10: eighth notes
   Invention no. 13: sixteenth notes
   Invention no. 14: sixteenth notes
   Invention no. 15: sixteenth notes

6. *Legato: long notes*
   Invention no. 6: eighth notes
   Invention no. 9: sixteenth notes

7. *Legatissimo: short notes*
   I found no short notes that sound well played legatissimo.

8. *Legatissimo: moderately long notes*
   Invention no. 1: sixteenth notes spanning an octave (measure 15)
   Invention no. 2: certain sixteenth notes spanning an octave or a seventh
   Invention no. 5: sixteenth notes spanning a seventh
   Invention no. 11: certain sixteenth notes spanning a seventh

9. *Legatissimo: long notes*
   Invention no. 9: sixteenth notes (Note the first five sixteenths, measure 1.)

Following is a brief discussion of each invention in terms of fingering and articulation.

Invention no. 1. Normal fingering may be used on the legato sixteenths, with shifts of hand location on the détaché eighths. Detaching the note before mordents and trills clarifies the ornament and allows time for *both* trill fingers to get to their notes before the first note is played.

Invention no. 2. A combination of normal, contracted, and expanded fingering is comfortable at this moderate tempo and with the predominantly legato touch. The legatissimo spots in measures 1–4 (and others similar to it) alleviate some of the pointillistic effect of steady sixteenth notes.

Invention no. 3. The détaché sixteenths in measures 1 and 2 require control at this speed; normal fingering is best. In measure 3, the fifth finger is a good choice on the A because it is already there. The shift of the hand necessary to play the B with the second finger is better done after the A than before, because there is more time. The fingering on the first two beats of measure 4 delays the C# slightly, but is possible because of its position at the end of the phrase.

Invention no. 4. The fingerings beginning measures 1 and 2 are ideal for the separation of the first sixteenth in each measure, because they are easy to do. Those in measures 3 and 4 in the left hand are, of course, more difficult but there is no help for that.

Invention no. 5. The first four notes of the subject are played détaché, which is difficult to do evenly. Therefore, a closed hand position, using the most reliable fingers, is needed. On the legato sixteenths, alternation of the hand between normal, contracted, and expanded hand positions will help to keep the fingers relaxed and agile (see left hand in measures 1–4 and right hand in measures 5–6). I omit the mordent on the third note of the subject; it seems redundant to me.

Invention no. 6. The thirty-second notes are difficult to play evenly because some weak finger combinations must be used. Nevertheless, the legato sixteenths alternating with the thirty-seconds provide enough relaxation to reduce the tension. All sixteenths and eighths are played legato and with expanded fingering when necessary, except for the tied-over sixteenths, which can be treated like rests and afford time to relocate the hand.

Invention no. 7. The feeling is predominantly legato and the three ornaments in the subject are unusual in that they seem to sound best if they follow legato notes. This calls for expanded fingering to get to the two mordents. There should be the shortest possible separation after the final note of each ornament, so short as to require legato fingering.

Invention no. 8. The most controlled right hand fingering of the opening broken triad is either 1 2 3 or 1 2 4, leaving the fifth finger to play the octave. The hand should be kept in normal position as much as possible, both on the détaché eighths and the legato sixteenths, even though more frequent shifts of the hand are necessary. In the right hand, measures 4–6 and in the left hand, measures 6–7, first beat fingerings differ from those of the following notes for ease in accenting.

Invention no. 9. This piece depends for its lyricism on a balanced mixture of legato and legatissimo sixteenth notes and détaché eighth notes, released slowly. Because of the importance of articulation, the hand position should be normal as much as possible, with frequent changes of hand location rather than expanded fingering to cover the leaps and stretches.

96

Invention no. 10. As in Invention no. 8, the use of 1 2 4 on these fast moving broken triads allows more control than 1 3 5, and saves the fifth finger for the high G. It also puts the hand in a slightly expanded shape to reach the high G in the second measure without having to overly shorten the preceding note. All of the short ornaments will be easier to hear if preceded by a short silence. All of the tied-over eighths in measures 7 through 12 should be treated as rests, allowing time for the fingers playing the following notes to get in place ahead of time.

Invention no. 11. Use normal fingering on the sixteenths. Shift the hand on long notes and in the separations between eighth notes.

Invention no. 12. The speed and frequent change of direction of the groups of sixteenth notes makes this piece very difficult to play *and* to hear clearly if the initial notes in each group aren't accented and played slightly détaché. They should all be practiced that way, in any case, for control and accent; then in performance some of this extra effort can be relaxed. The groups of conjunct notes are most easily played with normal and contracted fingering. There is no help for the expanded fingering on the disjunct sixteenths, but here the initial détaché note in each group gives a bounce which helps digital dexterity on the remaining five.

Invention no. 13. Expanded fingering serves both the legato and the détaché eighths.

Invention no. 14. The four consecutive détaché thirty-seconds are difficult to play evenly and therefore require normal and contracted fingering, with maximum use of the strongest fingers. The expanded fingering necessary for the legato broken harmonies in eighths and sixteenths affords adequate control at this moderate tempo.

Invention no. 15. Again, normal fingering with emphasis on the strongest fingers is called for on the first four détaché notes of the subject. The sixteenth notes in measures 8–9 are easiest with a shift of the hand for every eight notes and with every fourth note played détaché.

ORNAMENTS

The playing of ornaments deserves some special mention here even though Chapter 4 deals with them at length. Nowhere is precise, tension-free finger action more necessary than in playing ornaments. They should, of course, be practiced with all the possible finger combinations, in the event that the weaker combinations will be called upon to play them, but whenever possible the strongest fingers should be used to play them in pieces. The best fingers for playing trills and mordents in the right hand are the 3-2 combination, and in the left hand, the 1-2 and 2-3 combinations. The 1-2 combination, so useful in the left hand, is not equally so in the right because the fingers lie in reverse order; and since in both mordents and trills the upper note is accented and the lower note is played more lightly, in a right hand trill fingered 1-2 the thumb would have to play the light note, a somewhat awkward task for it. Early authorities who make this differentiation in trill fingerings between the two hands do not give the reason, but apparently they felt it was right because it worked.

The most difficult ornaments to play are the mordent and the half trill, because they are short, fast, and begin with an accent; and, if one of the notes does not "speak," the music is blemished. Therefore, care must be taken to learn the knack of playing these short ornaments cleanly and accurately. The secret is in the manner of preparation: Take an instant before the actual execution of the ornament to relax the hand and to place *both* fingers on the surface of the keys they are to play. Most short ornaments need to be preceded by a short silence in order to be heard clearly anyway, so taking the time for this brief preparation is no problem.

Once the fingers are on the surface of the keys they are to play, there are other subtle adjustments possible with fingers, hand, or wrist that can put the two fingers to be used in the best position for the job. Finding the exact position that is most relaxed for any particular situation is actually easier to do than to describe, but I will give a few pointers to let the reader know how to experiment so that he can do it for himself. Many ornaments are of course played with the hand exactly parallel to the surface of the keyboard and the fingers parallel to the keys, but it is usually an advantage either to turn the wrist laterally or rotate it slightly to equalize the leverage of the two fingers concerned or improve it altogether. In a right hand trill played with the second and third fingers, for instance, it is usually easier to play if the wrist rotates the hand a little towards the thumb; and if such a trill involves an accidental to be played with the second finger, the hand should be turned so that the fingers will be at a slight angle with the keys, and the second finger should be extended as well. If the trill is to be played with the third and fifth fingers, the best position may be obtained by rotating the wrist toward the outside of the hand and extending both fingers. Each person must find the positions that suit him best and should experiment to find the most comfortable, tension-free position. Play a long trill with the hand and fingers in various slightly different positions. If the hand can remain relaxed in any position for twelve to fourteen reverberations, the position will probably do handsomely for three or four.

If a note is missed in either a mordent or a short trill, it is apt to be the third one, because that note is a repetition of the initial, accented note; the finger may fail to relax enough to let the key come up far enough to repeat. The result, a hole in the ornament, may be remedied by attending to that upper finger.

ARPEGGIOS

If the reader feels a bit apprehensive about playing arpeggios on the harpsichord, he should first of all be reassured that long sweeping arpeggios are not ordinarily a part of harpsichord music, and, even if they were, their composers would not have expected them to be played like Chopin's, which were written after the damper pedal had come into use. Baroque keyboard arpeggios are usually limited to two octaves, and most of these move in a direction where the hand passes *over* the thumb, as I have already noted, with a few exceptions in such pieces as the Goldberg Variations and some Scarlatti sonatas.

The usual type of rapid arpeggio that the harpsichordist can expect, then, covers two octaves and either descends in the right hand or ascends in the left. This means that there is a spot in the middle where there will be an enforced détaché note and an unavoidably heavy thumb note. Both, however, are quite easily incorporated into the musical line as an accent—an accent which is usually musically necessary. If the tempo is moderate, even this problem vanishes, because the whole arpeggio *can* be played détaché and often is.

Arpeggio fingering is usually the same on the harpsichord as it would be on the piano. But a little more care must be taken to avoid the lumpiness that results if the arm takes over the duties of any of the fingers. As with arpeggio playing on any keyboard, accuracy and evenness of timing are the main essentials, and the notes before and after the shift of the hand from one octave to another must be played most deliberately. If no attempt at legato is made, and instead the note before the break is accented and released as quickly as possible so as to allot a little extra time for the more cumbersome hand movement which follows, the accent will give the ear the illusion of greater duration than the tone actually has and help cover up the slight gap that follows.

CONCLUSION

There are no correct or incorrect fingerings for the harpsichord. Some fingerings work better than others because of the distinctive physical characteristics of the instrument and its music; but the choice of fingering should be determined by what yields the best results rather than by an attempt at authenticity for its own sake. Good intentions are apt to be sabotaged if the player does not feel at home carrying them out. Early fingering practices were natural to early players, but they are not to us, and anyone who has learned modern fingering would have to do a ridiculous amount of unlearning to replace his techniques with the earlier ones.

In addition, I think we must admit that there is such a thing as progress in the development of keyboard technique. Just as one of the inventions of the nineteenth century was the idea of invention itself, so in virtuoso musical performance the idea existed that technique could be advanced to more and more astounding levels. Any player of a keyboard instrument in our day inherits the considerable advances of the nineteenth century without ever thinking about them; they have been incorporated into quite ordinary pedagogy on the instrument.

The wisest course, then, would seem to be to use the old methods to help us understand how the composer intended his music to be played and then to choose the means at our disposal, old *or* new, that best carry out his intentions. A performance of a piece of music is, after all, a practical matter; with all our progress it is perhaps still, as Saint-Lambert said in 1702, a matter of "convenience and the best way." The practical musician will consider just about anything as a possible solution, as Handel allegedly did. In *Hans Brinker and the Silver Skates* an astonished organist who had just heard Handel play declared that what he had done was impossible, that "no ten fingers on earth can play the passages you have given." "I know it," Handel replied coolly, "and for that reason, I was forced to strike some notes with the end of my nose."[10]

4

ORNAMENTATION

HISTORICAL PERSPECTIVE

Although the harpsichord should not be considered a historical instrument any more than other early instruments that are still used, some historical study is necessary to perform the music written for it. Certain important conventions were forgotten or greatly modified during the period of over a century when the harpsichord dropped out of the musical scene. These conventions must be known to play the music as the composers hoped it would be played. Since most of the conventions involve matters as fundamental as notation, the performer simply cannot know which notes to play and when without knowing the various kinds of notational shorthand used—in short, he must know ornamentation.

Ornamentation in baroque music was not mere decoration added to music that could be expressive without it or merely a way to compensate for expressive inadequacies of the harpsichord—since it is used in other instrumental and vocal music. To be sure, keyboard music is much more profusely ornamented than any other. Ornaments are an integral part of the musical conception. C. P. E. Bach, the great authority on keyboard playing of the eighteenth century and pupil as well as son of an even greater authority, makes this very plain:

> No one disputes the need for embellishments. This is evident
> from the great numbers of them everywhere to be found. They are,

in fact, indispensable. Consider their many uses: They connect and enliven tones and impart stress and accent; they make music pleasing and awaken our close attention. Expression is heightened by them; let a piece be sad, joyful, or otherwise, and they will lend a fitting assistance. Embellishments provide opportunities for fine performance as well as much of its subject matter. They improve mediocre compositions. Without them the best melody is empty and ineffective, the clearest content clouded.[1]

A performance of early keyboard music given without a knowledge of its ornaments is, in a very real sense, not a performance of that music at all.

Putnam Aldrich, in his excellent brief discussion of ornamentation in the revised edition of the *Harvard Dictionary of Music,* remarks that there have been throughout the history of music three kinds of ornamentation: "that left entirely to the improvisation of the performers," "that in which definite ornaments are indicated by some sort of written sign," and "that in which the ornaments are written out in notes."[2] From the nineteenth century until very recently, ornamentation in so-called serious music was almost exclusively of the third type. Some earlier composers, notably J. S. Bach, also wrote a great many ornaments out in notes, especially those that were absolutely integral to the thematic material in which they appeared. But in the music for the harpsichord there is a great profusion of ornamentation of the second type, indicated by various shorthand signs that constitute a notational language unfamiliar to modern players. As we shall see the language is not always completely explicit, for at times it merely indicates limits within which a performer is expected to add ornamentation. Even so, the language must be known in order to know what the limits are.

This chapter is concerned almost entirely with this second kind of ornamentation, some of which is apt to be so unfamiliar to the reader that it will take a distressingly large number of pages to give even a simplified, practical introduction to the subject. But in this area an introduction that is too simplified is not apt to be a true introduction, because it would be misleading and would necessitate un-learning later on.

A keyboard player, especially a pianist, schooled in the music and performance practices of the nineteenth and early twentieth centuries has some initial un-learning or adjustment of ideas and habits to do before feeling at home with baroque and earlier music. In writing of "inequality" *(notes inégales),* Robert Donington remarks:

> Of all the differences between ordinary Baroque habits of performance and ordinary modern habits of performance, the most

radical is their leaving so much more to the performer. It is our tacit assumption that the composer has first claims; it was their tacit assumption that the performer has first claims.[3]

A modern player often feels uneasy about playing notes that aren't there, like ghostly decoration, and hence plays them almost surreptitiously with results that are at best unconvincing. Or, if he has confidence in an ornament, he tends to apply the nineteenth century conception of ornaments, especially trills, as adding brilliance and plays them in a way that makes them leap out of the music, drawing attention to themselves rather than filling out or strengthening the musical line. Unfortunately also, the ornaments known by most modern players have been learned piecemeal, as isolated phenomena rather than as parts of a conventional musical language, whose application is often left to the taste of the performer. As a result, the modern performer often uses the ornaments he knows mechanically, without an adequate sense of stylistic coherence and propriety like an American tourist using French phrases from his guidebook. Most distressing is the nineteenth-century practice of playing ornaments *before* rather than *on* the beat, which omits the dissonance that many ornaments were intended to produce in baroque music and alters baroque rhythmic patterns—which may sound lumpish and jerky to ears accustomed to the smoother flow of ornaments played before the beat.

It must be noted, however, that until recently there was no easy way to get a very clear understanding of ornamentation as a whole. The problem in studying early ornamentation, as noted by Thurston Dart, is not that there isn't enough information but that there is too much.[4] Practically everyone wrote treatises on the subject, recording conventions that were in flux throughout the baroque period. From 1550 to 1800 musicians in Spain, Italy, France, England, and Germany produced over two hundred such treatises, with a good deal of disagreement among them. But ornamentation is to a great extent a matter of taste, and, although a codification of taste is impossible, the fact has never discouraged anyone from making the attempt. I may be making the attempt myself in these pages.

Arnold Dolmetsch concluded in 1916 that it was simply impossible to form any systematic generalizations from the variety of particulars contained in these treatises.[5] There are some ways, however, in which this mass of material may be divided into some general categories. Musicological research of the late nineteenth and early twentieth centuries, especially by Edward Dannreuther and Arnold Dolmetsch, collected a body of material for study of ornamentation that turned out to be literally overwhelming, and it has been only very recently, notably through the work of Putnam Aldrich and

Robert Donington, that we have begun to see the forest that the trees make up.[6] The patterns of order now beginning to emerge are not, I think, invented ones imposed on disparate materials but rather a rediscovery through analysis of patterns existing in the past in the form of general conventions, so well known or tacitly understood that it would perhaps have been difficult to set them down, even if it had been thought necessary to do so.

Comparing sixteenth-century ornamentation with that of the eighteenth century reveals an interesting development. The earlier ornamentation was melodic or rhythmic in function or both; but it was not until the main part of the baroque period that ornamentation with a harmonic, i.e., dissonant, purpose came into full use. Examples of melodic ornamentation can be seen in the ubiquitous sixteenth- and seventeenth-century divisions, many of which were written out in large notes and others put in by the performer without benefit of signs. And the main function of the ornamentation indicated by the two signs in virginal music is probably to supply accent, according to Thurston Dart[7] and Howard Ferguson.[8] Though there is no contemporary evidence to support their conclusions, they as well as others think that the two signs in the *Fitzwilliam Virginal Book,* the / and //, referred to mordents, plain or inverted, slides and short trills beginning on the main note, appoggiaturas, acciaccaturas, or springers, all of them short, crisp, accentual ornaments.

As the period progressed and tonality became more stable, there was greater and greater emphasis on ornamentation with a harmonic, dissonant function. One indication of this can be seen in the lengthening of the appoggiatura from the standard early baroque appoggiatura of moderate length to the long one characteristic of the main baroque. The same trend toward dissonance in ornamentation is evident in the development of the trill. Most sixteenth- and seventeenth-century sources seem to indicate a strong preference for trills beginning on the main note, while the eighteenth-century trill invariably begins on the upper auxiliary.[9] The length of time it hovers on that dissonant note before resolving onto its main note varies with the length of the main note and the character of the passage, but the dissonant auxiliary is always there in a more or less prominent capacity.

As the tendency grew toward greater dissonance in ornamentation, the earlier purely melodic or rhythmic functions were retained and gradually incorporated into the dissonant context of the harmonically oriented ornamentation, the more complex examples of which approached the floridity of the earlier free ornamentation of Frescobaldi and others. And whereas many of the early ornaments were sprinkled with some abandon through the music, to be added or not as a matter of taste or even whim, the later ornamentation grew in importance to become an integral part of the music.

The composers themselves felt this very strongly, and many of them wrote out fairly elaborate tables and instructions on how to perform the ornaments in their music. The French were particularly meticulous about this and quite distressed when performers didn't pay enough attention to their admonitions. In the preface to his third book of clavecin pieces, Couperin speaks out strongly against performers who ignore the directions he has taken such pains to give them in the playing of his ornaments and calls their negligence "unpardonable."[10] Such impatience in print must have been prompted by some fairly sloppy playing of his music.

Arnold Dolmetsch and others have mentioned the ways in which an ornament may affect the melody, rhythm, or harmony of a passage, but it was not until recently that writers on ornamentation have made a full assessment of the functions of ornaments and a detailed enumeration of their characteristics in each functional category. This is a valuable guide for, as Donington remarks, "If we know what an ornament is put there to do, we are more than half way to knowing what to do with the ornament."[11] He lists the three main functions, melodic, rhythmic, and harmonic, and a fourth of lesser importance, the coloristic. Ornaments that are primarily melodic in function may appear either on or between beats, are little accented, and are long and smooth enough to fill in all or most of the duration of the main note; turns are an example. Ornaments that are primarily rhythmic in function usually appear on the beat (or on a syncopation), are sharply accented, and are short, taking little time from their main notes; mordents, slides, and acciaccaturas are examples. Ornaments that are primarily harmonic in function *must* appear on the beat, are firmly accented, and are long, "long enough to delay their resolution on their main notes expressively, and at times to push those main notes right off their own beat and into the space afforded by an ensuing rest."[12] Cadential trills and long appoggiaturas are the main examples. It is possible for an ornament to have more than one function at a time, but where this is the case, one function is usually paramount and the others subordinated to it.

Like the animal kingdom, the great profusion of ornaments is more easily understood if it is classified and considered categorically. Relationships among different kinds of ornaments can then be more readily seen and their functions more easily understood. There are various ways in which ornaments can be classified. One is that used by Robert Donington in his invaluable book *The Interpretation of Early Music,* where ornaments are grouped into four families: (1) the appoggiatura family, (2) the shake family, (3) the division family, and (4) compound ornaments.[13] This grouping is based on the form and content of the various ornaments.

Another grouping might reflect more directly the historical development and general musical function of the ornamentation: (1) ornaments that embellish single notes of importance, such as the ornaments that came into prominence in the late seventeenth century and flourished in the eighteenth century and (2) ornaments that fill in the spaces between important notes, such as ornaments that flourished largely in the sixteenth and seventeenth centuries.

This is not to say, of course, that there were no ornaments embellishing single notes in the earlier period or ones filling spaces between important notes in the later period. Short accentual ornaments do embellish specific notes in the music of the English virginalists, although they are not integral to it; and there is a good deal of melodic ornamentation found in the music of the later period, which is similar to that in the divisions but usually written in large notation. It is the ornamentation of the first category that is the most characteristic of the main part of the baroque, whereas the divisions account for much of the particular flavor of sixteenth- and seventeenth-century music.

The reason for categorizing ornaments historically lies in the music itself. As Dolmetsch remarked, appoggiaturas and shakes have meaning only in the context of *concordant* harmony,

> which they transform and enrich by adding to one of the elements of the chord the flavor of the discord next above it: the fourth to the third, the sixth to the fifth, the seventh to the sixth, the ninth to the octave.
>
> The divisions, on the contrary, do not alter the notes of the subject or counterpoint. They repercuss and embroider them, they fill the spaces between them with passing-notes, but they have to start from and return to them. It is possible, and indeed frequent, to play both the subject and the division together, an impossible thing with the ornaments of the succeeding period.[14]

For my purposes, I think it simpler to consider ornamentation according to the historical-functional categories—ornaments that embellish notes as opposed to those that fill in between notes—because this grouping seems to me to make it easier to focus more direct attention on what the ornaments do musically. In this grouping the family of compound ornaments in Donington's classification can be assimilated to two other families, since ornaments like the trill that begins with an appoggiatura and ends with a turn can be discussed functionally under trills with prefixes and suffixes. The serious student should of course consult Donington's book, to which I am heavily indebted, as is indicated by my use of his "families" in modified form.

We shall now get to the details. I will concentrate on ornaments of the first category: those embellishing single notes. These are more common and the signs for them most mystifying to the uninitiated. I will also include a short discussion of ornaments in the second category, the divisions, which I hope will supply some helpful background for them. Divisions, however, involve conventions of improvisation, and a full discussion of that matter is beyond the scope of this little book. If the interested player steeps himself in the traditions of other kinds of ornamentation, he will probably find the improvisation for divisions coming to him quite naturally.

ORNAMENTS THAT EMBELLISH SINGLE NOTES

Appoggiaturas

The ornaments that may be classified as appoggiaturas include: (1) the appoggiatura proper (which includes the early appoggiatura of indeterminate length, the long appoggiatura, and the short appoggiatura), (2) the passing appoggiatura, (3) the double appoggiaturas (which include the simultaneous double appoggiatura, the slide, and the disjunct double or compound appoggiatura, (4) the acciaccatura, and (5) the appoggiatura combinations. I will discuss one of these appoggiatura combinations—the appoggiatura with mordent. The other combination, the appoggiatura with trill, will be treated in the section on trills.

The appoggiatura had such an impact on the music of the entire baroque period that one cannot help but wonder what that musical era would have been like without it. Its influence pervades the whole period and its development from a primarily melodic ornament to a strongly harmonic one is entwined with concerns of fundamental importance to the history of music at that time.

C. P. E. Bach's rather eloquent testimonial about it enables us to glimpse a contemporary estimation of its worth:

Appoggiaturas are among the most essential embellishments. They enhance harmony as well as melody. They heighten the attractiveness of the latter by joining notes smoothly together and, in the case of notes which might prove disagreeable because of their length, by shortening them while filling the ear with sound. At the same time they prolong others by occasionally repeating a preceding tone, and musical experience attests to the agreeableness of well-contrived repetitions. Appoggiaturas modify chords which would be too simple without them. All syncopations and dissonances can be traced back to them. What would harmony be without these elements?[15]

This ornament, which gave baroque music so much of its characteristic flavor and the far-reaching effects of which supplied so much of the poignant expressiveness of nineteenth-century music, had its spiritual origins in the suspensions of sixteenth-century polyphony. Practically speaking, however, its keyboard application emerged from much more humble beginnings, as a lute player's grace. The lute player's appoggiatura was short, and Thomas Mace's directions (1676) on how it should be played on the lute give us a clue as to why it had to be short: so that the main note, which followed the appoggiatura on the same string, would be audible.[16]

For this reason and others the early baroque appoggiatura was never long; it was not until later on in the period that the long appoggiatura became the standard form. While there were various factors contributing to the lengthening of the appoggiatura, one certainly was the spread of the ornament from the lute to the harpsichord and other keyboard instruments, on which the longer appoggiatura *could* be heard, and heard well, as a dissonance against a simultaneously played bass. And as tonality became progressively more stable, the expressive power of an ornament, which would supply sonorous dissonances to emphasize the sweetness of the new concords, was recognized and used.

The word appoggiatura can be derived from the Italian word "appoggiare," meaning either "to lean" or "to support." Traditionally, commentators have stressed the "leaning on" aspect of the word. But it seems to me that, whatever accepted etymological opinion may be, there is a question here of what is leaning and what is being leaned on. For surely the dissonance produced by the appoggiatura serves to *intensify* the main note to which it is attached and hence supports the main note. So if anything is leaning on anything, it is the main note which is leaning, because it is supported by the appoggiatura. And, with all due respect to tradition, it makes better sense to consider the appoggiatura as supporting the main note because, while the ear is hearing the appoggiatura, the mind is surely hearing the main note. Whatever the literal derivation of its name, however, there is little doubt that the appoggiatura is really an intensifier. And the common usage today of the one term where there were formerly many is all to the good.

Throughout the baroque, terminology for the appoggiatura was profuse and varied and tended to resemble the impressions the blind men had of the elephant. Many of these terms describe a characteristic of the ornament which, apt and even salient as it was, was not the essential feature. Some composers were concerned with distinguishing whether the appoggiatura appeared from above or below: Purcell, in his *Lessons* (1696, posthumous), uses the terms "backfall" and "forefall"; D'Anglebert (1687) uses "cheute descendant" and "cheute montant"; and J. S. Bach in his table for Wilhelm Friedemann's book in 1720 calls the two "accent fallend" and "accent steigend." Rameau in 1724 uses two entirely different names, "coulez" for the descending appoggiatura and "port de voix" for the ascending. Other terms in use indicated primary concern with still other characteristics of the ornament: terms like "half-fall," "beat," "Vorschlag," "Vorhalt," "portamento," and, of course, "appoggiatura."

Like the terminology, the notation of the appoggiatura also lacked standardization in the seventeenth and eighteenth centuries, although there are not as many different signs for the same ornament as there are terms. But there are enough of both to seem unnecessarily confusing to today's performer unless he is aware of the various stages in the history of this ornament, from its beginnings as a piquant spice through its development into staple fare. Marpurg's assessment in 1765 of the then-current practice in notation of the appoggiatura gives some shape to the seeming disorder:

> It is notated either by certain signs or by little subsidiary notes, or properly written out. The first notation is no longer usual, or can only be used with the very shortest appoggiaturas. Formerly, we used for it a simple cross, a hook before the note, or a small, slanting line. When, later on, long appoggiaturas occurred, we began to introduce the small, subsidiary notes, and with them the second notation of this ornament.[17]

As the appoggiatura became more refined, many composers felt that its actual length should be notated. C. P. E. Bach writes:

> Because of the variability, such appoggiaturas have been notated of late in their real length. Prior to this all were written as eighths. At that time, appoggiaturas as diverse as ours were not yet in use.

Today, we could not do without the notation of their real values, for the rules covering their length in performance are insufficient to cover all cases, since all types appear before every kind of note.[18]

This must not have been an entirely satisfactory solution either, because, while the "real length" of the appoggiatura was given, that of the main note was not, as in the following example from C. P. E. Bach.[19]

The problem was solved in the nineteenth century, of course, with the absorption of appoggiaturas into regular notation, another illustration of Donington's statement that "the impromptu figuration of today becomes the written figuration of tomorrow."[20]

All appoggiaturas from early through late baroque, regardless of their length, are played along with the accompanying bass note, *on* the beat, taking their value from the main note to which they are attached. This is a very important point and one that cannot be stressed too much to the modern player who is used to playing appoggiaturas *before* the beat, in the nineteenth-century manner, and lets this practice run over into his playing of baroque music. An additional factor which *visually* tempts such players is that the little note looks so insignificant in the score that they take it at face value and sneak it in just before the beat. If a player thus tempted will remember that playing the appoggiatura before the beat changes it from an ornament with a harmonic function to one with a melodic function and therefore cuts its effectiveness to practially nothing, he is more apt to follow the rules for baroque performance and play the little note (or sign) boldly and squarely *on* the beat.

Let us now turn to a consideration of the ways in which the appoggiatura can move to its main note. This movement is relatively free from restrictions, and C. P. E. Bach sums up the possibilities and gives representative examples:

> We can readily see . . . that at times appoggiaturas repeat the preceding note (a), at times they do not (b), and that the following note may lie a step above or below, or it may be separated from the ornament by a leap.[21]

Contemporary authorities also make the point that the purpose of the appoggiatura is to connect notes; therefore, it is always slightly separated from the note preceding and slurred into the note following it. If the player will follow these instructions, playing it as if it were notated as follows, he cannot help but carry out another characteristic of all appoggiaturas, that it should be louder than its ensuing note.

The three kinds of appoggiaturas that can be considered under the heading of the appoggiatura proper are the essential members of the family, and we will consider them first. The standard appoggiatura in the early baroque was the appoggiatura of moderate length; in the main part of the baroque the standard form was the long appoggiatura. Along with the long appoggiatura, as a kind of companion or complementary form of the ornament, the short appoggiatura developed and was used for purposes for which the long form was not suited. The earlier appoggiatura of moderate length did not immediately go out of fashion completely as the other more extreme forms took over, but it was no longer the *standard* appoggiatura.

Available as it was, then, in the short and the long lengths, the appoggiatura of the main and late baroque became a versatile and refined ornament indeed. In the main baroque, the long appoggiatura became a short rhythmic-harmonic force in the music, while the short appoggiatura served a more melodic-rhythmic function, although it provided fleeting dissonance as well.

Long Appoggiaturas

The rules affecting the length of the long appoggiatura in various contexts are few and simple, and agreement on them seems remarkably unanimous among contemporary writers. Donington sums them up concisely:

> From the last years of the seventeenth century onwards, we meet evidence to suggest that the standard appoggiatura now took half the length of an undotted note, two-thirds of the length of a dotted main-note; all the first of two tied notes in compound triple time; and all of a note before a rest.[22]

The following examples illustrate these four rules. The examples are mine, and I have supplied a bass part to make its relation to the appoggiaturas clear.

Sometimes the standard appoggiatura was prolonged, especially during the eighteenth century. C. P. E. Bach comments on this:

> With regard to the rule covering the length of appoggiaturas, there are a few situations in which the ornament must be extended beyond its normal length because of the affect. Thus it may take up more than half the value of the following tone.[23]

This is his example; the interpretation is mine but follows his instructions:

One sign that was seldom used to indicate an appoggiatura of *any* length was the eighth-note with the diagonal slash through its stem ♪ . This sign, common in nineteenth- and early twentieth-century editions of baroque music, is usually incorrect, and when the student encounters it he might question the validity of the whole edition and seek a more reliable one.

The long appoggiatura is not difficult to define because its duration in various contexts can be described in terms of simple arithmetical units. Because the short appoggiatura, on the other hand, has a much narrower range of variation, the rules for its length cannot so easily be described arithmetically, and thus it becomes more often a matter for the ear to settle. Donington's statement about the short appoggiatura defines its limits:

> The short appoggiatura varies in length from the shortest performable, at the minimum, to a quarter or more of its main note according to the context, the maximum being, however, always shorter than would sound like a long appoggiatura in that context.[24]

So many contemporary writers stress the fact that the ornament should be played as short as possible, frequently alluding to it as the "unvariable" appoggiatura, that it must have been played very short most of the time.

Agricola, writing in 1757, is one who stresses this point:

> Some appoggiaturas are quite short, and no matter what the value of any notes they precede, or what the tempo, they are of *uniform* value. They absorb as little as possible of the duration of the main note. Yet it is understandable that they occur mostly only before short notes, because *their purpose is to increase the animation and brilliance of the melody.* [The italics in this sentence are mine.] If therefore in a fast tempo an appoggiatura should precede each of the four following melodic figures:

> These appoggiaturas should be executed not as sixteenth notes but as thirty-seconds, in order that the listener may not hear the following figures instead:

> which would be against the intention of the composer, if otherwise he be accustomed to write correctly and precisely.[25]

C. P. E. Bach agrees with Agricola. He says, "In execution some appoggiaturas [long ones] vary in length; others [short ones] are always rapid."[26] His terminology in itself suggests his meaning: while he refers to the long appoggiatura as either merely an "appoggiatura" or "variable"[27] appoggiatura, he calls the short appoggiatura "unvariable."[28]

C. P. E. Bach's summary of its uses follows with his example:

> It is wholly natural that the unvariable short appoggiatura should appear most frequently before quick notes (Ex. a). It carries one, two, three or more tails and is played so rapidly that the following note loses scarcely any of its length. It also appears before repeated (b) as well as unrepeated (c) long notes. Further, it is found in caesurae before a rapid note (d), and in syncopated (e), tied (f), and slurred passages (g). . . . Example h with an ascending appoggiatura is better when the ornament is played as an eighth. For the rest, [and here he again draws attention to the shortness of all the other examples] the short appoggiatura remains short even when the examples are played slowly.[29]

He adds other examples:

> In an Adagio their expression is more tender when they are played as the first eighth of a triplet rather than as sixteenths. . . . Appoggiaturas before triplets must also be played quickly so that the rhythm remains clear (d) and distinguishable from that of (e). When the appoggiatura forms an octave with the bass it is played rapidly because of the emptiness of the interval (f). On the other hand, it is often prolonged when it forms a diminished octave (g). It remains short when it is substituted for a cadential trill (h).[30]

Among the examples given above, it is interesting to note that there are two exceptions to his stress on the shortness of the short appoggiatura: one occurs in an adagio, the other in the dissonant diminished octave. The conclusion we can draw from this evidence is that the short appoggiatura is usually played very, very short. I would like to add, however, that wherever it seems to have a jarring effect, or otherwise seems out of place, it should be lengthened appropriately.

I have listed the habits of the short appoggiatura in detail because it is mainly by their habits rather than by their appearance that they can be recognized. Their notation is, unfortunately, not always different from that of the long appoggiatura. We are told that they are written with one, two, or three tails, but since the long appoggiatura also frequently as one tail, it is only the two- or three-tailed appoggiatura that we can be sure about. Since composers are more prone to write one tail than several, much of the responsibility is still left with the performer. Lest all this discussion about the short appoggiatura put undue emphasis on *its* importance, as compared to the long appoggiatura, I would like to remind the performer that, since the preferred appoggiatura in the eighteenth century was the long one, he is safer to use it when in doubt.

The passing appoggiatura is really not an appoggiatura at all, although it was called by that name in the eighteenth century. It is a passing note, as shown by the following definition and examples from Johann Joachim Quantz's famous treatise on flute playing:

> *Passing appoggiaturas* occur when several notes of the same value descend in leaps of thirds. . . .

When performed they are expressed as illustrated. . . .[31]

They can be confusing, however, because they look like normal appoggiaturas. Authorities of the mid-eighteenth century disagree so violently on whether or not this ornament even has a right to exist, except in very limited circumstances, that I shall not attempt to resolve the matter here. It seems to have been in vogue for a very short time and probably attracted the annoyed attention of contemporary writers because it was overused, usually in the wrong places. (C. P. E. Bach refers to is as "repulsive.")[32] For the most part, I think the student can safely ignore it until he has enough experience to feel strongly about where to insert it properly.

Now that we have discussed the various forms of the appoggiatura that involve one accessory note, I would like to give an example written by Quantz to illustrate them:

Quantz makes it clear that he wants his readers to use the example in a practical manner:

> If you wish to be convinced of the necessity and effectiveness of appoggiaturas, play this example first with the designated appoggiaturas, then without them. You will perceive very distinctly the difference in style.[33]

The following example is my interpretation of Quantz's example but carries out his intentions:

17

Now that the reader has carried out Quantz's wishes by playing this example with and without appoggiaturas, he should play it once more, this time placing all of the appoggiaturas just before the beat as a player used to nineteenth-century editions might do. This should convince him that they belong *on* the beat.

Double Appoggiaturas

Now that we have covered the forms of the appoggiatura which involve *one* accessory note, let us turn briefly to the forms of the ornament which involve two: double appoggiaturas. There are three kinds of double appoggiaturas: (1) one in which two appoggiaturas occur simultaneously (the simultaneous double appoggiatura), (2) one in which the accessory notes are conjunct (the slide), and (3) one in which the accessory notes are disjunct (the disjunct double appoggiatura).

The simultaneous double appoggiatura acts like a single appoggiatura, except that it consists of two notes a third or a sixth apart.

The slide was in common usage from the end of the sixteenth century throughout the baroque. It may make its approach from a third above or below, and should be played rapidly and, like other appoggiaturas, on the beat. The most frequent misdemeanor musicians commit with the slide is to play it before the beat, which weakens its strongly rhythmic character. It can be notated in various ways:

A form of the slide, used by the French clavecin composers and applicable only to the keyboard, is that in which the first note is held:[34]

The disjunct double appoggiatura is not a very important ornament, since its use is limited chiefly to the gallant style,[35] but it is encountered occasionally. This ornament differs from other appoggiaturas in that even though it is played firmly on the beat, it is played more softly than the main note.

C. P. E. Bach tells us that:

> The compound appoggiatura may be applied to a note in two ways: First, the preceding tone is repeated and succeeded by the step above the principal note; second, the tone below and the tone above are prefixed to it. . . . Both types are clearly recognizable in the illustrations. . . . The first type is less rapid than the second, but both are played more softly than the principal tone.[36]

Actually, this last suggestion is an impractical one, especially on the harpsichord, and, as Donington suggests, the appoggiatura no doubt often took the accent.[37]

The matter of the acciaccatura involves semantic distinctions more than anything else. Most discussions of this ornament seem confusing, including, unaccountably, Donington. The confusion originates, it seems to me, because eighteenth-century writers on the ornament use the word "acciaccatura" to describe the musical effect and the word "mordent" to describe how to play it—except for Geminiani who uses the word "tatto" (literally, "touched") for the technique instead.

Actually, the real definition of acciaccatura could be "a mordent-like ornament played in a chord to introduce dissonance into it." Considered from a technical point of view, the ornament is a mordent; from the harmonic (listener's) point of view, it is an acciaccatura. There is much confusion on the point, but, if this distinction is kept in mind, the matter can remain clear.

The practice of inserting dissonant tones into arpeggiated chords was a common one well before the mid-seventeenth century, but the first known account of this practice that has come to light is that in Francesco Gasparini's *The Practical Harmonist*,[38] a manual for students written in 1708. He devotes part of a chapter to playing acciaccaturas and carefully describes how this is to be done. He begins with the manner in which the consonant chord is played:

> In order to perform the accompaniments of recitatives with some
> degree of good taste, the consonances must be deployed almost like
> an arpeggio, though not continuously so.[39]

Then he proceeds to the manner of playing the dissonant note or notes, using the word "mordent" to describe the technique:

> In breaking a full chord as I have described, one can touch
> fleetingly in the right hand on the semitone just below the upper
> octave. For example, in harmonizing G . . . the upper octave is
> played by the ring finger, and so one strikes the F-sharp with the
> third finger. Play it with a certain quickness, in the form of a
> mordent, sounded on, or rather a little before the beat and released

immediately, so that it adds a certain grace rather than offending the ear. It is called a mordent because of its resemblance to the bite of a small animal that releases its hold as soon as it bites, and so does no harm. This same mordent may also be played next to the key that forms a third in the right hand. . . . For the sake of clarity, I shall illustrate this as best I can in tablature. Notice that all the notes placed between the barlines are played together at a single stroke.[40]

Note that he has designated the dissonant notes played "in the form of a mordent" with the letter "m."

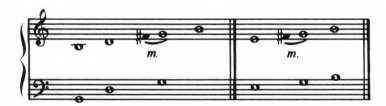

Then he continues with other examples of dissonant notes, now using the word "acciaccatura" for the first time:

Sometimes a certain dissonance is used which consists of an acciaccatura of two, three or four notes one close upon the next.[41]

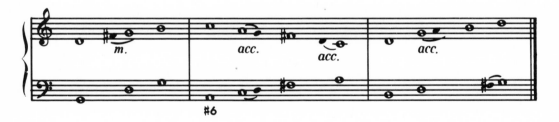

At this point it becomes apparent that, without informing his reader of his intent, Gasparini has decided to use both "mordent" and "acciaccatura" for the dissonant notes here, "mordent" for those which are a half step away from their notes of resolution and "acciaccatura" for those a whole step away. This particular distinction between the two terms for the dissonant notes is not found elsewhere, and Gasparini himself is not wholly consistent about it, as an examination of his "m" and "ac" marks will reveal.

Francesco Geminiani also distinguishes between the ornament itself (acciaccatura) and the manner in which it is played ("tatto") when he says in *A Treatise of Good Taste in the Art of Musick* (1749):

> The Acciaccatura is a Composition of Chords as are dissonant with respect to the fundamental Laws of Harmony; and yet when disposed in their proper place produce that very Effect which it might be expected they would destroy.

He continues by saying that every performer should master this "delicate and admirable secret" by using the examples he has included in the book:

> The Example which follows, has however something in it peculiar, as it serves to specify a signature called Tatto, which has a very great and singular Effect in Harmony, and which is perform'd by touching the key lightly, and quitting it with such a Spring as if it was Fire.[42]

It seems clear here that Geminiani uses "tatto" as others use "mordent."

C. P. E. Bach never talks about the acciaccatura at any length, but merely gives an example of "an arpeggio with an acciaccatura."[43]

The acciaccatura in J. S. Bach is either written out in full or indicated by diagonal markings similar to the slide marks in the above example.

C. P. E. Bach treats the ornament resulting from the same technique

Gasparini and Geminiani have described as "a very short mordent," notating it thus as does Marpurg.[44]

There has been some question about whether the thick dissonant bass chords that appear in some Scarlatti sonatas should not be played in the manner outlined above by Gasparini and Geminiani, because of the acciaccatura-like notes they contain. Ralph Kirkpatrick argues convincingly in favor of playing them as solid chords, supporting his contention with an illuminating analysis of Scarlatti's harmony.

> The acciaccatura of Scarlatti's harpsichord pieces, . . . is based on a different principle, one generally not of momentary decoration or spicing, but rather an organic principle, one of internal pedals and superposition of chords. Hence Geminiani's prescriptions for short playing of acciaccaturas are not generally applicable to Scarlatti. . . . In many cases there is every evidence that the clashing notes, as representing internal pedals or organic strands of harmony, should be sustained as long as possible.[45]

On the arpeggiation of Scarlatti's chords, he states:

> Many a chord will sound richer and fuller when imperceptibly broken than when all the notes are struck at once. Yet the softening of certain chords in Scarlatti should not be overdone; especially some of the acciaccatura dissonances sound all the more startling and intentionally brutal when struck all at once.[46]

In the nineteenth century the term "acciaccatura" came to mean the same as "grace note," but that meaning is not appropriate to the harpsichord repertoire.

Appoggiaturas in Compound Ornaments

Appoggiaturas frequently appear in combination with other ornaments, and there are two particularly common examples of this: (1) the prolonged appoggiatura from above followed by the trill, which is discussed with other forms of the trill, and (2) the long appoggiatura from below followed by the mordent. The appoggiatura-mordent combination was such a common one in the eighteenth century that some authorities declared it to be indispens-able. All composers used it extensively, and Couperin includes it among the relatively few ornaments in his table. His term for it is "port de voix simple."[47]

As the example shows, the ornament is played on the beat; the appoggiatura take its full value before it is followed by the mordent. C. P. E. Bach says of this ornament that the mordent should be performed lightly, so that the appoggiatura can diminuendo into its resolution, as all appoggiaturas should do.[48]

APPOGGIATURAS IN THE MUSIC OF THE ENGLISH VIRGINALISTS

There are only two signs for ornaments in the *Fitzwilliam Virginal Book,* the single slash and the double slash, and there are no surviving contempo-rary English treatises on keyboard playing. Although we cannot be certain of the exact meaning of these two signs, Thurston Dart has suggested that the slide from below and the appoggiatura were probably two interpretations for the single slash, and the acciaccatura was probably one interpretation for the double slash.[49]

Trills

Trills are the most common of all ornaments and the most indispensable to the harpsichordist's art. Quantz went so far as to say that "if an instrumentalist or singer were to possess all the skill required by good taste in performance, and yet could not strike good shakes, his total art would be incomplete."[50]

Trills are also the most complex of the ornaments since they are capable of the most variation. Basically, the trill is nothing more than the alternation of the main note with an auxiliary note a semitone or a whole tone above it. But the number of repercussions, the kind of prefix which precedes them, and the kind of suffix that connects them with the rest of the phrase are all variables that depend on the expressive purpose of the trill itself and the musical context in which it appears.

A trill may be so short as to be a mere accent, or it may be as much as several measures in length, standing apart from the musical line itself to add a considerable dash of color to the musical fabric. Or it may be any of a number of lengths in between, appearing as an integral part of the musical phrase melodically, rhythmically, and harmonically. It is this last type of trill, the one of variable length, that is the hardest to describe, to teach, and to learn, because its successful performance depends ultimately on the musicality of the player.

Much confusion has resulted from verbal and tabular explanations of the trill, both in baroque treatises and in those of the twentieth century. In the baroque period there were several contributing reasons for this: one was the use of many different symbols, terms, or both, for the same thing; another was imprecise or impressionistic notation, which made no attempt to convey the rhythmical flexibility of a trill or even to set down the approximate number of repercussions required. (Often an unrealistically large number of repercussions was shown for the time alloted to them.) And, finally, whenever musicians and composers, baroque or modern, talked about trills or attempted their classification, they used overlapping categories that further clouded and complicated the subject.[51]

But whatever the disparity in meaning of the profusion of signs, words, and notes that were used to convey the subtleties of variation in the ornaments generally classed as trills, musicians of both the eighteenth and the twentieth centuries all seem to be concerned with the same main points: (1) the length of trills; (2) the parts of trills which have prefixes and terminations; and (3) the rate of movement of trills and whether steady or accelerating. This discussion will bear on these points.

The signs used in this chapter will be only the most common ones, which are listed below. Once the student is used to interpreting these, he will find it very little trouble to absorb the other less common ones.

1. The commonest signs for the trill are: tr, t, ∿ and ⌁ . (The number of bumps in the wavy line does not necessarily indicate differences in length.)

2. The prolonged appoggiatura is most often indicated by the vertical slash at the beginning of the trill sign: ⌁ . The little note before the main note ♩♩ is also often used. It is important to remember about this sign that it does *not* mean that the appoggiatura is repeated.

3. The sign for the ascending turn as prefix is the curved line from below as the beginning of the trill sign: ⁓ .

4. The sign for the descending turn as prefix is the curved line from above, placed similarly: ⁓ .

5. The sign for the turned ending is either the slash through the bumpy trill sign ⁓ , two little notes, or two notes in regular notation, appearing after the dotted note.

6. The sign for the note of anticipation as the ending is not a sign in the usual sense but is simply the shorter note in regular notation which follows the dotted note. The value given to this note is such as to fill out the beat and is most often either an eighth or a sixteenth note. The player should bear in mind that the note after the dot is part of the ornament, and its exact value should be that appropriate in the ornament rather than its literal notated length. Even though it may be written ♩. ♫ , it is often played as ♩.. ♫ , or even shorter.

For the purpose of clarity in this discussion, I will talk about trills in order of length, beginning with the shortest trills (the half trill and the Trillo) and proceeding to the longer trills. I will consider any trill that is longer than the six-note Trillo to be a full trill. Rather than coin any new terminology of my own (for there is too much already), I will try merely to describe trills and let them speak for themselves in the examples.

HALF TRILLS

The shortest possible trill consists of two rapid repercussions with a stopping point on the main note. C. P. E. Bach calls this trill the "least dispensable"[52] and the most difficult to play. It is known as the short trill, the half trill, or the Pralltriller, all terms meaning the same thing. The signs used are the same as for other trills. It may begin on the beat on the upper auxiliary:

Or it may appear as a tied trill with the upper auxiliary introduced on the previous beat and tied over:

In fast passages where there isn't time for the two complete repercussions, the half trill may omit the upper auxiliary at the start and begin on the main note. The result is a three-note ornament resembling the early baroque upper mordent.

In baroque music however, this ornament should be regarded as a shortened form of the half trill rather than as an inverted mordent (or Schneller), which was introduced by C. P. E. Bach only at the very end of the period and does not represent standard baroque practice at all.[53] See my example below:

Long Half Trills

The trill which is next in order of length after the half trill consists of six notes. It is known by various names, the commonest of which is J. S. Bach's "Trillo" from the only table he ever wrote, that in the *Clavierbüchlein vor Wilhelm Friedemann Bach*, 1720;[54] and the most accurately descriptive is Donington's "long half-trill." Its symbol is the same as that for other trills. It is played:

This trill is particularly useful in cadences or on any note where the half trill would sound truncated.

Full Trills

All trills which are longer than the half trill and the Trillo may be regarded as full trills, and this body of complex and infinitely varied trills will be the subject for the remainder of this discussion. (I use the term "full trill" rather than Donington's "continuous trill" because it is the logical counterpart of "half trill.")

First, a distinction must be made between trills that mainly add brilliance and color to the musical line and those that are an integral part of it. Trills which are there chiefly to add color or brilliance achieve their effect by standing out from the line, but trills that are a part of the melodic line have to be set in such a way as to enhance the line as a whole.

The first type of trill is simple, for it is all of one piece, with no definable beginning, middle, or end. Walter Emery calls it a "plain" trill,[55] which is just what it is, consisting entirely of rapid repercussions played at uniform speed. Though it may be of any length, from as few as eight notes to several measures long, it looks basically like this:

An example that shows how this simplest of all full trills fits into a musical context may be seen in Bach's Invention no. 4, measures 18–22:

There is no need for the player to do anything with *this* trill but to play steady repercussions, because Bach has focused attention on the main note so well by means of the repeated C's beforehand and the stop on the tied sixteenth note afterwards that its identity is unmistakable.

The second type of full trill may be considered as an integral trill and is the most complex of all ornaments, because it is the least "ornamental" in the literal sense of the word. Unlike many other ornaments, which are more or less stereotyped and predictable, trills can assume various shapes and appear almost anywhere. They may occur in any melodic context and they may be approached from either direction, whether by step or by leap or from a repeated note. Because of the trill's multiplicity of approaches as well as its various guises, care must be taken to allow the main note that it graces to establish itself enough to make the proper sense in the phrase.

The three-part structure of the integral trill achieves this purpose very well. The three parts consist of (1) the preparation or prefix, (2) the repercussions, and (3) the termination or suffix.[56] In practice these parts are continuous; they are separated here only for the purpose of discussion.

The preparation is the most important of the three parts of the trill. For the trill is there to intensify the expression by means of dissonance, aided by increased melodic and rhythmic activity, and the preparation must introduce the dissonant note convincingly. The nature of the preparation determines whether the trill begins suddenly and dramatically or smoothly and quietly.

There are a number of ways in which the preparation can set up the trill, depending on the amount of attention the entrance of the trill should have.

1. The repercussions can begin immediately, on the initial appoggiatura, without its being prolonged.

2. The initial appoggiatura can be prolonged, to a greater or lesser degree.

3. The previous note (if a major or minor second above the main note) can be tied, becoming the initial appoggiatura.

4. An ascending turn can serve as the prefix.

5. A descending turn can serve as the prefix.

The first three points describe appoggiatura beginnings which make the entrance of the trill explicit; the last two points describe turns as prefixes, which tend to cover up the approach to the trill. The prolonged appoggiatura is the most angular and dissonant of the preparations and consequently has a more dramatic effect, while the turns are more graceful and allow the trill to slide into the musical line in an unobtrusive manner. The appoggiatura is frequently used where the trill is approached by leap, and the turn where the trill is reached by step. The ascending turn is more suitable as a prefix in *ascending* stepwise passages, and the *descending* turn in passages descending by step.

For a greater degree of accent on the appoggiatura, the previous note can be cut short, as in this example from Bach's Invention no. 4, measures 18–19:

Where a smooth beginning to the trill is desired, the approach should of course be legato, as in this example from Bach's Invention no. 2, measure 2:

Whereas the preparation or prefix introduces the trill, the termination aids the transition from the trill proper back into the melodic line; it reinforces the main note on the way by stopping on it or, less directly, by turning around it. The termination may consist of a stopping point on the main note, a connection with the note following the trill, or both.

There are a number of terminations for trills:

1. The trill may end with the stopping point on the main note, with no connecting notes inserted between the stop and the following note.

2. The arrival at the stopping point may be followed by a note of anticipation.

3. The arrival at the stopping point may be followed by a pair of closing notes, which connect the trill with the following note. (Occasionally there are three or more notes after the stopping point, which should be treated in the same way as the usual pair.)

4. The trill may go directly into a turn which proceeds at the same rate of speed into the following note.

5. The trill may end with a turn which stops on *its* last note before continuing on to the following note. (Variants of this termination can occur when the stopping point on the last note of the turn is followed by a note of anticipation.)

Note that no. 5b is a combination of no. 5 and no. 2 and that no. 5c is a combination of no. 5 and no. 3.

Nos. 1, 2, 3, and 5 tend somewhat to set the trill off from the musical line by the pause on the main note after the movement stops. On the other hand, the termination by turn which proceeds nonstop into the following note allows the trill to weave itself back into the musical fabric with no fuss at all.

Now that we have taken the three-part trill apart, let us attempt to put it back together again. Since there are five kinds of preparations and five kinds of terminations that may be combined with an indeterminate number of repercussions played either at uniform speed or accelerating, it is evident that there are far too many possible combinations to set them all down here. Therefore I will merely suggest some of the possibilities:

1. The trill beginning with the unprolonged appoggiatura and ending with the note of anticipation.

2. The trill beginning with the prolonged appoggiatura and ending with the note of anticipation.

3. The trill beginning with the appoggiatura tied over and ending with the note of anticipation.

4. The trill beginning with the unprolonged appoggiatura and ending with the stopping point on the main note.

5. The trill beginning with the unprolonged appoggiatura and ending with the turn going directly into the following note.

6. The trill beginning with the prolonged appoggiatura and ending with the turn going directly into the following note.

7. The trill beginning with the unprolonged appoggiatura and ending with the turn stopping on its last note.

8. The trill beginning with the unprolonged appoggiatura and ending with the stopped turn followed by the note of anticipation.

9. The trill beginning with the ascending turn and ending with the turn as its closing notes.

10. The trill beginning with the descending turn and ending with the turn as its closing notes.
The minimum number of notes for this last trill is ten, for any fewer notes would result in a double turn, which makes no sense at all.

RHYTHM AND SPEED OF TRILLS

It is up to the player to determine what the actual rhythm of the trill is to be, whether the trill is short or very long. In order to do this he must take into consideration the tempo of the piece, whether the trill is to be even or accelerated, the trill's speed, and how long the dissonant note is to predominate. It helps, in determining the degree of dissonance, to try notating your trills in simplified form as appoggiaturas. Thus, a long half trill, which is written: [musical notation] and played: [musical notation] is equated with an appoggiatura that takes up half the value of the main note. And a half trill written: [musical notation] and played: [musical notation] is equated with an appoggiatura that takes up only one-fourth of the main note. Or the full trill in example no. 1 on p. 139 can be equated with an appoggiatura that is three-fourths the length of the main note. Variations are endless.

Compared with the amount of material written in the eighteenth century on other aspects of playing trills, almost nothing was written on their rate of movement. Couperin, however, did clearly state his position on this point:

> Although shakes are indicated by notes of equal value in the Table
> of Graces in my first book [1717], they must nevertheless begin
> more slowly than they end; but this gradation should be imper-
> ceptible.[57]

Although there is a lack of written evidence to prove it, I cannot help but think that trills were frequently accelerated in the eighteenth century just because it is the natural, musical way to play a trill that is an integral part of the musical phrase. It also makes the main note stand out more clearly.

It should be noted from the foregoing examples that acceleration occurs automatically as a consequence of the stopping point on the main note. In addition to this means of slight acceleration, however, there are other more prolonged accelerations possible which can occur over a larger portion of the trill. Two representative examples are notated below:

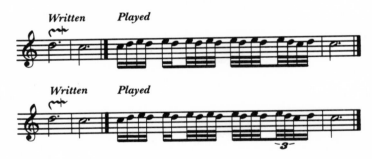

Long cadential trills, such as the following example from measure 15 of Bach's Invention no. 9, require acceleration to avoid squareness in the graceful contours of the piece. Three possible ways of playing this trill are given below. The variations occur as a result of the length of the appoggiatura (upper auxiliary) before its resolution. In example no. 1 the resolution is on the second half of the first beat. In example no. 2 the resolution is on the beginning of the second beat. In example no. 3 the resolution is delayed until the second half of the second beat, making the appoggiatura three-fourths the length of the main note. In spite of the acceleration, example no. 1 is still too angular and uninteresting, partly because the resolution comes too soon and partly because the repercussions begin exactly in the middle of a beat and on a consonance. It is better for the repercussions to begin between two bass notes, as in nos. 2 and 3, rather than with any of them.

Played (3)

Many full trills sound better played at uniform speed than accelerated, of course. Long, fast, coloristic trills, like the one already excerpted from Bach's Invention no. 4 and those in Inventions 10 and 12, are examples of trills which add excitement and brilliance. On the other hand, trills can convey a feeling of calmness or placidity by a relaxed, even movement —those, for instance that consist of eight notes and end with closing notes or a turn like the one in the opening measures of Invention no. 2 or those that begin with the ascending turn and end with closing notes or a turn like the one at the beginning of the Allemande from the French Suite no. 5:

Written

Played

All of these examples are rather clear-cut instances of either accelerated or steady trills. There are many others that are not so obvious and that require the performer's decision as to what the trill should accomplish. Without more conclusive documentary evidence to fit every conceivable situation, however, the most reasonable solution for the performer is to do as eighteenth-century musicians undoubtedly did—to try the trill at uniform speed or as an accelerating trill and decide which sounds best in the musical context.

Another matter in trill playing which has consistently been of concern to musicians is the question of the speed at which trills should be played. All writers substantially agree that they should generally be played rapidly. But when baroque musicians spoke of a rapid trill, they did not mean the kind of speed that often reduced nineteenth-century trills to an indistinct blur. However great the *impression* of rapidity, the notes should still be distinct, a point that Quantz goes to some trouble to make clear:

All shakes do not have to be struck with the same speed; in this matter you must be governed by the place in which you are playing, as well as by the piece to be performed. If playing in a large place which reverberates strongly, a somewhat slower shake will be more effective than a quicker one; for too rapid an alteration of notes is confused through the reverberation, and this makes the shake indistinct. In a small or tapestried room, on the other hand, where the listeners are close by, a quicker shake will be better than a slower one. In addition, you must be able to distinguish the character of each piece you play, so that you do not confuse those of one sort with those of another, as many do. In melancholy pieces the shake must be struck more slowly, in gay ones, more quickly.

Slowness or quickness, however, must not be excessive. The very slow shake is customary only in French singing, and is of as little use as the very quick, trembling one, which the French call chevroté (bleating) . . . a moderately quick and even shake is much more difficult to learn than the very fast trembling one, and . . . the latter must be considered a defect.[58]

Quantz is speaking of singing here in the last sentence, but the same could also be said of harpsichord playing. I think that the moderately fast shake, if played evenly, actually *sounds* faster than one that is quite fast. In a moderately fast shake, the listener hears every note individually. In a very fast and *uneven* trill, on the other hand, the ear hears the unevennesses as accents, each of which groups several notes together and hence slows down the *apparent* speed.

Another factor that the player must keep in mind in determining the speed of trills is the range in which it occurs. Here Quantz is so explicit, and his remarks have so much practical application for anyone playing the harpsichord, that I would like to quote him in full:

With regard to the speed of shakes in general, it might also be mentioned, perhaps unneccessarily, that you must adjust to the height and depth of the notes. Taking the four octaves of the harpsichord as the gauge, I believe that if the shake is struck at the speed described above in the octave C' to C'', it can be struck a little more quickly in the octave above; in the octave below it can be struck a little more slowly and in the lowest octave still more slowly. In the case of the human voice, I might further conclude that the soprano could execute the shake more quickly than the alto and, in the proper proportion, the tenor and bass could execute it more slowly than the soprano and alto. Shakes on the violin, viola, violoncello, and double bass could correspond to the shakes of the four voice parts. On the flute and oboe the shake could be executed as quickly as the soprano executes it, and the shake on the bassoon could have the same quickness as the shake of the tenor. I grant everyone the choice of accepting or rejecting this notion. Although some may censure subleties of this sort as useless I will be satisfied if only a few persons of refined taste, ripe critical sense, and much experience are not completely opposed to me.[59]

Although trills add a great deal of rhythmic and melodic interest to the music, it is generally acknowledged that their most important function is to create harmonic interest by producing dissonance. The cadential trill is a particularly characteristic example of the importance of this function. Donington stresses the importance of dissonance in the cadential trill:

Cadences are an inescapable feature of baroque style, and rather than trying to escape them, it is better to carry them off with conviction, including the almost inevitable trill. That means not only starting the trill in standard baroque manner with its upper note, but *accenting, and often prolonging, that upper note with great assurance and emphasis.* Many modern performers who are aware of the need to start baroque trills with the upper note still do not realize that the *entire stress* should go to it, the remainder of the trill functioning as the merest resolution of the strong discord thus introduced.[60] [Italics mine.]

This is an important point, and if we consider the trill as a series of reiterated appoggiaturas, as many writers do, Donington's instructions for playing the trill should certainly be followed, for they make the identification of the appoggiatura with the trill very explicit. To accomplish the accenting of notes on the harpsichord, however, so as to put the entire stress on the upper, dissonant, note, requires some special consideration, since the harpsichord cannot produce dynamic accents that are strong enough to stand out noticeably in a trill. Therefore, the accents must be accomplished, or at least aided, by other means: by slightly prolonging the note to be accented (an agogic accent) and by grouping the notes so that the upper auxiliary not only falls on the beat but is also the first note on each subdivision of that beat.

If the trill is a long one, an agogic accent at the middle point in addition to the rhythmic subdivision indicated above achieves just as convincing an accentual effect on the harpsichord as the dynamic accent would on the piano. The literal notation of this means of accenting a long trill might look something like this:

The continued repetition of the upper auxiliary on the natural divisions of the beat also reinforces and intensifies the dissonance:

This occurs quite naturally in plain trills, but, in trills with the prolonged appoggiatura as prefix or in any accelerated trill, the arrival at the upper auxiliary on these points in the trill has to be deliberate. Here is one suggested example, which includes both the prolonged appoggiatura and the acceleration:

Small dynamic accents are also possible on the harpsichord and can be used so long as the player doesn't expect too much from them. Trill practice on the harpsichord should routinely incorporate the dynamic accent, not so much for its effect on the listener, for it will not produce a very audible accent at a distance, but because it can be heard—and felt—by the player. A trill of eight notes or longer, and especially if it is very rapid, should be accented at the middle point, and if the trill is much longer, the notes beginning smaller subdivisions should be accented as well:

Long trills, especially if they are very rapid, are much easier to play (because easier to conceive) if divided into manageable groups of notes in this way. And from the listener's standpoint, they acquire a degree of clarity and rhythmic vitality that is apt to be lacking in a trill played merely as so many beats worth of rapid reiterations and accented only at the beginning.

Turns

The turn is an ornament that consists of either four or five notes which turn around the main note. It remained remarkably stable from its sixteenth-century examples, as a group of changing notes, to the nineteenth century, when it became a part of the written-out melodic line. The most common form of the turn in the seventeenth and eighteenth centuries contains four notes, begins on the beat on the upper auxiliary, passes through the main note to the lower auxiliary, and moves back again to rest on the main note. Until about 1750 these four notes were of equal length and took up the whole time value of the written note over which the sign was placed.[61]

In the twentieth century, perhaps partly because of its distinctive sign, the turn has usually been considered an ornament in a class by itself; but in the eighteenth century it was regarded as similar to the short trill, for which it may actually be substituted in tempos too fast to play the short trill clearly. C. P. E. Bach called it "a normal, suffixed trill in miniature,"[62] and told his readers that if they regarded it in this way, they would understand how to use it:

> It may replace the trill in those cases where the latter is difficult to perform owing to the presence of another voice in the same hand. . . . The substitution may be made only on a relatively short note, for others cannot be completely filled in the turn.[63]

For convenience in discussion, turns may be thought of in two groups: accented and unaccented turns (Donington's terms). Accented turns begin on the beat and consist of three forms: (1) the ornament known simply as "the turn" (the commonest form, as mentioned above); (2) the inverted turn (very unusual); and (3) the geschnellter Doppelschlag[64] (simply a five-note turn beginning on the main note, also uncommon in the early eighteenth century).

The sign for the accented turns is placed directly above the note.

The unaccented turn is played on the second half of the beat, carrying the motion into the following beat. C. P. E. Bach states that this turn, for which the sign is placed a little to the right of the main note, goes well (1) on fairly long notes, (2) over ties, and (3) after dotted notes.[65]

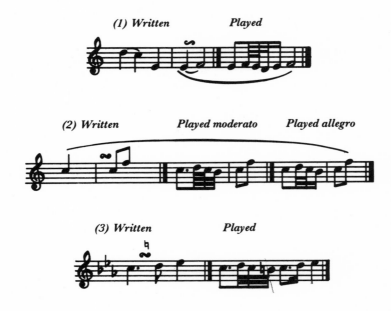

All turns have a melodic function, but the plain turn and the inverted turn have a harmonic function as well, because the initial note is usually dissonant to the harmony note with which it coincides. It is a mild dissonance, however, compared with that provided by any of the longer appoggiaturas or any form of the trill that begins on the upper auxiliary.

The turn is distinctly a keyboard ornament, a fact which is reflected in C. P. E. Bach's statement that, in spite of the great value of this ornament, its symbol is seldom found except in keyboard music. It adapted itself so well to the keyboard, in fact, that it often tended to overuse, which Bach deplores:

> . . . this lovely ornament is almost too obliging. It fits almost everywhere and consequently is often abused. Many seem to believe that the sum and substance of the keyboardist's art consists in introducing turns at every slightest instance.[66]

The turn is often combined with the short trill. This may occur (1) in the compound ornament known as a "double cadence," frequently used by J. S. Bach and his contemporaries:[67]

Or, (2) it may occur as a shorter compound ornament without a name, used frequently by Couperin, and also included by C. P. E. Bach in his *Essay.* Couperin does not include this ornament in his *Methode,* so we must try to imagine what he had in mind for it. Because he most often uses this ornament on quarter notes, the following execution would seem to combine the two ornaments in the most feasible manner:

C. P. E. Bach, on the other hand, regards this ornament in a rather special way as an ornament with a snap; this is consistent with his instructions on the playing of many other turns.

> The turn allies itself with the short trill when its first two notes are alternated with extreme rapidity by means of a snap. The effect of the combined ornaments can be most easily realized by thinking of a short trill with a suffix. This trilled turn introduces a unique charm and brilliance to the keyboard. It is a miniature but lively, enclosed and suffixed trill with which, however, it must not be interchanged, for there is as great a difference between the two as

there is between the short trill or the turn and the normal trill. It
has no distinctive symbol.[68]

Mordents

Arnold Dolmetsch has defined the mordent so succinctly and described
its essence so aptly that I would like to quote his definition here in full:

> This ornament consists of the rapid alternation of a note with the
> next note below it. The interval may be a semitone or a
> whole-tone, according to the scale. The main note is played first,
> and bears the accent. There may be one or more repercussions. As
> this ornament does not alter the melodic or harmonic character of
> the principal note, but rather emphasizes it, it is equally suitable
> to the early contrapuntal and to the later harmonic music. The
> note above the principal is sometimes used instead of the note
> below; the ornament then becomes very similar to the common
> modern shake, but this form had become obsolete in the 18th
> century.[69]

The player should make special note of Dolmetsch's last sentence which
states that the form of the mordent using the upper note, namely the inverted
mordent, ♪♪♩. was not used in the baroque part of the eighteenth century.

The term mordent means "biting," and if the player keeps this in mind,
he will find it easier to play the ornament convincingly. The mordent can be
played in three ways: as a single mordent, as a double mordent, or as a longer
mordent of a greater number of repercussions, to be determined by the
player. The sign is the same for all three forms.

The single mordent is by far the most common of the mordents, and the form from which its name no doubt originated.

Because it emphasizes the melodic note instead of altering it by adding dissonance to it the mordent is a particularly useful accentual ornament on the harpsichord. Composers have used it constantly to clarify the main note and make it more easily heard. J. S. Bach's use of the mordent in the Inventions is typical. If the student would gain an understanding of this ornament and a knowledge of how it differs from the trill, he should study its use in the Inventions. He will find that it is used to bring out notes in passages ascending by step (nos. 3, 5, 10, 15); in ascending leaps (nos. 1, 7, 11); to emphasize main harmony notes (nos. 5, 7, and 12) where the subject is able to acquire the rhythmic and melodic clarity it needs largely through the use of the mordent on the tonic, third, or fifth; and to intensify repeated notes (no. 12). Although Bach doesn't indicate it specifically, the long mordent is very effective on the long notes in no. 3 (measures 26–27 and 30–31), where it sustains the main note, lending the brilliance of a long trill without the dissonance such a trill would add. These particular long notes need reinforcement and clarification rather than dissonant piquancy, and the long mordent is suited to that task.

C. P. E. Bach points out that the mordent is the ornament most often used in the bass, particularly in octave leaps, and that it is also very appropriate in middle notes in chords, where on long notes the mordent may be prolonged with satisfying effect.

Because of the incisive accentual nature of the mordent and its ability to clarify notes to which it is assigned, the player will help it carry out its purpose fully if he will shorten the note before which it appears, introducing a short rest, so that, when the ornament is played, it will not be muddied by any leftover sound from the previous note. The following example from the first measure of Invention no. 5 illustrates this point:

The double mordent has two repercussions and is also played quickly. It does not have quite the explosive effect of the single mordent, and hence it is suitable on longer notes where the single mordent would sound too abrupt and die out too quickly to give the effect of a sustained note. The Sarabande from Bach's French Suite no. 5 is a typical example of the proper place to use double mordents. The notes on the first beats in measures 1 and 5 and the second beat in measure 6 all need the double mordent to make the piece sound quiet, graceful, and sustained, as a sarabande should. Not all of the mordents in the piece should be played double, however, or the movement becomes stultified. After the mood is set, some of the remaining mordents should be single ones. The mordent in measure 2 of this Sarabande is preceded by a sign for an appoggiatura from below. This common combination (see the section on the appoggiatura) is perfectly applicable here in this context of grace and elegance.

In measure 5 of the Loure from the same suite the mordent will sound less rhythmically jarring if it is played double.

In the Bourrée, however, the single mordent is just what is needed on the first beat of the first full measure to start the piece with the required rhythmic vitality.

The long or continued mordent is not found as frequently as either of the shorter mordents. It has the brilliance of a long trill without the trill's extended dissonant sound, as we have seen above in Invention no. 3. The long mordent is also much more rarely used than the long, coloristic trill, but certainly one of the most exciting uses of this ornament is that in the Gigue of Bach's English Suite in D minor, the second half of which is permeated by the brilliance of mordents from one measure to three measures in length.[70]

Unlike the long trill, the long mordent has no termination but merely comes to an abrupt stop on its main note. It needs no termination because the sound of the main note has been clearly heard all the way through the playing of the ornament. One cannot help but compare it to the trill in this respect: In the trill the dissonance is most clearly heard because it is on top; in the mordent, though the note below the main note *is* dissonant, it is not nearly as emphatically heard because it is underneath the main note.

The most common sign for the mordent is ✤ . Couperin includes all three forms of the mordent in his table of signs, though he calls the ornament by its French name, *pincé*. Rameau, on the other hand, uses a symbol that resembles a comma, placing it after the note: ♪, .

C. P. E. Bach and others mention a short short form of the mordent, which is discussed briefly in the section on the acciaccatura. I mention it here because it really is a mordent that has been squeezed together, and as such, it could be useful in a fast passage, or on a short note where there would not be time for even the most adeptly played single mordent. It is played thus:[71]

The mordent is the simplest of all ornaments to talk about. But like the half trill, it requires care and quick fingers (and a properly regulated harpsichord) to play it well.

There are two ornamental signs in the music of the English virginalist composers, the single slash / and the double slash // . These marks appear above or below the note, through its stem, and, in chords, often through the head of the note itself. There is no contemporary treatise which explains these marks, so their interpretation has been left to conjecture, which must continue to serve the purpose until future investigation of the internal evidence or other information supplies more reliable answers.

There has been some agreement among twentieth-century musicologists as to possible specific meanings for these signs. The most frequent suggestion is that the single slash indicates a quick slide from the third below and that the double slash, indicates a mordent, trill or acciaccatura.[72]

The mordent would of course be *either* of the two early baroque forms of that ornament, the upper and the lower; and both the mordent and the trill probably serve this purpose best in their simplest, shortest forms. In addition, the player should heed Thurston Dart's reminder that:

> Merulo (1592) and Diruta (1593) make it clear that at this time all mordents and many trills began on the main note (not on the upper or lower auxiliary), and they were not always played on the beat. Here are two great differences between the practice of the early and late baroque period, worth preserving in modern performances.[73]

Other possibilities regarding the meaning of the signs are (1) that they are often put there merely to call the player's attention to some distinctive point (see note 7 for this chapter); or that (2) they do not stand for specific ornaments (as the + did not in later music) but for types or families of ornaments, and that within these limits the signs might perhaps be translated as ornaments "ad libitum" to emphasize or reinforce the note to which they are attached. The art of ornamentation was in a comparatively rudimentary state at that time, and composers had much less fixed ideas about what specific ornament to apply on a given note. Consequently the performer was left with a great amount of freedom to rely on his own taste within certain conventional limits. What the performer of the sixteenth and early seventeenth centuries would think appropriate is, of course, unknown to us, because the tradition is lost, and therefore we have to rely on information made available by musicological scholarship in order to try to re-create the tradition.

In attempting to re-create this tradition, however, the player must be careful not to confuse one tradition with another. The usual instinct of one who is familiar with music of the late baroque, for instance, but who has played relatively little earlier music, is to use the dissonant ornamentation so suitable in the late baroque and so out of place here. The player must keep in mind that the purpose of the early keyboard ornamentation was to supply accent, to fill in gaps between important notes and to lend emphasis and flourish to cadences. We must rely on educated speculation for our ideas on much of the accentual and melodic ornamentation, but cadential passages that are written out supply many models for cadential ornamentation. Many of these passages are quite florid and some of them include ornaments such as the trill with the turned ending, which continued as a part of the musical language into the eighteenth century.

ORNAMENTS THAT FILL SPACES BETWEEN NOTES

Thus far our attention has been directed to ornamentation of the first classification mentioned near the beginning of this chapter: that which embellishes individual notes. Now we will very briefly consider the second kind of ornamentation: that which connects notes. This ornamentation, called division (or diminution, figuration, or glosas), is less refined and formalized than the first type and consists chiefly of a variety of scale-like fragments, leaps, arpeggios, and the like, although it may also sometimes include short melodic formulas embellishing single notes. Having a connective function, appearing now in one voice, now in another, its effect is often pervasive.

This kind of figuration was such a common feature of music from the sixteenth century until well into the eighteenth that everybody indulged in it, some with taste and even genius and some with no taste at all. When well done it must have been a rare and exciting spectacle for the audience, judging by the willingness of music lovers to travel long distances to hear improvisation by Sweelinck, Frescobaldi, Buxtehude, and others of similar caliber. When badly done, on the other hand, it elicited comments like Zarlino's contemptuous statement about singers who, "wishing to be thought worthier and wiser than their colleagues, indulge in certain divisions that are so savage and so inappropriate that they not only annoy the hearer but are ridden with thousands of errors."[74]

There were many treatises written on improvised divisions, the earliest of which is Diego Ortiz's *Trattado de glosas sobre clausulas y otros generos de puntos en la musica de violones* (1553), which Donington credits with the best sixteenth-century examples of free ornamentation. Fray Tomás de Santa Maria wrote another, *Libro llamado Arte de tañer Fantasia* (1565), which is relatively accessible because musical examples from it are reproduced in the Appendix to Harich-Schneider's *The Harpsichord,* pp. 7–8.[75]

A special application of the term "divisions" refers to the predominantly English practice of combining a harpsichordist playing a ground bass with a solo flute or viol playing a descant or division over it. The most important treatise giving instruction on this technique of playing "divisions upon a ground," and which Donington says contains the best examples of seventeenth-century divisions, is Christopher Simpson's *The Division-Violist* (1659).[76] The entire section from this book that applies to harpsichord playing is reproduced in Dolmetsch's *The Interpretation of the Music of the XVII and XVIII Centuries,* pp. 323–39.

It is not the purpose of this book to give instruction in the performance of divisions, for the ability to do this well depends on a thorough absorption of the conventions of extemporization and ornamentation. The student who would like to gain an insight into this tradition, whether merely for a keener appreciation of its problems or for the purpose of attempting some improvisation himself, should acquire a copy of the accessible and reasonably priced Dover reprint of *The Fitzwilliam Virginal Book* (2 volumes) and read through or study the numerous pieces in it which employ written-out divisions. A random selection of a few pieces in which the divisions are particularly profuse and florid include: Orlando Gibbons's "The Woods so wilde," William Byrd's "John come kisse me now," Thomas Morley's "Goe from my window," John Bull's "Walsingham," and Peter Philips's "Pavana Pagget" and "Fantasia," all from the first volume. There are countless others throughout both volumes of this book, which the student can discover for himself.

After thoroughly familiarizing himself with this musical idiom, the student should then try his hand at embroidering simple folk tunes in like manner, avoiding any attempt to learn or memorize specific figurations or to apply them literally. This practice is entirely consistent with instruction in late renaissance and baroque manuals, such as Thomas Morley's *A Plaine and Easy Introduction to Practicall Musicke* (1597), which directs the composition student to begin his study with sightreading and continue it with "descant," or improvised vocal counterpoint, before composing on paper. The seventeenth- and eighteenth-century music student customarily learned to compose by extemporizing at the keyboard, which for him was a practical matter of improvising harmonies above a figured bass. For a fuller appreciation of the whole tradition of extemporization, of which the playing of divisions was a part, and its significant role in the musical life of the baroque period, see Dart's chapter on extemporization in his *The Interpretation of Early Music.*

5

TEMPO AND RHYTHM

TEMPO

The first practical consideration of any player is that of tempo. Determining the intended tempi of baroque compositions again becomes a matter of deciphering notation. And while more and more editions are coming out that translate the old tempo markings into modern terms, most players will feel on safer ground if they acquire some background appreciation of the problems.

Tempo notation was in a period of transition from the sixteenth to the eighteenth centuries, from the old barless proportional system to the modern system that is based on the constant relative value of notes, has a time signature indicating how many notes of a given value are in a measure, and has a tempo marking indicating how fast they should go. Time signatures were in use by the end of the seventeenth century, but, instead of the single purpose they now have, they were intended to do double duty, to indicate tempo as well as meter. Composers were obsessed with the need for clarifying and standardizing the whole procedure and published a number of tables explaining these tempo-meter markings during the final years of the seventeenth century and the first half of the eighteenth.

Purcell's table from *A Choice Collection of Lessons* (1696)[1] and Michel de Saint-Lambert's table in his *Principes de Clavecin* (1702)[2] were among the first, and J. J. Quantz was still working on the problem in the 1750s, using the pulse rate as a point of reference. Numerous attempts were also made to measure the beat by mechanical means. Father Marin Mersenne initiated the pendulum idea in 1636; his efforts were followed by many other unworkable or cumbersome inventions, some of grandfather clock proportions, culminating in the appearance of Mälzl's metronome in 1816, which settled the matter.[3]

Following the enforced adherence to the old mathematical proportions governing tempo in the sixteenth century, the growing relaxation of the rules in the seventeenth century delighted many musicians, particularly the Italians, who, always ready for something new, were the first to indulge in freely chosen changes of tempo within a composition. Indeed, they seemed to revel in seeing how far they could go, if the constantly shifting tempi of the toccatas of Frescobaldi and others are any indication. As a descriptive aid they initiated the vocabulary of words intended to denote mood, which gradually took on tempo meanings as well and which are still in use today as general guides to tempo.

A stabilizing factor amid all this was the growing popularity of the instrumental dance suite and with it the enormous influence of dance rhythms. The original tempi were those of the dance floor, but as the suite movements acquired more and more sophistication, with the addition of melodic elaboration and irregularities of phrase structure, these tempi became greatly modified. And, in an effort to create some semblance of order from threatening chaos, tables of dance tempi appeared. It is not surprising that there is some lack of agreement among these tables, but they are at least some help in determining comparative speed of movement. Curt Sachs reproduces several of these in his *Rhythm and Tempo* and adds a kind of composite table constructed from four eighteenth-century sources, which he believes shows the standard tempi of French dances in the first half of the century.[4] Howard Ferguson reminds us that in using these tables the performer should know that French harpsichordists often applied the beat to quarter notes rather than to half notes, and sometimes even to eighth notes.[5] One does begin to wonder whether the main benefit today's player might get from consulting these tables is the confidence to disregard them knowledgably.

One conclusion that can be drawn from all of this information, however, is that baroque tempi were not slow and sober. Evidence from all sides indicates the opposite to be true: C. P. E. Bach, for one, states that his father's tempi were "very lively,"[6] and Forkel reinforces this observation when he says that "in the execution of his own pieces he [Bach] generally took the time very brisk."[7] Curt Sachs comes to the same conclusion when he observes that all the tempo tables "show one impressive fact: the vast majority of tempi were speedy, light and gay."[8]

In the end, the player must rely on his own musical judgment and remember that the music must feel comfortable at whatever tempo he chooses. In addition, he must take into consideration that tempo is also dependent on articulation and that a highly articulated performance will sound more lively, because there is more detail to listen to than in a legato one played at the same tempo.

RHYTHMIC NOTATION

The notation of rhythm has always been a difficult matter, much more so than the notation of pitch, and different eras have attempted to solve the difficulty in various ways. Rhythmic notation must always fall short of absolute precision, first of all because it is dependent on a system of mathematical multiples for its written communication, which while it has the virtue of simplicity cannot possibly convey the infinite refinements of real fluidity of movement in time. The problem has always been to make the notation specific enough to convey the necessary detail, while keeping it simple enough not to interfere with ease of reading. In our day we have gone so far toward mathematical exactness that the resultant complexity sometimes makes even mere comprehension an all-engrossing task; baroque musicians on the other hand valued spontaneity in reading and performance to such an extent that they were content with simplicity at the cost of specificity.

The simple solutions they adopted regarding some rhythmic problems may seem to us no solution, for they leave more to the performer's judgment than we are accustomed to. But once we learn the notational conventions they relied on to communicate certain rhythmic patterns, I think it must be agreed that the notation becomes readily accessible, freeing the player's attention for the other things he must be alert to in performing this music.

Inequality

Baroque rhythmic notation often left the performer with a great deal of freedom, ranging from the mere modification of certain aspects of the written notation to the virtual carte blanche he had in the unmeasured prelude. These modifications became more or less codified as notational conventions under the classification of "inequality"—usually referred to as *notes inégales* as noted earlier. These practices are applied to certain pairs of conjunct notes, and have the effect of lending grace to passages that would otherwise sound stiff and foursquare or of heightening the excitement of already moving passages.

There are three types of *inégales: lourer, couler,* and *pointer.* In the first two, notes that look equal are played as unequal; in the third, notes that are dotted are played with an exaggeration of the notated inequality. One might describe the effect of *lourer* as persuasion, that of *couler* as hesitation, and that of *pointer* as exhilaration.

In the *lourer* classification, the most common of the three, ♫ becomes ♫♩ or ♪.♪ . Generally, only notes of one particular value in a given piece of music are eligible for inequality, and this is determined by the tempo and time signature. After a little experience with *notes inégales,* the player will have little difficulty in deciding which note values sound right played unequally; he will soon find that if he tries to adjust notes that already move at too fast a rate, the movement will become jumpy and restless, while if he tries to alter notes that go too slowly, the movement will be awkward and mannered. If he bears in mind that the reason for the alteration is to impart a lilting rhythm to notes that would otherwise proceed dully or stiffly, he will be on safe ground. As an aid, however, it may be helpful to state the guidelines set up during the baroque period, when the rules stipulated the note values ordinarily affected within given time signatures. A table showing this correlation follows:[9]

							Note value
$\frac{3}{1}$							𝅗𝅥 𝅗𝅥
$\frac{3}{2}$							𝅗𝅥 𝅗𝅥 and 𝅗𝅥̄𝅗𝅥
2	3	$\frac{3}{4}$	$\frac{6}{4}$	$\frac{9}{4}$	$\frac{12}{4}$	¢	♫
$\frac{2}{4}$	$\frac{3}{8}$	$\frac{4}{8}$	$\frac{6}{8}$	$\frac{9}{8}$	$\frac{12}{8}$	C	♬
	$\frac{3}{16}$	$\frac{4}{16}$	$\frac{6}{16}$	$\frac{9}{16}$	$\frac{12}{16}$		𝅘𝅥𝅲𝅘𝅥𝅲

Eighths and sixteenths are those which seem to be most frequently played *inégal* in baroque music.

Since the main problem the novice is apt to have in deciding which notes to play *lourer* is their plain-clothes appearance (notational clues are given for both *couler* and *pointer*), it may be helpful to state the cases in which the notes are played just the way they look:

1. When the words *notes égales, martelées, détachées, mouvement décidé* or *marqué* are placed over a piece or a passage.

2. When dots or short lines are written above the notes.

3. In disjunct motion.

4. In triplets.

5. In allemandes, as well as in other pieces where grace and charm would be out of place.

6. In syncopated passages.

7. In passages containing many rests.

8. In repetitions of the same note.

9. In notes appearing in accompanying parts. The performer must use his discretion to decide what is accompanying. Imitative passages or passages of more than ordinary melodic interest, even if not strictly imitative, may seem important enough to be eligible for inequality.

10. In fast tempi. There are borderline cases, of course, in which the performer must decide, as he must in, say, Couperin's "Les Moissonneurs."

11. In slurred passages. Slurred pairs of notes are played *couler,* while a slur over *more* than two notes indicates that they should be played evenly and legato.[10]

The *couler* classification is the least frequently found and is very easy to recognize because the pairs of notes are marked ♪♩ or ♪♩ . Here the rhythm becomes short-long: ♪♩ . If the first note is played very short, like a Scotch snap, the effect is sharp and arresting (as in Couperin's "Le Gazoüillement"); if it is played less short, the effect is to soften and hold back the movement.

In the *pointer* (or *piquer*) classification, the first note of a dotted pair is lengthened so that ♩.♪ becomes ♩..♪ . The dot in baroque music is in any case considerably more flexible than it was to be in the nineteenth century, and the performer of this music should always feel free to lengthen or shorten it a little, as befits the expression of the passage.

Finally, in all three types of *notes inégales* the degree of inequality is left up to the player, who must by careful listening and exercising of his rhythmic judgment develop his musicianship to the point where he is able to play all such passages convincingly.

The surest way to become comfortable with *notes inégales* is to use them. I would advise the reader who has not reached this state to study and play all of the pieces in Howard Ferguson's three volumes containing French music, listed in Appendix B. He has given such clear and explicit directions that the performer who consults and absorbs them will be able to proceed with much greater confidence on his own.

Duplet Against Triplet

Another notational problem which frequently causes confusion is that of equal or dotted duplets in one voice against triplets in the other. Having become used to the legitimate two-against-three cross-rhythm, as well as other notational refinements which arose in the nineteenth century, a modern player is apt to be literal minded in playing an example like this one from the Allegro of Handel's F major Sonata for Violin and Harpsichord:[11]

Actually, the source of the confusion is the baroque use of binary time signatures for ternary ones: 4/4 for 12/8, 3/4 for 9/8, and 2/4 for 6/8. If Handel had written this movement in 12/8 instead of in 4/4 time, the duplets could quite easily have been accommodated to the triplet figures, making his intention clear:

Bach seems to have been less content with the old conventions than some other composers, however, attempting greater precision in rhythmical notation as he did in notation of ornamentation. One may find numerous examples in the two books of the *Well-Tempered Clavier,* for instance, of time signatures such as 9/8, 12/8, and 12/16 (and one each of 6/16 and 24/16) that do allow for exact notation of triplet relationships.

Sometimes this must have seemed more trouble than it was worth, and Prelude no. 5 (*Well-Tempered Clavier,* Book II) is one interesting example of Bach's combining the old practices with the new. He begins the piece with a time signature of 12/8 to accommodate the note values to the triplet subdivision of the pulse that is to prevail throughout. Then he momentarily breaks the flow with a subdivision of that pulse into *two* in measures 2 and 4, notating *those* measures as if the time signature were 4/4:

Actually, if he had wished, he could have conveyed his exact intentions by retaining the dot after the quarter note and adding a bracket over the eighth notes ♩♩ for extra measure, although the slur is a clear indication that he did not want the eighths played unequally. And if he had, he could have carried consistency even further into the many measures like measure 5, where he reverts to easy convention and assumes that the player will assimilate the dotted duplet into the triple. (Any thought this figure might be regarded instead as a case of over-dotting, with the sixteenth note following the dot played against the final sixteenth in the other voice, is clearly out of

the question, unless the performer chooses an irritatingly ponderous tempo.)
It is perfectly clear what Bach means here; the notes are easily read when we
know the rules.

Another interesting example is the first *double* of Rameau's "Les Niais
de Sologne,"[12] written in a time signature of 2, in which pairs of equal
eighths move against triplet eighths throughout. Harpsichordists have been
known to attempt this as an impossible *tour de force* of two-against-three
perpetuo moto, when the duplets should simply be accommodated to the
triplets, thus: ♩♩ . There are many other examples in baroque music.

Unmeasured Preludes

The type of rhythmic notation that allows the player the greatest
amount of freedom is of course that of unmeasured preludes, odd-looking
pieces written as an unbarred succession of white stemless notes held together
to some extent by phrasing marks of various lengths and, later in the period,
sometimes interspersed with rhythmic notation. The unmeasured prelude is
derived from the extemporaneous nature of the lutenist's art and consists
chiefly of the arpeggiated figures characteristic of lute pieces. And sometimes
the prelude is part of a long piece, the rest of which is barred. (See Rameau's
Prelude in A minor, which prefaces a barred gigue section.)[13]

There are no contemporary accounts telling us how to play these
preludes. However, Howard Ferguson has supplied us with some practical
directions on realizing this type of notation, together with suggested
realizations of two preludes, one by Louis Couperin and one by Louis Nicolas
Clerambault, in the two volumes of his *Early French Keyboard Music* (Oxford,
1969). After studying these thoroughly, the reader should then turn to other
unmeasured preludes and experiment with them. They are found in great
abundance in Louis Couperin's *Pièces de Clavecin*[14] as well as in the works of
other French harpsichordists.

6

REGISTRATION

Many players coming to the harpsichord for the first time are delighted to discover registration, which they feel they must use because it is there. Some players never get over this and overuse, or misuse, these enticing "attachments" for their surface appeal and as a compensation for the lack of the piano's instant dynamics, indulging in too frequent changes which soon tire, bore, and confuse the listener. This sound-effects approach to registration fails to recognize its main purpose, which is to clarify the musical structure through variation of tone quality and quantity.

The essential registration on a harpsichord can be contained on one manual. The basic registers are two eight-foot stops, which can be used as contrasting colors and in combination. To these basic stops other features are often added, such as a four-foot stop, tuned an octave higher; a buff stop, which damps one set of eight-foot strings; sometimes a third eight-foot stop with soft leather plectra; and, of course, the sixteen-foot stop. But with only two eight-foot stops we can get an enormous variety of sound, especially from a harpsichord scaled on historical proportions, because the principal eight-foot stop has a great tonal variety throughout its compass.

Some harpsichords have a second manual, which usually consists of one eight-foot stop equipped with a buff. The second manual adds another dimension to the expressive possibilities of the harpsichord, but it is not an essential feature; most of the music written for the instrument can be played without it. In fact, the second manual was originally used to transpose, and the "expressive" second manual was introduced only comparatively late in the period.

The various registers can be operated either by hand stops or by a more elaborate pedal mechanism. Most harpsichords in the baroque period were equipped with hand stops, which meant the composer had to provide time—in the form of rests—for the performer to change the stop if he wished a change of color anywhere but at the end of a section. Some early instruments had the hand stops located far enough around the side that the player could not reach them from his playing position at all.

Perhaps I can best illustrate the tonal resources at the player's command by attempting to describe the different sounds available on the "typical" eighteenth-century harpsichord of French or Flemish design. These same sounds are similar to those of a modern historically oriented harpsichord, such as those made by Hubbard or Dowd, so they are at the disposal of today's players, too.

The principal eight-foot stop has the richest degree of variety, because the jacks are placed at the optimum plucking point on the strings. Its qualities, which vary from one part of its range to another, might be described as full, dark, and sonorous in the bass, as mellow in mid-range, and as fluty or even bell-like in the extreme treble. The differences among them are noticeable enough that an uninitiated listener might think they come from different registers. This makes the mechanical changing of stops much less necessary than it otherwise would be.

The second eight-foot stop, sometimes referred to as the "nasal" eight, has an edgy, more penetrating sound which contrasts very noticeably with the rounder sonority of the principal eight-foot and which results from the jack being closer to the end of the string. In contrast to the principal eight-foot, its tone quality is more uniform from one end of its range to the other.

The character of the two eight-foot stops will determine the character of a harpsichord, and two eight-foots such as those I have described—interesting by themselves and distinct from each other yet complementary—will provide the player with a wealth of resources for fine definition of voices as well as great coloristic variety with a minimum use of stops. The principal eight-foot should be voiced to sound a little louder than the nasal eight-foot.

The addition of the buff stop, which partially damps the strings very close to the end with little pads of felt or leather, produces a plucked, lute-like tone quality, as well as a softer tone than the strings will produce without the buff.

The four-foot stop has quite another tone quality than either of the eight-foots. It might be described as sweet and lyrical, although rather unsubstantial in the lower and middle ranges and tending toward the shrill in the extreme treble. It is occasionally effective as a solo stop, but it is mainly used in combination with either or both eight-foots to lend brilliance and sharpness of outline. The combination of either eight-foot with the four-foot has a transparent lustre and vitality; the combination of both eight-foots with the four-foot has brilliance and power, although there is some loss of clarity, compared with the eight-foot–four-foot mixture.

The total tonal possibilities on an instrument with just three sets of strings that are playable from one manual are more than adequate. When referring to specific sets of strings to designate registrational combinations, I will designate the principal eight as 8_1, the nasal eight as 8_2, and the four as simply 4. In general discussion, I will abbreviate eight-foot as 8' and so on. Using this terminology, the options open to the player on a one-manual instrument with three sets of strings would be indicated as follows: 8_1; 8_2; 4; $8_1 8_2$; $8_1 4$; $8_2 4$; $8_1 8_2 4$; 8_2 + buff—a total of eight possibilities.

We can regard a harpsichord with the sounds just described, then, as possessing a basic working palette that is adequate for most purposes. Many eighteenth-century and present-day harpsichords have additional features, however, that extend their range of expression. Probably the most useful and desirable extra is a second manual, not just because it increases the number of tonal possibilities but because it also allows the player to use two different tone qualities at once. When registration is indicated for a two-manual instrument, the lower manual will be designated as I and the upper manual as II. The figures above the horizontal line will show the manual and registration played by the right hand; those below the line will show that played by the left. Thus, $\dfrac{\text{I } (8_1 4)}{\text{II } (8_2)}$ shows that the right hand is to play the $8_1 4$ on the lower manual, and the left hand the 8_2 on the upper manual. If both hands are to play on the same manual, the indication will simply be: I $(8_1 4)$ or II (8_2) and so on.

The following additional tonal combinations are possible with a two-manual instrument which has two 8's and a 4' playable from the lower manual, and the nasal 8', (one 8' coupled) equipped with buff stop that is playable from the upper:

$$\frac{\text{I } (8_1)}{\text{II } (8_2)} \qquad \frac{\text{I } (8_1)}{\text{II } (8 + \text{buff})} \qquad \frac{\text{I } (8_1 4)}{\text{II } (8_2)} \qquad \frac{\text{I } (8_1 4)}{\text{II } (8 + \text{buff})} \qquad \frac{\text{I } (8_1 8_2 4)}{\text{II } (8_2)}$$

In addition the 4' stop can be played an octave lower as another solo 8' quality, against the nasal 8' or against the nasal 8' buffed. Still other combinations are possible, but impractical because of the difficulty in hearing them. The following are examples:

$$\frac{\text{I} \ (8_1 8_2 4)}{\text{II} \ (8_2 + \text{buff})} \qquad \frac{\text{I} \ (8_1 8_2 + \text{buff})}{\text{II} \ (8_2 + \text{buff})}$$

The simultaneous use of two manuals is an advantage of greater consequence than the multiplicity of stop choices, because it allows differentiation of the horizontal elements in the music, whether they are melody and accompaniment or two individual polyphonic lines. Pieces specifically written for two manuals, such as certain of the Goldberg Variations, can cross and re-cross each other with a freedom impossible in single-lane harpsichord traffic. An additional bonus with a second manual is that some delightful sound effects can be produced with the alternation of the same pitch on the two manuals, an effect similar to the alternation on a violin of the open string with a stopped string on the same pitch. Examples of this occur in Rameau's "Les Cyclopes" and the fourth variation of his "Gavotte et Doubles," as well as in Couperin's "Le Tic-Toc-Choc" and various other pieces written by the French clavecin composers.

Other extra features extend the range of dynamic and tonal possibilities in still different ways. Some harpsichords are equipped with leather plectra that can be voiced for a half-stop position, producing a softer tone as well as the normal-size tone. Half-stops on all registers raise the number of possibilities geometrically.

Some harpsichords are made with more than three registers, which may include one or more of the following: 1) the 16′ stop, found chiefly on German instruments in the baroque period; 2) the lute stop, of English origin and extremely nasal in tone; and 3) the *peau de buffle* (buffalo hide), a nicety invented by Pascal Taskin in 1768[1] made of soft leather that produced a partially damped lovely soft sound. The 16′ stop is the most commonly found of the three today, although it is becoming less popular than it was a few years ago. Both the lute stop and the *peau de buffle* have limited usefulness, the lute stop because of the distinctive quality of its nasal snarl and the *peau de buffle* because it cannot be heard well in large halls.

The feature which facilitates the use of all the registers is, of course, the pedal mechanism to operate the stops. Much has been said about whether or not the pedals are necessary or desirable, and I don't propose to take sides here. It seems likely, however, that, in an age of convenience such as ours today, the pedal will endure because it is convenient. Like many conveniences it can also be a nuisance, particularly if the owner wants to transport his instrument. But if you are willing to put up with this and increased cost, there is no reason why the pedal should be eschewed, so long as the player does not use it to produce unstylistic effects in baroque music. In playing contemporary music, on the other hand, the player should be free to use it in any way he finds helpful in carrying out the composer's intentions.

It might be helpful here to consider briefly the use of registration on a modern production instrument, such as a Neupert or a Speerhake. The tone of these instruments is smaller, less resonant, and more uniform in quality than the historically oriented harpsichords just described because of their heavier construction and longer scale.[2] For these reasons, the player may want to make more frequent changes of register than would otherwise seem necessary. Two particularly effective combinations on instruments of this type that are equipped with a 16′ stop are the 16′4′ mixture (an organ-like quality) and the 16′ + buff (the theorbo effect). The 16′ played an octave higher and the 4′ played an octave lower will also serve as additional 8′ qualities to alleviate some of the sameness of the two existing 8′s.

Ultimately, good registration depends upon a thorough knowledge of the music together with exercise of perception and good sense, and the final result will vary somewhat from performer to performer within the boundaries of good musical taste. The *bon goût* which Couperin constantly refers to should be the final judge in our day as it was in his.

The pedals usually found on concert instruments today make changes of registration so easy that the player is often tempted to use much more registration than the composer ever dreamed of. Since most baroque music was written for instruments with hand stops, one clear principle of registration is that registration of this music should be of a kind that is possible with hand stops in order to be consistent with the possibilities the composer had in mind. Baroque music often contains rests at points where a change of registration is desirable. On the other hand, if a change of registration by hand would be impossible without dropping out notes in the piece, one probably shouldn't change registration at that point even though it would be possible to do so with the aid of pedals.

Registration has two main purposes: one is to enhance the music by giving it additional surface interest and color, and the other is to make the structure more explicit. Coloristic use of registration on the harpsichord is of rather incidental importance while structural use is fundamental.

Coloristic registration is anything that draws attention to itself as an *effect.* The most common and available effect—often too tempting to resist—is the buff. Other out-of-the-ordinary sounds produced from the basic registration are either the 8′ stop played an octave higher as a 4′ solo or the 4′ stop played an octave lower as an 8′ solo. The 16′ stop, if there is one, can be played as a solo 8′, or it can be used to produce the theorbo or organ effects already mentioned. And of course the special extra registers like the lute stop and the *peau de buffle* yield their unusual sounds. We do not expect a brilliant array of colors from a harpsichord, however, and even these comparatively few choices are more than the player needs most of the time.

Some excesses of registration are prompted by considering the harpsichord like the organ. It is especially easy to do this if the harpsichord has a 16′ stop. Unlike the organ, however, which is really a whole band of instruments of boldly contrasting colors and timbres, the harpsichord is a single homogeneous instrument in which the tonal colors are not strikingly contrasted, but finely modulated as in a string quartet.

The most essential function of registration on the harpsichord, then, is that of reinforcing the musical structure. For the purposes of our discussion, it may be helpful to think of the musical structure of a given piece in terms of mass and line. Mass refers to the sections or parts of a movement, which follow each other in time; and line refers to the horizontal elements, which exist simultaneously—the individual, interweaving polyphonic lines or simply melody and accompaniment. Registration may be used either to set off sections from each other or separate the horizontal elements. Changes which take place at sectional divisions require only one manual; changes which differentiate lines require two manuals.

We can best illustrate how registration can clarify musical structure by applying a few principles to some of the most common baroque forms. These forms fall into two chief classifications: repeat forms, which include variation form, binary and ternary forms, and the rondeau, and continuation forms, which include imitative forms such as the fugue.[3]

REPEAT FORMS

First we will consider registration in the repeat forms. Since a one-manual harpsichord with a disposition of two 8′s (one with a buff) and 4′, is usually adequate for these pieces, my suggestions will be applicable to such an instrument. If the player learns maximum use of modest resources, he will be able to transfer with ease to more elaborate accommodations.

Variation Form

It is difficult to generalize about registering variations, because there are so many different kinds of variations in the baroque. The main distinction for our purpose here, however, is that between sectional variations such as Sweelinck's "Mein Junges Leben Hat Ein End" or Rameau's "Gavotte et Doubles" and continuous variations such as abound in the *Fitzwilliam Virginal Book*. Sectional variations retain the melody and harmony of the theme; continuous variations preserve only the harmony. In the sectional type, each variation should have a change of registration suitable to it and that will in addition contribute to the unity of the piece as a whole. The cumulative excitement of Rameau's "Gavotte" for instance, is reflected in the registration. The theme would be best stated on a single 8′, the first three variations in gradually increasing volume. The fourth variation should be played on the softest possible combination; two manuals are required—the principal 8′ against the buffed nasal 8′ is particularly effective. The fifth variation should be played with an 8′ and a 4′, and the sixth with maximum volume and brilliance—two 8′s and a 4′.

In continuous variations more freedom of choice is left to the player, making the task more delightful and more difficult. In the English figural variations, which may consist of a few or a great many short sections, the player may want to alternate rather freely between the two 8′s and add an occasional buff, but announcing each new strain or its repetition with a new registration leads only to a motley effect. He should remember that the instruments for which these pieces were written were very simple and then register accordingly. One useful and appropriate registrational practice in these pieces is to play either 8′ stop an octave higher as a 4′, for it is reasonable to suppose that English virginalists did the same thing. The player should take his cue from the plan of the individual piece and determine what overall effect is desirable from the structure and the figurations themselves. The numbering of the sections as in the *Fitzwilliam Virginal Book* will serve as a guide to structure. He must observe, for instance, whether the piece waxes and wanes with each variation or whether the effect is one of generally increasing momentum and excitement from beginning to end. The player may of course feel free to delete some sections, if he wishes.

Binary Form

In short pieces in binary form, such as the individual movements in a dance suite, one registration is usually appropriate for both halves. In addition, the simple harmonic structure of such movements remains most clear when the tone quality is constant. Repeats, however, would ordinarily be varied with a change.

The character of the register should match the mood of the individual piece; the bright nature of courantes and gigues suggests an 8'4' combination, while the quieter, more lyrical sarabande may be more suited to a single 8' stop. A change of registration from one piece to another frames each dance separately.

Here is one suggested registration for Bach's French Suite no. 6:

		Repeats:
Allemande	8_1	8_18_2
Courante	8_14	8_18_2
Sarabande	8_1	8_18_2
Gavotte	8_14	8_18_2
Polonaise	8_2	8_2+buff
Menuet	8_1	8_2
Bourrée	8_18_2	8_2
Gigue	8_14	8_18_24

The player may make repeats or not as he chooses.

The Scarlatti Sonatas

Scarlatti wrote all of his sonatas in binary form, but since his treatment of the form differs from that in the dance suite, we will consider these sonatas separately. The key to an intelligent and musical registering of Scarlatti sonatas is the disposition of the harpsichords for which the composer wrote most of them. Ralph Kirkpatrick concludes that most of the sonatas were composed for a harpsichord with one keyboard and two 8' stops, one probably voiced very softly and the other more loudly, so as to differentiate between lyrical and brilliant passages.[4] This is certainly the simplest, most basic registration possible. Kirkpatrick states that "unequivocal cases of writing for two manuals are extremely rare in Scarlatti," that the frequent hand-crossings are not necessarily facilitated by using two keyboards, and that, though there are a few sonatas that would be difficult to play on one manual, all but three of them (sonatas K. 21, K. 48, and K. 106) are *possible* on one manual.[5]

Some of these sonatas can be played with no registration changes at all because Scarlatti has virtually "registered" them with his dynamic manner of writing. He does this in various ways, but chiefly by his orchestral negotiation of the entire compass of the keyboard range and by his variation of the density of the texture from a Mozartean transparency to Lisztian sonority. No composer for the harpsichord has achieved a wider range of expression with such a minimum of means.

Here are suggested registrations for three Scarlatti sonatas. The changes are very simple but entirely adequate; anything more elaborate simply gets in the way:

Sonata in F minor (K. 239, L. 281)
$8_1 8_2$ throughout

Sonata in C major (K. 132, L. 457)
First half (measures 1–37) 8_1
    Measures 35–37, left hand 8_2+buff
Second half
    Measures 38–57 8_2
    Measures 58–77 8_1
    Measures 75–77, left hand 8_2+buff

Sonata in D minor (K. 141, L. 422)
First half
    Measures 1–18 $8_1 8_2$
    Measures 19–52 8_1
    Measures 53–85 $8_1 8_2$
Second half
    Measures 86–125 8_2
    Measures 126–61 $8_1 8_2$

In the Sonata in D minor, note how the built-in crescendo effects at measures 39–51, 53–72, 113–124, and 126–144 come through without the benefit of registration changes.

Ternary Form

The simplicity and symmetry of the A-B-A form should be matched with a simple, symmetrical registration. The tone quality of the two A sections should be either identical or recognizably similar, and the B section recognizably contrasting, the degree of contrast to be determined by the musical context.

Rondeau Form

The rondeau form is A B A C A D . . . A. This is the instrumental form most frequently used by the French clavecinists in the seventeenth and early eighteenth centuries. It consists of a recurring refrain and contrasting couplets, each couplet emphasizing a different but related key. As in ternary form, the A sections are usually best played with the same, or at least similar, registration with the couplets in contrasting registrations. If the first rondeau section is repeated, as it usually is, the repeat should be varied, just as it would be in repeats in binary form.

If the instrument has enough stops, each couplet could be played with a different tone quality, but this is not necessary nor even desirable. The essential contrast is that between couplet and refrain, rather than that between the couplets themselves.

Here are registration suggestions for several pieces in rondeau form from François Couperin's *Sixième Ordre:* The arrow (↑) means the passage should be played an octave higher than written; the (↓) an octave lower than written.

"Les Moissonneurs"

$$\frac{A}{8,4} \quad \frac{A\text{(repeat)}}{8,4}\uparrow \quad \frac{B}{8_1} \quad \frac{A}{8,4} \quad \frac{C}{8_2} \quad \frac{A}{8,4} \quad \frac{D}{8_1} \quad \frac{A}{8,4}$$

"La Gazoüillement"

$$\frac{A}{\mathrm{I}\,(4\downarrow)\;\overline{\mathrm{II}\,(8_2)}} \quad \frac{A}{\mathrm{I}\,(4)\;\overline{\mathrm{II}\,(8_2)}} \quad \frac{B}{8_2+\text{buff}} \quad \frac{A}{\mathrm{I}\,(4)\;\overline{\mathrm{II}\,(8_2)}} \quad \frac{C}{8_2} \quad \frac{A}{\mathrm{I}\,(4)\;\overline{\mathrm{II}\,(8_2)}} \quad \frac{D}{8_2}$$

(Echo, m. 7-8: +buff)

$$\frac{A}{\mathrm{I}\,(4)\;\overline{\mathrm{II}\,(8_2)}}$$

"Les Baricades Mistérieuses"

$$\frac{A}{8_2} \quad \frac{A\text{(repeat)}}{8_2+\text{buff}} \quad \frac{B}{8_2} \quad \frac{A}{8_2+\text{buff}} \quad \frac{C}{8_2} \quad \frac{A}{8_2+\text{buff}} \quad \frac{D}{8_1} \quad \frac{A}{8_2+\text{buff}}$$

CONTINUATION FORMS

For our discussion here a practical distinction must be made between two-voice polyphony and polyphony of three or more voices. Two-voice polyphony lends itself very well to performance on two manuals, one voice taken by each hand. Polyphony written in three or more voices, on the other hand, is usually *not* readily playable on two manuals, because of the difficulty of writing so that the voices are divisible between the two hands. There are a few pieces, such as the fugue from Bach's Toccata and Fugue in C minor and the fugue following the Chromatic Fantasy in which some sections are possible on two manuals; but it is evident that in these Bach took special care to write so that the voices could be divided in this way.

Polyphony in Two Parts

Most two-part polyphony can be played on one manual, and Bach's many two-part pieces illustrate this very well. Suggestions for registration of his Two-Part Inventions follow below. Each piece may be played on a single registration with changes from each one to the next so that all fifteen Inventions can be played continuously as one composition.

No. 1	8_1
No. 2	8_2
No. 3	$8_1 8_2$
No. 4	$8_1 4$
No. 5	8_2
No. 6	8_1
No. 7	$8_1 8_2$
No. 8	$8_1 4$
No. 9	8_1
No. 10	$8_1 4$ or $8_1 8_2 4$
No. 11	8_2
No. 12	$8_1 4$
No. 13	$8_1 8_2$
No. 14	8_1
No. 15	$8_1 4$

If the Inventions are played on a two-manual instrument, there are a few changes that might provide additional interest. Since the subject is rhythmically homogeneous in Invention no. 2, the performer may achieve additional clarity of voice-leading if he uses two separate 8' stops; also, the trill in measure 13 is more conveniently played on separate manuals. In Invention no. 3 the echo effects in measures 7–8 and 49–50 stand out a little more if the registration is transferred to a softer 8' on the upper manual. Adjustments in articulation can be made, however, which will compensate for the awkwardness in the trills and bring out the echoes without having to resort to the second manual. The suspensions may be differentiated a little more in Invention no. 6 with two contrasting 8' stops; and in Invention no.

12, the little episodes in measures 7–8 and 16–17 recede into the background even more effectively if they are played on a softer 8′.

Some two-part music requires two manuals because of the crossing of the voices. Bach's Goldberg Variations is the most famous example of this kind of writing, and Bach himself marked certain of the two-part variations "for two manuals." (Pianists can play them on one keyboard only because the greater depth of the piano keys allows room for the hands to pass each other, but it must be said that they do it with great difficulty even so.)

When playing two-voice polyphony on two manuals, the clearest registration is usually a single 8′ stop on each manual. Other possibilities are an 8′4′ against an 8′, or two 8′s against one 8′, with the heavier registration in the voice which has fewer and longer notes. The player should always be careful, however, not to obscure one voice by an overly heavy registration in the other.

Polyphony in Three or More Parts

It is usually neither necessary nor possible to change registration in a multiple-voice polyphonic piece—unless, of course, it is sectional. Furthermore, the homogeneous texture of most fugues is more clearly projected by a single registration throughout, and the comparative brevity of the average fugue permits this without strain to the listener. Bach's *Well-Tempered Clavier* illustrates this point very well.

There are interesting exceptions. Very long or complex fugues may be made more immediately accessible to the listener through changes in the density and volume of the registration. The triple fugue from Book I of the *Well-Tempered Clavier*, no. 4 in C♯ minor, is both long and complex. It is interesting to note that Bach has written it in such a way that, although it can be played with one registration throughout on one manual, changes of registration are possible at crucial points in the structure, if it is played on two manuals. This is a difficult enough feat of composition that he must have intended to do just that. The points at which registration can be changed are: 1) at measure 35, the beginning of exposition 2, where the second subject is introduced; 2) at measure 49, the beginning of exposition 3, where the third subject is introduced; 3) at measure 73, the beginning of exposition 4, where a dramatic statement of the first subject in the bass marks the return to the tonic; 4) at measure 88, with the arrival at the key of the subdominant and the temporary lightening of the texture before the final section; and 5) at measure 105 and the dominant pedal point announcing the final return to the tonic.

TERRACE DYNAMICS AND ECHO EFFECTS

The harpsichord, and the organ as well, lends itself to the use of stops in such a way as to produce what has come to be called "terrace dynamics" —long stretches of loud and soft. Some baroque harpsichord music is written with this kind of registration in mind, and the classic example is probably Bach's Italian Concerto, where, to make his intentions even more explicit, Bach has given us "forte" and "piano" cues right in the score. The Italian Concerto requires two manuals, and the registration suggestions below are made for a two-manual instrument with two 8's and a 4' on the lower manual and a single 8' with buff on the upper. The forte sections should be played on the lower manual, either on the principal 8', the coupled 8's, the $8_1$4, or the $8_18_2$4; and the piano sections on the nasal 8' stop on the upper manual. Where the hands play on separate manuals, indications for the right hand appear above the line, those for the left below the line.

First movement

Measures 1–30 $8_1$4

Measures 30–52 $\dfrac{\text{I } (8_1)}{\text{II } (8_2)}$

Measures 52–90   I (8_18_2), except for echo in measures 67–68: $\dfrac{\text{I } (8_1)}{\text{II } (8_2)}$

Measures 90–129 $\dfrac{\text{I } (8_18_2)}{\text{II } (8_2)}$

Measures 129–39   II (8_2)

Measures 139–46 $\dfrac{\text{II } (8_2)}{\text{I } (8_1)}$

Measures 146–63 $\dfrac{\text{I } (8_1 4)}{\text{II } (8_2)}$

Measures 163–92   I $(8_18_2 4)$

Second Movement

Measures 1–76   *forte* passages: I $(8_1 4)$

                        piano passages: II (8_2)

Measures 76–92   II $(8_2 + \text{buff})$

Measures 92–126   I (8_18_2)

Measures 127–87   *forte* passages: I (8_18_2)

                        piano passages: II (8_2)

Measures 187–210   I $(8_18_2 4)$

Echo effects are related to terrace dynamics and are merely the echoing of a short phrase on a softer stop. Examples are measures 67–68 of the first movement of the Italian Concerto and measures 7–8 and 49–50 of Invention no. 3.

CONCLUSION

Registration provides the player with a wider dynamic range as well as a greater number of tonal qualities than he has on a single set of strings. Because they can be used singly or together, even the modest resources of an instrument with two 8' stops and a buff can supply considerable variety, and the facilities available on many concert-sized harpsichords are actually greater than the player needs or may want to bother with most of the time.

The player can use these tools, his collection of tonal qualities and quantities, in three basic ways: to decorate the surface with coloristic effects, to differentiate tonally between horizontal lines, and to separate the sections of a piece from one another. The first of these adds interest to the music but is not essential to the meaning; the second can be adequately done by other means—articulation and phrasing—and is possible with restricted registration anyway. The third, on the other hand, becomes a means of structural clarification and reinforcement; this is the prime function of registration. It is also essential to the harpsichordist's art, because it is his only means of fully revealing the shape of the larger forms.

Perhaps we can bring the real significance of harpsichord registration into perspective if we consider it an extension of articulation and phrasing, the other means of expression and organization the performer has at his disposal. Articulation binds notes together or separates them; phrasing links phrases or sets them off from one another as punctuation marks do in language. Registration divides the whole structure into its component parts and indicates the relationship of those parts to the whole. With articulation and phrasing, the player fits the little pieces together to form his building blocks; with registration he puts the blocks together according to the composer's architectural plan for the composition. If the piece is short and the structure simple, the player may not need to use changes of registration at all, relying solely on his fingers for the task; but if the piece is of sizable proportions and the structure is complex, he needs registration as a tool to erect the framework which supports the parts. In the end, then, proficiency with registration depends on the player's thorough knowledge of musical form and his ability to apply it intelligently.

7

ENSEMBLE PLAYING

A harpsichord player, like all other keyboard players, will soon find himself doing a good deal of accompanying and ensemble playing. With the harpsichord this often takes the form of continuo playing, with the cello doubling the bass line. Ensemble playing is a complex skill, and while it cannot be learned from a book, I would like to mention some problems and give a few suggestions on possible solutions here.

Continuo playing can involve the improvisation at sight of the realization of a figured bass, adapting the texture of the accompaniment to the needs of the particular situation. The term "basso continuo" was used in the baroque to mean literally a bass line that continued throughout the piece; "thorough bass," "through bass" and "general bass" were synonymous terms. In music written for one choir of voices or instruments, this line was simply the existing bass line; in music written for more than one choir, the bass was a composite one made up of the notes which were the lowest at any given point, a true bass of the harmony rather than an actual bass part. The terms "basso continuo" and "figured bass" are often used interchangeably, but actually the two are quite distinct. A figured bass is a continuo part with figures added to indicate what intervals the player should add above the bass to complete the harmony.

HISTORICAL PERSPECTIVE

The practice of playing an extemporized continuo from an *unfigured* bass line goes back farther than the introduction of figured bass, at least to the early sixteenth century. At that time harmonic practices were so simple that figures were not necessary, and the continuo player would habitually play from the bass line of the full score, which explains the absence of special organ or harpsichord parts. After 1600, however, harmonic innovations rendered the old rules inadequate,[1] and Viadana, Peri, and Caccini invented and developed the practice of putting figures and signs below the bass notes as an aid to the player.[2] The figures were a simple, adequate means of telling the player what to do and served the purpose very well until the practice of thinking in intervals gave way, after Rameau, to thinking in terms of harmonic functions.

The organ and the harpsichord, with the frequent addition of a cello, came into such standard use as continuo instruments in the eighteenth century that we now tend to think of continuo playing almost entirely in terms of these instruments. This was not always the case. In the renaissance the assembly of instruments used for continuo parts was varied and imposing. Sixteenth-century accounts of music making for family and ceremonial use during the reign of the Medicis in Florence, for instance, show a splashy use of accompanying instruments, with trombones, archlutes, bass viols, and multiple harpsichords supplying the bass line.[3] The scorings, often for what seems now an ostentatious display of instruments to accompany relatively few voices, might be written off as merely the conspicuous consumption of a prince who might well have a harpsichord and a chest of viols in every room in his palace. But other works written for less incidental occasions show an equal delight in sound for its own sake, as well as a sensible inclination to use whatever happened to be handy at the moment.

In the seventeenth century, larger instrumental groups used multiple continuo instruments (though not all at once) that must have fulfilled some of the same purposes as the percussion section of a modern symphony orchestra: providing arresting changes of coloration along with a solid beat and reinforcement of the harmonic foundation. The continuo section for the score of *Orfeo* (1607), for instance, contains nine of the thirty-nine instruments in the orchestra. The exact number and nature of continuo instruments used was often determined by the size and disposition of the group to be accompanied. Agazzari attempts to formalize this practice in his book on continuo playing (1607) by recommending specific instruments for the various-sized groups: a lute, chitarrone, theorbo or harp for a group of two or three instruments; a small positive organ or a harpsichord for a group of six or seven; and a large organ or harpsichord or both for a group of sixteen to twenty. Quantz thought there should be one harpsichord for every six violins in the orchestra, and, while the proportions proposed no doubt changed from one authority to another and as opinions and conditions changed, our modern custom of having only one harpsichord for an entire orchestra would have been unthinkable in the eighteenth century. In recitatives, however, a single harpsichord would be used.[4]

Out of this profusion of continuo instruments, then, the organ and the harpsichord emerged as the chief ones, a position they have again assumed today. Of the two the harpsichord is more useful as an all-purpose continuo instrument because of its greater flexibility and of course its portability.

SCORES

When asked to play accompaniments on the harpsichord, the player who has come to the instrument from the piano soon discovers that there are a few problems that he did not have before. The first problem is the score that is handed to him, which may fall into one of these several categories:

1. Piano accompaniments.

2. Piano-vocal scores. The *Messiah,* edited by T. Tertius Noble (G. Schirmer, 1912), is a familiar example.

3. "Realizations" specified for piano or harpsichord but written with the ghost of a piano in the background and playable only on the piano.

4. Piano-organ arrangements intended for rehearsal with piano and performance with organ. The Watkins Shaw edition of the *Messiah* (Novello, 1958) is an example.

5. A realization actually playable on the harpsichord with or without figures. Sometimes the right hand notes appear in small print, making it easier for the keyboard player to improvise his own harmonization from the bass line if he wishes. The cembalo part to the *Messiah* edited by Schering-Soldan (Peters, 1939), is an example of a playable realization without figures and written in notes of uniform size.

6. A bass line with figures.

7. A full score with figured bass such as an eighteenth-century player would have used.

The complexity of the problem is made evident by the fact that a work like the *Messiah* is still available in several entirely different keyboard versions. From the player's point of view, he seems to have either too many notes (in the case of the piano accompaniment or piano-vocal reduction) or too few (the figured bass line) but seldom just enough. He soon finds that even the so-called realizations are not real but approximations, for they can't be taken literally.

What is the performer to do? First of all, if he is given a piano accompaniment or a piano-vocal score, he should replace it with anything else, for the most difficult task is to ignore a bristling profusion of notes. If he *must* use an unabashed piano score, he can often make do by thinning out the left hand octaves and the thick right hand chords that require the damper pedal and by keeping the hands closer together than they are apt to be in the piano score. A piano reduction is in many ways the most difficult to use because the homophonic passages are too thick to play literally and the harmonies resulting from the conversion of the lines in polyphonic passages are often not readily recognized at sight. Even the bass line is often hard to distinguish at first reading. If the player is familiar with the work, he may be able to play from the reduction, with some practice; if he doesn't know the work, there may be no alternative but to extract the bass line and supplement it with figures or enough skeleton harmonies to get by at the keyboard. Whichever of these two solutions he resorts to, he will probably end up playing partly by ear and partly from memory, kept on his course with the aid of his own mental or written notes. The simpler he makes the part, the more comfortable he will be with it.

The performer can work with a realization if he does not follow it literally but regards it as a kind of blueprint and devotes some time to learning proper styles of continuo playing. More and more simple, usable realizations are being published as the need has been recognized, and this kind of almost bare harmonization can be of great practical help as an intermediate step to sole reliance on the figured bass line.

FIGURED BASS

The harpsichordist who wants to become proficient at playing continuo parts will want to learn to play either from the full score or from the figured bass line, and if he does, he will be on safer ground because such a score is generally available. First of all, the player must be able to interpret the figures into the proper intervals or chords above the bass. There are just a few of these and they are simple, logical, and easily learned:

1. *No* figure below a note indicates that the triad is to be played.

2. A figure below a note indicates the interval to be played above the bass note in the key signature of the piece. In the key of F major, for instance, a 6 written below B♭ would indicate G, and a $^6_5$ written below E would indicate B♭ and C.

3. Chromatic alterations are shown by a sharp, a flat, or a natural sign put before or after the figure, by a diagonal slash through the figure, or, less frequently, by an apostrophe.

4. A sharp without a figure placed below a note calls for a major third; a flat similarly placed calls for the minor third. A natural sign is used to indicate the appropriate alteration of the note from what the key signature would designate it to be.

5. A horizontal line following a figure or set of figures shows that the right hand holds the initial harmony even though the bass notes move.

6. A diagonal slash where there is no figure indicates the repetition of the same interval above the changed bass notes: 6 / / = 6 6 6.

7. Two or more figures in succession show melodic rather than harmonic changes (appoggiaturas or passing tones). 4 3, 6 5, or 5 4 3 are quite commonly indicated.

8. The words "tasto solo" or "O" indicate that only the bass notes should be played.

The next step is to take any figured bass line and practice realizing the figures in simple four-part style, playing the bass note with the left hand and the realization in close position with the right. When the player is able to do this readily at sight, he will have become proficient in the simplest kind of accompaniment, the so-called organ style[5] of figured bass playing, which consists of chordal progressions. This is the style used in the accompaniment of works with chorus and orchestra and is exemplified in the Peters edition of the cembalo part to the *Messiah.*

A second style of accompaniment, which is arpeggiated, was called "lute-play" during the baroque period. It is appropriate for the thinner textures of music for soloists or small ensembles. It is also used in recitatives in which the harpsichord accompanies the soloist, often with the cello doubling the bass line. Such an accompaniment provides the singer with a firm harmonic foundation as well as rhythmic and dynamic support through the percussive attack peculiar to the harpsichord and the spacing and tempo of the notes in the arpeggiations. Transparent in texture, it also provides a welcome relief from the thick, rich consistency of the rest of the work and, by the simplicity and economy of its means, focuses attention on the soloist and the words he is projecting.

The third style of figured bass playing, sometimes referred to by contemporary authorities as the "finer accompaniment,"[6] is the most difficult to learn, and the player should become quite secure in the other two styles before he attempts it. The finer accompaniment amounts to a more or less free improvisation using the harmonies indicated by the figures as the basis for figurations, motifs, imitations, and even ornamentation. It is the kind of playing called for in the accompaniment of soloists and smaller ensembles and varies with the peculiarities of each situation: the volume of the individual voice or instrument, the number of instruments, the density of the rest of the composition, the size and acoustics of the hall, and the character of the harpsichord itself. It is because of these variables that a realization cannot be written out that will be satisfactory on all occasions; therefore the player's job is to adapt the accompaniment to the demands of the situation, which he can learn to do only by tireless practice with various kinds of ensembles and soloists, acute listening, and the constant use of his critical faculties. The first two styles of continuo playing, while they embody a great deal of craft, can be done well by anyone willing to learn that craft, but the finer accompaniment requires an artistry as well and raises accompanying to the level of an art.

Three examples of thoroughbass improvisation that survive in written form—two from J. S. Bach and one from Handel—reveal the art at its highest level. The Bach examples are the second aria from *Amore Traditore,* a solo cantata, and the second movement of his B minor Sonata for Flute and Harpsichord. The Handel example is Sonata for Viola da gamba and Harpsichord (Handelgesellschaft ed., xlviii, 112–17).[7]

The three styles of continuo playing just enumerated—organ style, recitative style, and the finer accompaniment—are intended here mainly as convenient categories to aid the player, and, while one particular style may be used to the exclusion of the others in any given piece of music, the player who has learned all of them will frequently and unconsciously move back and forth from one to the other, with the exception of recitative playing, which usually limits him to a few rather modest techniques.

The following set of guidelines, which includes basic suggestions as well as more advanced ones, will help the player to adapt his realization to the particulars of each accompanying situation. They summarize Wilfrid Mellers's comments on the rules applying to a free homophonic realization such as would be found in the works of F. Couperin, but they seem remarkably close to what a good musician with common sense would do today.[8] The practices apply to all possible variations in bass movement, tempo, texture and dynamics, range, dissonance, ornamentation, and arpeggiation.

1. The hands are to be kept close together and in mid-keyboard. For special effects they may play at the extremes of the keyboard compass.

2. In simple chordal realizations the left hand plays the bass note, the right fills in the harmony, three or four notes being the norm.

3. Ordinarily, one chord is played for each bass note, assuming a moderate tempo and a fairly disjunct movement of the bass.

4. When the bass moves conjunctly only alternative notes require accompaniment.

5. In triple time or when the tempo is fast only the first beat of the measure requires accompaniment.

6. In extremely fast tempi, only the first beats are to be played and accompanied, leaving the rest of the bass notes to the cello or other continuo instrument ("basses de Viole ou de Violon").

7. If the voice to be accompanied is slight (i.e., a light singing voice or a soft instrument, such as a recorder), or if the texture is thin, the right hand harmonies may be reduced to two notes.

8. In choral or concerted music where many voices or instruments are used, more notes are needed; the left hand should provide them by doubling one or more of the right hand notes.

9. The continuo player may use dissonances often and rather freely, whether indicated or not—sevenths and ninths where appropriate and even added seconds, sixths, and sevenths to enrich the texture. They should not be doubled, however, except for the second. Their resolutions could either be normal or by means of ties and retardations.

10. Notes common to two successive chords are tied.

11. Ornaments may often be played in the continuo, especially trills.

12. In exposed textures contrary motion between the hands is expected,

but in the playing of full harmonies, especially where the other instruments would cover up the harpsichord, the usual rules on consecutives are not to be enforced. The progression from the diminished to the perfect fifth, for example, was not only permitted but considered admirable.

13. Arpeggiation is appropriate only in recitatives where the movement is free; in arias the harmonies should ordinarily move in notes half the length of the bass notes.

ARPEGGIATION

I would like to add a few remarks on the technique of arpeggiation here, for smooth ensemble playing depends on this perhaps more than on any other single skill. The player must first decide whether to arpeggiate a chord or play it solid. He may have read various arbitrary maxims on the necessity of arpeggiating each chord at least a little, but he will soon find whether or not to arpeggiate is a practical decision to be made on the basis of tempo. Arpeggiation is impractical or downright impossible at certain tempi, and when this is the case the chords must be played solid. When this is necessary, the technique of releasing the notes becomes very important, because a sustained, cohesive effect depends on it. The release of notes in solid chords, played at rather brisk tempi, should be staggered in such a way that the right hand notes are released upward, the uppermost note last, an instant before the bass note. If the left hand has played two or more notes, their release should be staggered as in the right hand, but downward, bass note last. Arpeggiated chords should be released in the same manner.

If the player is going to arpeggiate, he must also decide:

1. How many notes to play.

2. Whether to arpeggiate slowly or rapidly.

3. What the rhythmic pattern is to be for each arpeggio. (A limp or sloppy arpeggio will sound even worse on the harpsichord than it does on the piano.) The rhythm may be in evenly spaced notes or accelerated. An example of one common rhythmic motif is:

4. Whether the arpeggio begins or ends on the beat. If it begins on the

beat, its rhythm must not interfere with what the soloist is doing; if it ends on the beat, it is usually played quickly so that the beat is clearly felt on the final note.

5. The direction of the arpeggio. The most usual practice is to begin with the bass note and play upward. Sometimes, however, especially at final cadences or at other places where there is a long interval to fill in with harmony notes, the arpeggio may go up and back down again, or even up, down, and back up again.

RELATED PROBLEMS

The player will soon discover there are related practical problems that concern him, and I would like to include a few observations on them. The kind of instrument the player has will affect the way he plays. An instrument patterned after the very lightly constructed Italian instrument, which has a rapidly decaying tone, is ideal for small ensembles, because it allows great freedom to play more elaborate continuo parts with more notes. On a heavily voiced instrument with a pervasive tone, such as those made following French or English traditions, he will have to thin out the textures to keep from obscuring other instruments in a small ensemble, especially soft ones like the recorder. Such an instrument can of course be voiced down so it isn't quite so loud. And sometimes simply lowering the lid and using the short stick will suffice. A totally closed lid should be avoided if possible because it gives a choked sound. An instrument with a closed bottom, like those built on historical principles, can't have its lid closed too. (A piano lid can be closed because its bottom is open.)

The style of playing of fellow musicians in the ensemble will naturally affect the continuo player. When he is accompanying instrumentalists accustomed to playing loud in the nineteenth-century tradition, the continuo player won't have the problem of obscuring anybody; in fact, he may not even be heard. He can play all the notes he pleases but will probably still be drowned out except for the percussive rustle of his attack, which in a strange way does impart a kind of transparency even to very thick textures.

Another matter relating to ensemble playing is that of tuning to other standards than A = 440. Orchestral instruments can play at A = 440, although their players sometimes prefer the pitch to be a trifle sharp. Recorder players, on the other hand, may require that the harpsichord be tuned several beats below pitch. So the harpsichordist should be able to tune up or down a few beats to fit the needs of the situation.

Ensemble playing requires a greater flexibility in dynamic variation within the phrase than is ordinarily needed. This can be accomplished by varying the thickness of the texture. When accompanying light voices or instruments, especially in their less resonant ranges, the player may have to thin out the harmonies to two or three voices on the beats and a single line between beats. And when he is playing with chorus and orchestra he will want to play thick chords in the right hand and octaves in the left much of the time.

Changes of registration should be kept to an economical minimum; fussy registration takes too much of the accompanist's attention and is apt to be useless anyway. In accompanying a small sound, alternation between the soft and loud 8' stops, with an occasional use of the buff, will provide enough variety. The accompaniment for a large group of players can include a greater range of dynamic levels, but the use of the two 8' stops, or an 8' and a 4', will be appropriate most of the time, with two 8's and the 4' used in the loudest sections.

It is a great help to use enough electrical amplification to slightly reinforce the tone without altering it, particularly in performances with large groups. If two small portable speakers are available, one may be placed so that it is directed back toward the other musicians and the other toward the audience. If only one speaker is used, the requirements of the situation will dictate its placement, but the player should remember that the raised lid directs the sound away from performers stationed behind the harpsichord, so that sometimes they hear nothing at all from it unless the sound is re-routed to them by amplification. Even in the performance of works with a small chamber group, the other players will be able to proceed more confidently if the harpsichord sound is amplified just enough so that they can hear without straining their ears.

A cello or viola da gamba is commonly used to double the bass line, and a bassoon is particularly appropriate to do so in wind ensembles. In either case the ensemble between harpsichord and cello, or whatever, should be so precise that the result is *one* sound. Occasionally, the bass line may contain very rapid figures that may become obtrusive if doubled. If so, the cello might play the main harmony notes and the harpsichord the bass line as written. Or it is sometimes effective if the cello plays the quick figurations in the bass line and the harpsichord takes the harmony notes.

In this chapter I have tried to alert the player to some of the problems of continuo playing, so that he can proceed a little more methodically to acquire proficiency in the craft. What is needed to learn the skills, however, is systematic practice, which he can best get by using the only modern method available, Hermann Keller's *Thoroughbass Method,* translated and edited by Carl Parrish and published by Norton in 1965. The book begins with the practice of thoroughbass playing in simple four-part style, note against note, and continues with extensive musical examples from the seventeenth and eighteenth centuries. It also contains a short but invaluable bibliography on the subject.

There is an enormous literature on the subject, most of it written in the seventeenth and eighteenth centuries, and most of it still in the original languages, although translations are now appearing at a good rate. Two of these works, available in translation, contain valuable suggestions. They are C. P. E. Bach's *Essay on the True Manner of Playing Keyboard Instruments* and J. J. Quantz's *On Playing the Flute* (1752). The player should also consult F. T. Arnold's monumental work, *The Art of Accompaniment from a Thorough-Bass,* now available in a Dover reprint (1965) and the excellent section in Robert Donington's *The Interpretation of Early Music,* pages 222–305. In addition, Thurston Dart's *The Interpretation of Music* contains informative and fascinating observations on continuo practices in each of the periods discussed in his book.

If the task of improvising an acceptable continuo part from a figured bass line seems bewildering or overwhelming, one should remember that what baroque listeners loved most was not the brilliant, complex, finished accompaniment coolly made up on the spot, but rather the fresh and vital *feeling* of an improvisation from the whole group of performers. Baroque music lovers savored spontaneity in ensemble playing as they did in freely improvised ornamentation and expected their musicians to give performances that were alive—as our age has expected spontaneity from jazz players, and, more recently and in a different way, from aleatory music. Robert Donington's words convey the spirit of the ensemble player's art so well that I would like to let him say it here:

> They [baroque musicians] believed, and modern experience confirms, that it is better to be accompanied with buoyancy than with polished workmanship. An accompanist who can give rhythmic impetus to his part, adapt it to the momentary requirements of balance and sonority, thicken it here and thin it there, and keep every bar alive, can stimulate his colleagues and help to carry the entire ensemble along. This is not merely to fill in the harmony; nor is it merely to make the harmony into an interesting part; it is to share in the creative urgency of the actual performance.[9]

8

TUNING

A harpsichordist must learn to tune his own instrument, unless he is rich or has a resident tuner. Unlike pianos, which will stay in tolerable tune for months even through a change in seasons and relative humidity, all harpsichords except those with metal frames *and* soundboards must have at least a touch-up tuning every week or so. In summer when the humidity changes suddenly, a harpsichord that was in good tune in the morning may be out by afternoon unless the room is air-conditioned. J. S. Bach tuned his harpsichord every morning.

TUNING KEYBOARD INSTRUMENTS

Fortunately, tuning a harpsichord is not nearly as difficult as tuning a piano. A harpsichordist with some experience at tuning can do the job in about forty minutes on a full-sized concert instrument that has more than 180 strings. According to Forkel, Bach tuned his in fifteen minutes. The harpsichord's light strings and low tension make unnecessary many of the piano tuner's special mechanical tricks that compensate for friction or tension as the strings are pulled up or let down. And the clean sound of the light, plucked string is much easier to hear than the more muffled sound of the thick, often-covered piano string, which is struck into vibration by a soft felt-covered hammer. You don't have to guess at the fundamental frequency in the low bass as you do on a domestic grand or an upright, which have greatly foreshortened bass strings. And of course there are fewer strings on the harpsichord.

The traditional method of tuning starts by tuning one string to a standard, a fork, and then tuning the fifth above that string smaller than a pure fifth to the right number of beats, then the fourth below the fifth larger than a pure fourth, then the fifth above the third string (A up to E, E down to B, B up to F#, F# down to C#, and so on) until tuning has proceeded all around the circle of fifths and all notes in the octave have been tuned. As soon as thirds become available, the tuning is checked with them.

Unfortunately, the method is easier to describe than for the beginner to practice, because slow beats are hard to hear, and if he gets off somewhere in the process of going around the fifths, he probably won't know it until he comes back to the octave. If he makes a mistake in an early fifth, he will have to start all over again. It takes experience and usually some instruction to learn to hear the beats so that mistakes don't occur. And hearing the beats seems to be very hard for some people, because beats don't really beat in any obvious way but often appear as a sort of wavering change in tone quality. If the tone quality can't be heard to waver at about 1½ times every second in the fifth above A = 440, all the rest of the fifths in the circle will be off. You should try to work up to the traditional method, but it is frustrating to start out with it unless you have a teacher.

The method I shall advocate here is one that will enable you to get your instrument reasonably well in tune right off and will still let you train your ear. This method uses three forks at pitches spaced at equal intervals around the circle of fifths. With forks pitched at A, C#, and F, you will have only three fifths to tune between reference points, so if you make a mistake in one of the fifths you can correct it before you have gone all the way around the circle. Three forks equally spaced also provide accurate thirds with which to check new thirds as they appear in the tuning. The spacing I suggest requires forks other than those usually available at music stores, but they are available from a piano tuner's supplier. You could use the commonly available A, Bb, and C forks, but this combination leaves a large segment of six fifths in the circle without any reference point to check against.

The three-fork method is not perfect because, I regret to say, tuning forks are not perfectly accurate. Even high quality forks have an advertised accuracy of one-twentieth of one percent—which at A = 440 amounts to over two vibrations per second! In the three-fork method, these two vibrations will have to be distributed over four fifths, putting each one out by half a vibration. Most good forks would probably not be out this much and would be more accurate than a fifth a beginner could get by ear, using one fork as a starting point. The beginning tuner should console himself with the fact that in measurements of pianos tuned by professionals, tuning is quite good in the two octaves above middle C but beyond this range octaves get progressively "stretched" so that the extreme treble comes out to be very sharp and the bass very flat. Even the scientifically designed Strobotuner is not absolutely accurate, but its intervals are consistent with each other, or more so than those in unselected forks. Forks can be adjusted by this standard to be consistent with each other: to lower the pitch of a fork, thin both prongs equally with a file where they join the stem; to raise it, shorten the prongs.

I would like to offer a practical hint for the use of forks with a harpsichord. Since a harpsichord has no damper pedal, striking the fork, pressing the key, and turning the hammer is a three-handed job. A simple device can eliminate the need for the third hand and greatly amplify the faint sound of the fork so it can be heard all over the house; it is the cigar box resonator in Figure 4. Glue a small block of wood (1″ x 1″ x ½″) in the center of the bottom of a cigar box, drill a hole the size of the stem of your fork through the outside of the bottom, insert your lowest pitched fork and strike it while the cover of the box is closed. As the fork is sounding, gradually open the cover to the point at which the sound is loudest (it will actually be about ten decibels louder than with the cover closed) and measure the gap between cover and box. Install a small piece of wood that swings out to hold the box open to that point. The box with the cover open to maximum loudness is actually a cavity tuned to the frequency of the fork. It will not be as loud with other forks but will still give good volume. You can make a striker to hit the fork from a piece of wood, wrapped with felt so it does not produce extraneous noise. The cigar box must be a good solid one, especially for forks at lower pitches, or you will hear only the jangle of upper partials. A box made of eighth-inch plywood that is 5″ x 4″ x 8″ will give a good fundamental at any pitch. The fork must be firmly seated for good results.

I strongly urge use of the resonator because without it the sound of the fork is so faint and dies so quickly that it is very hard to be sure when the strings are accurately tuned to it. The resonator box is also handy for storing forks and hammer. If you want to save yourself the trouble of making the box, you may buy it instead. They are available from Vitali Import Company, 594 Atlantic Blvd., Maywood, California 90270. The resonance case with an A fork (steel) and striker is $13.00; with an aluminum fork it is $21.00.

As one last comment on equipment, I might mention the two kinds of tuning hammers, the T-hammer and the goose-neck; historically they were

Figure 4.   Cigar box resonator.

combination tools for stringing and tuning.[1] The goose-neck is a bit easier to use because it provides better leverage, but most harpsichord makers seem to prefer the T-hammer, probably because it exerts no lateral pressure on the pins. Both kinds of hammers and other harpsichord supplies are available from Tuners' Supply Company, 94 Wheatland Street, Somerville, Massachusetts 02145 and from B & G Instrument Workshop, 318 North 36th Street, Seattle, Washington 98103. A star-tip hammer is best because it allows greater flexibility in positioning on the pin, although it is slightly more expensive.

THE THREE-FORK METHOD

Now let us get down to the actual tuning, using the three-fork method. In going around the circle of fifths, you will have to tune not only fifths but some octaves because to start with it is best to stay within approximately the same octave. Figure 5 shows the circle of fifths and the progression used in setting the temperament in the notes between middle C and F# at the top of the staff, given in ordinary notation. Figure 6 represents graphically the beats for fifths, fourths, and thirds for a span of two octaves. Note the exponential rise of the beats in the guide.

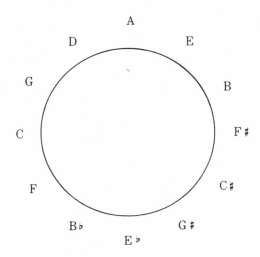

Figure 5. Circle of fifths with the progression used in setting the temperament in notes between middle C and F#. Filled-in notes are those already tuned with forks; enharmonic notations are in parentheses.

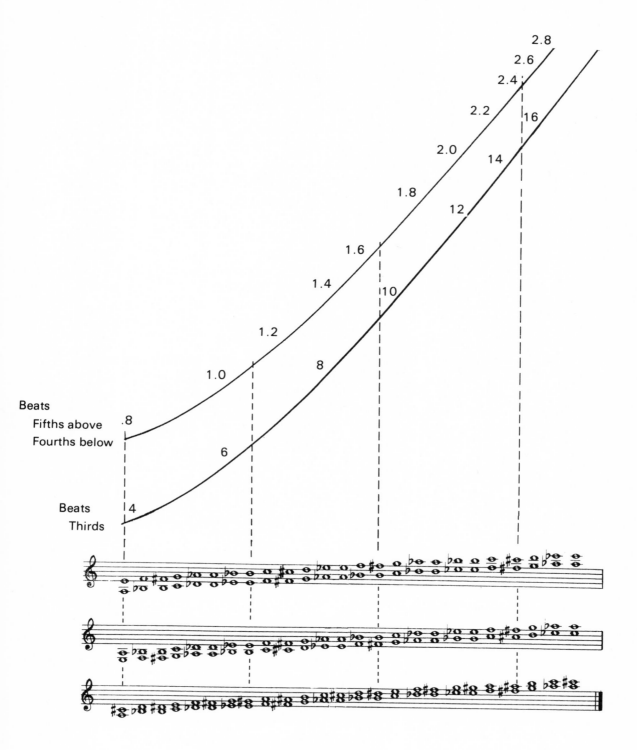

Figure 6. Tuning guide.

It doesn't matter which set of 8′ strings you use to start with (you will recall that they sound at pitch), but the principal register is probably easiest to hear, having fewer upper partials than a more nasal register. But be sure to locate the proper set of pins. You might want to mark the ends of all A, C#, and F pins *carefully* with a bit of model enamel of different colors to make them easier to locate. The paint won't run if you apply it with a Q-tip cotton swab; be sure you do not overload the swab.

Tune A (440) first. Start by striking the fork on the resonator, or on the knee if the resonator is not used, then turn the pin slowly counterclockwise so as to *loosen* the string a bit, listening for the increasing rapidity of beats as the pitch of the string goes down. Make this standard practice, because it helps you to be sure that you have the right string and keeps you from turning the wrong pin to tighten the string and thus perhaps break it. Turn the hammer gently, because harpsichord strings are very thin (from .008″ to about .025″) and will break if violently wrenched. Do not make the pitch scoop below and around the note of the fork the way string players do when tuning because in doing this you are almost sure sooner or later to break the thin treble strings.

Strike the fork repeatedly and gently tighten the string. As it approaches the pitch of the fork, the beats will get slower, finally getting so slow that you can't really hear them as beats but as a very slight waver or as a sort of spacious, echo-like quality in the tone. Finally, when your string is exactly at the pitch of the fork, this quality will disappear and the sound will suddenly seem to drop into focus. At first the sound of fork and string exactly at pitch may seem a little dull or flat compared to echo-like sound just off pitch, and it may even seem a little flat in pitch, but it is correct. Learning to hear the beats will probably take a bit of practice, because most people are so accustomed to listening to the tones producing the beats that they can't hear anything but the tones.

When you get this focused sound, gently turn the wrench clockwise to move a little above pitch, then counterclockwise to go below it, and then return to pitch once more to be sure that you have exactly the right point. For a variety of reasons different strings on an instrument will have slightly different qualities, which show up when you are listening critically to one note at a time. Some in the treble may have slight beats in one string alone, because of being plucked near the middle of the string, and poor instruments may have some extraneous or "wolf" sounds, so that the normal focused sound of the correctly tuned string may not appear as dramatically as it should; in this case you will have to settle for the most nearly focused sound you can get. You may hear some buzzes or sympathetic vibrations in other strings whose dampers aren't working properly, but you must learn to shut these out of your ears—or adjust the dampers. In an extreme case, you might lay some felt over the other strings to damp out extraneous noises.

Now, using the same procedure, tune C# (277.2) and F (349.2). After you have tuned them, check them again with the forks to make sure that pulling them all up to pitch, in a very flat instrument, has not altered the pitch of the first ones. If the instrument is very flat, it may take several complete tunings to get it to stay up to pitch. New strings drop in pitch for a week or more even with constant retuning.

Next tune the octaves of your reference notes, A = 220, C# = 554.4, and F = 698.44, getting the focused sound like that of the unison, with no beats.

You are now ready to begin setting the temperament, the part of the job requiring the most skill. With A, C#, and F exactly in tune with the forks, you have reference points distributed evenly around the circle of fifths, so you can't go too far wrong. You also have three major thirds as a reference for checking by thirds as soon as you get some new ones. Start by sounding A (220) and the E above it, tuning the E down, counterclockwise as always, until the beats get very rapid. Now gently pull E up, continuing to sound both notes, until you get to a pure fifth, which will sound a trifle hollow and dead to ears accustomed to the scale of equal temperament, will have the characteristic *terza suono,* and will have no beats. Again, as with the unison with the fork, the pure fifth will rather suddenly seem to drop into focus. Sounding both notes as often as needed to keep the sound in your ears, now raise E just above the pure fifth, bring it back down through the pure fifth to below that pitch, and bring it back up to pitch at the pure fifth. Do this to get your bearings so you will know which side of the pure fifth you are on when you start tempering that interval.

Now comes the crucial part, the actual tempering. At this part of the scale, the fifth between A and E should be smaller than the pure fifth by one and a half beats. In practice, you will eventually temper the fifth as much by the quality of sound as by trying to count beats. But initially, you might try to count beats, using a metronome set at sixty to give you the one second reference, or count as photographers do by saying "thousand-one, thousand-two," and so on. Let the pitch of E down very slowly while sounding A and E together until you think you hear a beat or waver, at just about one and a half per second. Try it several times, each time from the pure fifth to just below it, because you are making the fifth smaller. The reason for always going to the pure fifth for a reference is that the most common mistake among beginning tuners is to make an occasional fifth larger rather than smaller, as it should be. The larger fifth will sound just about the same as the smaller fifth but of course will throw everything off. The tendency of beginners seems to be to make their fifths too small. You might watch for this tendency. A fifth in equal temperament is not really much smaller than a pure one.

Now proceed from E to B, as before, noting the number of beats in the tuning guide. Then tune from B to F$^\#$, and tune the octave F$^\#$ below. Now comes the test to show whether your fifths—and octaves—were properly tuned. The fifth from the low F$^\#$ octave to C$^\#$ above it should have a beat of about one and a fourth per second (1.24). If it doesn't, don't tune the C$^\#$, which is your first reference, but retouch your F$^\#$, making sure that it is *smaller* than the pure fifth. Doing this may throw the fifth between B and F$^\#$ off, in which case an earlier fifth was off. What you are doing now, if these errors show up, is going backwards from your reference point at C$^\#$. Incidentally, you could have done your initial tuning clockwise around the circle from A-E-B and counterclockwise from C$^\#$-F$^\#$-B. I suggested going clockwise mainly because for a beginner it seems a bit confusing to make the fifth smaller first by lowering the top note and then by raising the bottom note, but if this doesn't confuse you go ahead.

When everything checks out, you will have tuned one-third of the octave. For the next segment, from C$^\#$ to F, proceed exactly the same way except for getting the different numbers of beats for the fifths given in the guide. In the first segment of the octave, we didn't develop any new thirds in addition to the ones we started with, but in the second segment we have A$^\flat$ to C and B to D$^\#$. You should have a smooth progression of thirds, with beats increasing smoothly, from A$^\flat$ to C, A to C$^\#$, to B to D$^\#$ (see the tuning guide).

Tune the third segment of the octave the same way as the others, consulting the notated progression. Now, however, you will have all the thirds between middle C and F an octave above to check against the table of thirds. Or you could simply play the following progression of chords to determine generally by ear whether everything sounds pretty well in tune.

If it does not sound in tune, you must go back to find out what went wrong, picking out the note or notes that sound sour in combination with others.

The great advantage of the three-fork method is that you can make a correction in one segment of the octave without having to retune the whole octave—if the initial strings tuned from the forks haven't been pulled out of tune in the meantime.

If all chords in the part of the scale you have tempered sound harmonious, you are now ready to tune the rest of the instrument, by unisons and octaves. First tune the principal, or whatever register you used to set the temperament, proceeding by octaves from the notes tuned between middle C and F$^\#$ an octave above. It doesn't matter whether you tune the bass or treble first. You should have little difficulty except possibly in the very high treble, where it is rather hard to tell whether the high tone is sharp or flat when it is sounded with the note an octave below. Sometimes it is easier to tune the upper note approximately by playing it and the lower note alternately and then tuning it so the beats disappear when the two notes are sounded together.

After one register is tuned all the way up and down, tune all other registers from this one, by unisons for the 8′ register and octaves for the 4′ register. You may find that the 4′ register is hard to hear if it is regulated to be soft. You may have to increase its volume just a bit for purposes of tuning, so that the loud sound of the 8′ register doesn't drown out the beats. If your instrument has a 16′ register, you should make sure that the lower bass tones are really being tuned an octave below your 8′ notes, for the pitch of the low covered (wound) strings is sometimes indistinct, especially on a shorter instrument.

The three-fork method of tuning I have advocated is admittedly amateurish and quite properly so, because this whole chapter is intended not as a treatise on tuning but as an expedient way for a beginner to get his instrument in tune while at the same time developing the rudiments of tuning technique. When you have gained experience, you may want to move on to the ordinary way of tuning with one fork, using a tuning theme such as the following, which goes up by fifths, down by fourths, and checks with thirds. The tuning guide will tell you how many beats to listen for at any point. Remember that tempered fifths are *smaller* than pure, fourths and thirds are *larger* than pure.

Some professional tuners prefer to tune by thirds, or by thirds and sixths. Because the thirds beat more rapidly than fifths or fourths, they may be easier for some people to hear and to count. If you want to try tuning by thirds, you could use a theme like the following, which employs a few fifths to move from one set of thirds to another. If you have tuned A, C, and F by using three forks, you will already have three correct thirds as reference points, so you can tell whether the beats of the thirds are progressing smoothly.

All information given on tuning in these pages is based on the international standard of A = 440. Historically, pitch has varied about two semitones above and below this standard,[2] but the whole matter is an extremely confused one, and conjectures as to what pitch A really was at any time are often extremely tenuous ones, at least before Handel's trumpeter invented the tuning fork in 1715. You may find other instrumentalists complaining that your pitch is low even though you have just finished tuning with a good fork. Instrumentalists seem naturally to want to raise pitch because it makes them sound more brilliant. On one occasion I was obliged to tune to A = 443 because the orchestra was used to the higher A. Some orchestras use a Strobotuner as a pitch standard—but the orchestral pitch will still rise on the stage. There should be no arguing with the standard set by a high quality fork, and A = 440 should be high enough for anyone, perhaps too high already.[3]

Tuning to other historical temperaments, like the mean tone system, is interesting, but hard to do accurately with forks. If you want to try another system of tuning and have access to a Strobotuner or are willing to construct a monochord (a historical tuning standard having one calibrated string), consult J. M. Barbour's *Tuning and Temperament: A Historical Survey* (East Lansing, Michigan, 1951); he gives a detailed treatment of the subject and gives monochord measurements for various temperaments. For suggested construction of a monochord, see Sigmund Levarie and Ernst Levy, *Tone: A Study in Musical Acoustics* (Kent, Ohio, 1968). George Sargent gives instructions for various kinds of tunings by ear in the journal *The Harpsichord* (published by The International Harpsichord Society, P. O. Box 4323, Denver, Colorado 80204).

A beginner trying to teach himself tuning deserves sympathy and consolation at times, and I would like to close this discussion with the thought that tuning by ear is an art and therefore allows room for subjective decisions. Good tuning approaches the *norm* of the equally tempered octave in which intervals are made up of successively raised powers of $\sqrt[12]{2}$, but in practice good tuning is what sounds good. An instrument with "stretched octaves" in treble and bass measurably deviates from the norm but still sounds good. What I have tried to do in this chapter is to provide you with some information on which to base subjective decisions as you learn to hear tones in a way unfamiliar to most musicians who don't have the tuning problem. If you can get three forks pretty well in tune with each other, you may find it comfortable to stick with using them. Very likely you will soon develop the skill and confidence to use one fork and trust your ear. If you wish more technical information on tuning, it is provided in Appendix C.

9

MAINTENANCE

The action of a harpsichord is extremely simple. Pressing a key lever pushes up a jack, which has a tongue in an elongated slot. The tongue pivots at its lower end but is stopped at its top end from swinging more than a certain amount toward the string. The tongue is held at its forward position by a spring. In the tongue, at right angles, is a plectrum, which plucks the string as the jack rides up because the tongue is stopped in its forward motion but goes past the string without plucking it on the way down because the tongue is free to swing away from the string. After swinging past the string the tongue returns to its forward position. Compared with the piano's enormously complicated system of levers and friction devices this is an extremely simple mechanism—nothing more than a mechanized miniature guitar pick. Unfortunately, it is rather delicate and much more inclined to get out of adjustment than a piano's mechanism in spite of the piano's greater complexity.

JACKS

Modern harpsichord makers have attempted to reduce the need for adjustment to a minimum by using marvelous materials like the new plastic Delrin (an acetal resin) for quills, jack bodies, tongues, and springs. As a quill, Delrin lasts almost indefinitely, unlike the crow, turkey, and vulture quills used in the historical period of the harpsichord. As a jack body, it is dimensionally stable under all kinds of heat and humidity conditions and is highly resistant to wear; it is also self-lubricating and therefore moves quietly with little resistance.

Even so, the jacks do get out of adjustment, mostly because some of the structural parts of the instrument swell, contract, or, in some instances, warp, since it is essentially made of wood. Delrin jacks themselves sometimes warp because the material has a "memory" and wants to reassume a bend it had at the time it was formed. But the harpsichord makers have provided various kinds of adjustments. The one most often used is a screw adjusting the amount of bite that the plectrum takes: the amount the plectrum sticks past the string when the register is engaged. The other adjustment is the end pin (sometimes called the pilot), which adjusts the amount the jack juts up and therefore adjusts the distance that the plectrum sits below the string when at rest. Another adjustment is used when a whole register is taking too much of a bite or not enough. This adjustment moves the whole slide and therefore all the jacks of a register to the left or right.

These adjustments are simple, since the mechanism is simple, and the way to make them can be readily seen by looking at the jacks themselves or at the slide mechanism. What is not so obvious is the proper amount of adjustment. Most people who construct harpsichords from kits adjust their instruments with far too much bite, perhaps with the mistaken idea that voicing it with a large bite will increase the volume. Up to a point, increasing the bite will increase the volume because doing so increases the displacement of the string when it is plucked and therefore increases the amplitude of its vibrations. But there is a limit, and getting the last few fractions of a decibel out of the instrument is accomplished at great cost to the quality of tone produced and to the touch that results. An instrument voiced too loud produces a harsh tone because of extraneous unmusical noise, and the touch becomes so stiff and hard that it is almost impossible to play most of the music written for the instrument, especially the delightfully ornamented music of the French masters.

The instrument can be voiced to be too soft, so that the plectra do little more than nudge the strings as they go past. With this kind of voicing, the touch is very light indeed, but the tone lacks depth and focus.

Within the limits suggested by the preceding remarks, voicing is a matter of taste and the player's strength, and it also depends partly on the shape, thickness, and material of the plectra. Ordinarily, the plectrum should stick out a little beyond the string and not merely brush past it. A short, stiff plectrum should stick out very little past the string, while a longer, thinner plectrum, especially if it is tapered (as plastic plectra usually are), may be quite a bit longer, perhaps sticking out 1/32″ past the string.

Adjusting the amount of bite in a hard plastic plectrum has a relatively small effect on the amount of sound produced, although it does have an effect on the stiffness of the touch. It is for this reason that half-hitches or soft stops on instruments with plastic plectra are rarely used—or even installed. But the amount of bite with leather plectra makes a real difference, and half-hitches in instruments with leather plectra—or the softer plastics, used on some instruments—are common.

An instrument adjusted for concert use of course will be voiced to the point of optimum loudness and perhaps sometimes even to a point just beyond, if the hall is large and some of the slight harshness of the loud sound can be tolerated in exchange for a little extra volume. For the home, however, the voicing should be modest.

Earlier I mentioned the end pins, which are threaded and screw into the bottom of the jack bodies. These adjust the amount that the key may be depressed before the plectrum touches the string. The touch on a harpsichord should be quite shallow compared with the piano but not so shallow as to be hair-triggered, for then the merest accidental brushing of a key will make it sound. Ordinarily the total key-fall of a harpsichord should be about 5/16″ before it meets the resistance of either a felt washer or "punching" under the key or of the jack bumping against the padded underside of the jackrail. The point at which the key depression causes the plectrum to pluck the string should be nearer the beginning of the stroke than the end to allow a certain amount of follow through in the stroke. Usually the string should be plucked when the key is depressed about 1/12″ or 1/8″.

But before the end pin is adjusted for the proper amount of key-fall for plucking, the amount of bite should be adjusted, because a long bite will require that the key be depressed farther before plucking than will a short bite: more of the plectrum must move against the string before passing it. So changing the amount of bite will also change the amount that the key is pressed before it will cause the string to be plucked. If the jack is to work properly, there are limits to the amount of adjustment possible for plectra and end pins, however, and there are two simple tests that will enable you to know whether you have exceeded either or both of these limits. To apply these tests, engage one register at a time and, beginning with one end of the keyboard, (1) repeat each key rapidly and (2) let each key up slowly.

If a key will not repeat, the problem could be one of four things: (1) the quill is too long; (2) the end pin is turned too far in, leaving the plectrum with too great a distance to travel; (3) the end pin is turned too far out, leaving the plectrum too little distance in which to gain momentum before it plucks the string; and (4) the spring that returns the tongue to its rest position is weak and does not return the tongue quickly enough. If the quill is too long, turn in the screw that regulates the bite of the quill about a quarter-turn. If the end pin is turned too far in, lengthen the end pin a turn or two or more if necessary by turning it counterclockwise. If the end pin is turned too far out, shorten the end pin a turn or two or more if necessary by turning it clockwise. If the spring is weak, it needs replacing.

If the key will not repeat on a subsequent stroke after being slowly let up, one of two things could be the matter: (1) the quill may be too long or (2) the end pin is turned too far out, leaving the quill too near the string in its position of rest. If the quill is too long, turn in the screw regulating it. If the end pin is turned too far out, turn it in (clockwise) one or two turns, more if necessary. Any end pin adjustment necessitates a slight adjustment of the damper (see my remarks on dampers below) so that it is lightly resting on the string in the jack's position of rest.

A sticking key can be the cause of either the failure of the jack to repeat rapid tones or to return the quill to its normal position so that it can repeat a tone after a slow release. If that is the case, however, it will be apparent from the fact that the key itself does not return to its normal position.

The sound of a harpsichord with more than one set of strings being plucked by more than one set of plectra gives the impression that all sets of strings are being plucked at exactly the same time. This is an illusion produced by the quick strokes of a competent player. On most harpsichords, even those in perfect adjustment, a slow stroke on the key, such as might be used on the piano, will show that the plectra pluck at different degrees of key depression. It is desirable that they do this, because having three and sometimes four sets of plectra plucking at exactly the same time would produce an intolerably heavy touch. So the plucking points follow each other in close succession, and it is up to the player to strike the keys quickly (rather than merely press them) to keep the sound clean.

The succession of plucks should, however, be close. Even a skillful player will have trouble avoiding a rather clattery sound if one string is plucked at a key depression of 1/12″ and another at 1/4″. And of course if some strings don't sound until the key is almost at the bottom, the player will not have the feeling of being able to follow through with the stroke and will be fighting the keyboard. So all registers should sound within a space of 1/8″ or so after the first string has sounded.

The order in which the registers sound is usually not crucial, but it makes good sense to have the combinations most often used sound closest together. On a large instrument, these two will be the 4′ and the principal 8′ registers. To bring out the brightness in a combination using the 4′ register, it is usually made to sound first, followed by the principal 8′, then the second 8′, and then the 16′ if there is one.

Especially in summer, you may find that a jack doesn't return fast enough for rapidly repeated notes. Various things can cause this: the jack may have warped a bit, or swelled if it is a wooden one; a key lever may be sluggish because of excessive friction with the felt in the hole where the key lever guide is located; or a key lever may have warped and be rubbing an adjacent one. A warped Delrin jack should be straightened, not sanded or filed. Earlier I remarked that this plastic has a "memory" of a previous condition to which it wants to return. One can stress it in an opposite direction to help destroy that memory. Bend the jack firmly in the direction opposite to the one it bows in, taking care not to hold it by the end pin or above the hole for the tongue, because these are weak points. The jack itself is very tough and will withstand a fairly harsh bend. When returned to its slot, it should move freely, but it will be out of registration. A swelled wooden jack will require a little careful sanding.

Neupert instruments have round metal jacks moving in a hole through a metal slide. If these stick, it is probably because of a slight amount of dirt in the hole, which is easily cleaned out with the small brush provided; it resembles a rifle brush. No solvents should be used, since the jacks and holes are chemically lubricated, and solvents would run down onto the key levers, causing possible damage to felts.

If a key lever is causing the trouble, first try working the key up and down while exerting a little sideways pressure. If the difficulty was in friction in the key lever guide, this will usually correct it. If, however, the friction is occurring because the key lever itself is rubbing against another one, you may have to take the keyboard out. But first remove the fallboard (with the maker's name on it), and look inside at the key levers of the manual in question to see if the space between the key levers has closed up or narrowed. You might try rubbing some sandpaper between the keys while they are still in the instrument.

If this doesn't work, the keyboard will have to be removed. Doing this may require so much courage for the uninitiated that it would be preferable to call a competent piano technician—or a harpsichord technician, if there is one available. Removing the keyboard must be done with great caution and on many instruments it requires removing all the jacks first. If jacks are removed, their order should not be mixed up, because they are individually adjusted. Usually they are numbered up from the bass. A piano technician who is going to work on harpsichords should study Frank Hubbard's *Harpsichord Regulating and Repairing* (published by Tuner's Supply Inc., Boston, Mass., 1963) before attempting very much repairing. This book was written especially for piano and organ technicians.

PLECTRA

Thus far we have considered adjustments built into the instrument that may be manipulated with screw driver or pliers. It may be necessary to alter the plectra themselves, if they were improperly made or otherwise turned out to be unsatisfactory. They may be too thick in an instrument to be used exclusively in the home. Or some of them may be too long, requiring the adjusting screw to hold the tongue too far back in the jack. Altering the shape or thickness of the plectra isn't hard but it must be done with care to avoid making nicks that will lead to breaks. The most useful tools for this purpose are a single-edge razor blade and an X-acto knife (no. 1) with the long tapered blade (no. 11) or similar knife available in stationery and office supply stores.

If an instrument has been properly quilled with quills of a durable material like Delrin, complete requilling will probably not be necessary for many years. But requilling is occasionally done; it is a rather exacting job and it is hard to find someone else to do it. The reasons for some of my suggestions will become clearer if we first consider briefly what happens when the quill plucks the string. When I say "quill," I of course include leather plectra too.

A piano string is set into vibration by a quick blow from a hammer, a violin string is rubbed by a bow, but a harpsichord string is plucked: first displaced, pushed out of the straight line it normally has, and then suddenly snapped free. With a given amount of damping in the snap and a given speed for the snap, the amplitude of the string's vibration and hence its loudness are determined by the amount it is pushed out of line. The snap should be quick so the string is completely free to vibrate as its length, mass, and tension dictate as soon as possible after its release; if it does not do so, it will lose some of its volume. A soft plectrum material like leather will release it just a little more slowly than a hard material and will damp the sound a little, suppressing some of the upper partials. With one qualification, the speed with which the string is displaced is not significant, since it is the amount and not the speed of the displacement that governs the volume and since the acoustical properties of the whole instrument almost entirely govern the tone. There is the qualification, however, that a string that is displaced so rapidly that its segments on both sides of the plucking point sag like a clothesline will produce a slightly different sound than one displaced gradually enough for it to form straight lines from the plucking point to the two ends. The very suddenly displaced string will have more upper partials and perhaps, speaking subjectively, just a little more volume. Harpsichordists use this feature occasionally for a climactic chord, striking the keys very fast and hard, but the basic touch is a quick light one that is pretty consistently the same. So in talking about quill action, we can fairly confidently disregard the speed of displacement and direct our attention to its mechanism.

The quill lets the string go because it bends, allowing the string to slip off. A perfectly stiff quill would simply push the string without letting it go. All harpsichord quills, therefore, have some flexibility and are really little springs. As the key is pressed, the quill bends, storing energy that will be released when it snaps free. In bending, it also displaces the string more slowly than would a perfectly stiff quill, because it is acting not only as a spring but as a wedge (or half of a wedge), pushing the string up and to one side. Since the change of momentum of the string results from the force exerted multiplied by the time it takes to exert it, the wedge feature of the bent quill, in slowing down the displacement, reduces the force required at the key lever.

Here we finally get to the relation between quills and touch. The touch of a harpsichord might be described in terms of the amount of force required to pluck the string and the abruptness with which plucking occurs. The two may be the same thing. At any rate, it is clear that a very stiff quill will require a force more rapidly exerted for a given displacement of the string than would a flexible one. And the action of plucking as felt at the key lever would be abrupt, whereas with the flexible quill it would be felt as a smoothly increasing resistance and a smooth letting go. With a really stiff quill, there may be a momentary lapse of control over the key as the quill abruptly snaps past the string, whereas with the flexible quill the key lever should remain under better control because the snapping off the string is done more by the spring action of the quill than by the finger on the key.

The quill might also be compared to a shock absorber, or perhaps a fishing pole, which helps the fisherman exert a smooth force on the fish to avoid breaking his line. Or it might be compared to a flywheel in an automobile, which stores energy from the explosions of the engine and transmits power smoothly. It allows the stroke on the key to be smooth and light while transmitting the energy of the stroke in a way that results in a sharp snap.

In general, the lighter the touch a harpsichord has, the easier it is to play, but the following things limit how much lightness can be achieved from making longer flexible quills: (1) the shallow key-fall, (2) the space between the strings, and (3) the distance the jack is able to drop while still letting the quill return to its rest position under the string.

In a quill that is a little over 1/8″ long, differences that seem small take on a good deal of significance, a fact which took me some time to appreciate. Changing the length of a quill by 1/64″ seems trifling until one recognizes that this is a change of 12.5 percent and a change of .05″ inches in thickness is anywhere from 30 percent on up. Small differences show up very noticeably in the action of the instrument, in the way it feels to play it.

Only a few years ago replacing a Delrin quill was a rather tedious and somewhat uncertain process because the Delrin used for plectra came in strips or sheets too thick for the purpose. Now, however, pre-cut Delrin plectra are available in three thicknesses (.016″, .019″, and .022″) from the B & G Instrument Workshop (see p. 193) at less than a cent apiece. The plectrum is cut to taper very gradually toward the end that plucks the string so that it can be firmly held in the tongue by friction when it is inserted from the back of the tongue. It is inserted into the tongue, and any part of it sticking out of the back of the tongue is cut off flush with it; then it is scraped toward the tip. The X-acto knife is good for cutting and trimming; the razor blade is best for scraping. Scraping should be done on the bottom side of the plectrum while the top side is held firmly against a thumbnail.

The finished quill, as I mentioned, is actually a little spring that stores energy released in the plucking action, and it should have some of the characteristics of a fishing rod, bending but also having a firm resistance. Like a fishing rod, it should be thinner at the tip than at its base at the tongue. It is hard to give exact measurements for its graduated thickness since it is so small, but it can be almost the thickness of the original material at the base but scraped to 0.01″ or less at the tip. The quill should start getting thin near the base and gradually get thinner towards the tip. This gradual thinning comes about quite naturally in the action of scraping, if one scrapes toward the tip, because when you set the razor blade against the quill you will want to avoid pushing the edge in so as not to get a nick, and you will find yourself exerting more pressure toward the tip. Very likely you will also find yourself rotating the blade a bit as you scrape and the right degree of thinning will result. Be sure to clean off any burrs, because a small burr can produce large effects in sound.

If you are requilling or adjusting a whole instrument, you may want to follow the suggestion of Frank Hubbard and work on all the C's first, then the D's and so on, to make the voicing of the instrument even over the whole keyboard. It is easily possible for infinitesimal differences in voicing to become progressively quite finite in the sixty-one notes in a standard harpsichord if you work from one end to the other.

Requilling a harpsichord fitted with leather plectra requires cutting rather than scraping. The very tip of the leather is tapered by a diagonal cut on the under side. The leather on the top of the quill must be smooth. Often if a leather plectrum seems to be plucking more loudly than its neighbors and can't be easily adjusted to conformity, it may be too stiff. Its stiffness can be decreased by flexing it up and down with the fingers. No amount of flexing has any permanent effect on Delrin.

Some instruments, like the popular German Neuperts, use a soft plastic which behaves rather like leather. This too must be cut, but the quill starts to taper at the base. The X-acto knife with the tapered blade is almost indispensable for cutting this material. Ideally, in shaping these quills, you should make your first cut correctly. If your instrument is equipped with quills of this material and if the instrument is voiced at all loudly, you will have occasion to develop skill in repair, because they break much more often than Delrin or leather.

One maker a few years ago used heavy nylon fishline for quills, which required no shaping to install but did require frequent replacement because they succumbed to fatigue at the base, grew weak, and eventually broke.

DAMPERS

Dampers require adjustment as the instrument changes with humidity and as the felt gets compacted or wears. A damper should be adjusted so that the end pin is just sitting on the key lever, so the jack starts to rise as soon as the key lever is pushed down even a little but also so that the damper immediately stops the string from sounding when the key is let up. A damper should, in other words, press down on the string but only so much that the compression of the damper felt allows the end pin to touch the key lever. If the jack is actually hanging on its damper, there will be a loss in control and a disconcerting gap in the key stroke before the jack starts up. If you replace a damper felt on a damper requiring glue, put the glue on the metal or whatever the felt is glued to, not on the felt, and use glue that won't penetrate the felt and produce a hard damper. Goodyear Plyobond or General Electric flexible silicone cement work very well. The silicone cement, which is very flexible but strong, could be used to stiffen the back side of a damping felt that is too floppy to work properly.

REPLACING STRINGS

Harpsichord strings, although very thin (ranging from about .025″ to .009″ or even less), usually will not break unless violently wrenched in tuning. But occasionally a string does break, and when it happens the first time most people seem to panic. Actually, replacing a string isn't hard if you observe a few rules.

The replacement string, of course, must be the same diameter and of the same material as the broken one. The maker of the instrument is the best source for a new string, because he will have the right material and will know the diameter from his stringing charts. Covered strings for 16′ registers must be obtained from the maker. Small coils of steel and brass harpsichord strings are available from Tuner's Supply Co. and from the B & G Instrument Workshop, which also stocks phosphor bronze strings, used in the extreme bass of some instruments. You can measure string diameters accurately enough with an inexpensive micrometer ($5 or less).

Be careful to hold the wire as you take it off the spool or loop, because it is very springy and when let go can easily get itself into a snarl that defies analysis. Measure off about six inches more than you need, *being careful not to get any kinks or even bends into it.* Almost any bend in a piece of brass wire will so weaken it that when it is straightened it will snap as it is being tightened. So uncurl it loosely.

Now remove the wrestpin, or tuning pin, by turning it counterclockwise and lay it down near its normal location. Then form a loop in the end of the string to go over the hitchpin by carefully wrapping the wire tightly around itself at least six times. Do not use pliers with sharp grooves in the jaws for this, because they may notch the wire and cause it to break. This part will be easier if you stick a large nail through the loop to hold it as you wind.

At this point you might want to get another pair of hands to help. Now loop the end of the string over the hitchpin, routing the string so that it goes on the proper side of the damping strip behind the bridge, and gently straighten the string as you pull it toward the location of the tuning pin. Watch very carefully for kinks as the wire uncurls. Insert the wire through the small hole in the pin and bend the wire at the end so you can hold it with the pin as you move on to the next step.

Notice how many turns of wire the neighboring pins have, and notice the down-draft (the amount the wire angles from the nut to the pin) and the height of these pins. Since a harpsichord tuning pin is a little less than 0.2″ in diameter, each turn takes about 0.6″ of string. The threads on the pin will pull it down into the wrestplank about .05″ per turn, or a little more than ⅛″ every three turns.

Insert the pin into its hole to see how much the pin will have to be pulled down by turning. The number of turns for a proper down-draft will probably be one or two more than the turns required to pull the pin down. Take the pin out of the hole and pull the string fairly tight, checking to see that it lies next to the proper jack as you measure approximately the amount of string needed to get the right down-draft. Bend the string in the hole of the pin in the right point, and wrap one or two turns around the pin in the proper direction. Set the pin firmly in the hole with your fingers or by tapping it with the tuning hammer while holding the wire so as to take up the slack. Then start turning the pin clockwise and feeding the wire to it so that a single layer of wire goes onto the pin. When the slack is taken out of the wire, but before it is tight, make sure that the wire lies correctly on the bridge, drops in front of the jack that will pluck it, and is not otherwise out of line. Then slowly turn the pin to bring the note up to pitch.

The string will almost immediately go flat, as it stretches or the loop slips on the hitchpin with a noose action, and it will continue to do so for some time, requiring constant retuning. To speed up the stretching, carefully pull it up a half tone or even a little more above pitch for a day or so.

I might add one more thing. Sometimes the holes in tuning pins have such sharp edges that they will cut a string as you start wrapping it. A sharp edge makes a sharp bend, which brass wire cannot tolerate. You might examine the pin to see if this is the case, and, if so, round off the edges with a drill somewhat larger than the hole or with a small round file.

Harpsichord technicians are hard to find except in large cities, and not many piano technicians are yet familiar enough with the harpsichord to undertake many repairs. Colleges and universities with harpsichords, however, will usually know of someone who could be of help, perhaps someone on the faculty or a piano technician who has studied the harpsichord to maintain the school's instruments. Most makers will also know of someone who is qualified, although for any major repairs they will usually prefer having the instrument returned to them. Each maker has his preferred means of shipping in such cases, and you should consult him about it. Do not have any repairs made other than the sort of routine maintenance described in this chapter without the maker's approval, especially if you have an instrument that you might later turn back to him on a larger one.

COMMON PROBLEMS

Following is a checklist of common difficulties with suggested remedies:

Beats heard on one string.

> A damper on another string may not be working. In the extreme treble, some notes simply produce beats, perhaps because of being plucked near the middle.

Buzzing string.

> The back of a jack is too close to the string because one register moves too far to its off position: Adjust the capstan screw limiting movement to the off position.

Jack won't return.

> A jack may be sticking in the slide because it is warped or has swelled: Straighten or sand (if wooden). A jack may be hanging on its damper: Adjust damper. The quill may be taking so much bite that it won't drop past the string: Adjust quill.

> The end pin may be set out too far so quill is too close to the string at rest position: Turn end pin in. A key lever may be sticking: Work it up and down or sand (see text discussion).

Jack returns but won't repeat fast enough.

> Jack may be sticking slightly or key levers may be rubbing: See Jack won't return.

Key goes down too far before note sounds (on one register).

> End pin is too far in or quill takes much too much bite or both: Adjust. If this happens in a key when the coupler is on, the coupler requires adjustment: Seek professional help if you don't have instructions on adjusting the coupler.

A key goes down more stiffly than its neighbor when two registers are engaged.

> Two quills are plucking simultaneously rather than successively: See text discussion and adjust end pin.

Mechanical thumping noise

> Jack rail is loose or felt on underside of jack rail under key is compressed.

One note sounds different than others.

There may be a blob of dust on the string. The quill may have a burr or be fatigued and weakened. A felt on the buff stop may be lightly touching the string.

Soundboard warps noticeably.

Humidity is too high: Move the instrument or de-humidify the room.

Strings break by themselves.

This rarely happens but is due to heat and/or humidity.

Strings break in tuning.

You are turning the pins too violently: See chapter on tuning.

Undamped tone even though the damper works on the note played.

A damper on another string isn't working, allowing a sympathetic vibration: Check dampers on other unisons and octaves, then fifths, and so on.

APPENDIX A:
Readings in Early Keyboard Fingering

1. C. P. E. Bach, *Essay on the True Art of Playing Keyboard Instruments* (1953), trans. and ed. William Mitchell (New York, 1949), chapter 1, "Fingering," pp. 41–78. Instructions with copious musical illustrations on how to play scales in all keys, double notes (including octaves), and chords. Discusses "turning" of the thumb, crossing the fingers, leaps, change of finger on the same key, sliding.

2. François Couperin, *L'art de toucher le clavecin* (1717), trans. Anna Linde, Breitkopf & Härtel (Wiesbaden, 1933). Couperin presents his ideas in diffuse and disorganized fashion, but we are indebted to him for the trouble he took to make his wishes known, and no performer should play his music without studying his instructions. The book includes the *Eight Preludes* (containing some fingerings), as well as a section on passages in the first book of *Ordres* with difficult fingering problems. Couperin advocates much finger substitution, changing fingers on a repeated note for more finely controlled articulation, and playing successive notes with the same finger, to produce the desired phrasing. He also seems to prefer the old scale fingering. Wilfrid Mellers's book *François Couperin and the French Classical Tradition* (London, 1950; Dover reprint, New York, 1968) discusses the interdependence of fingering and phrasing in Couperin's music, pp. 308–10.

3. Arnold Dolmetsch, *The Interpretation of the Music of the XVII & XVIII Centuries,* 2nd ed. (London, 1946), chapter 6, "Position and Fingering," pp. 364–418. A fairly comprehensive survey of fingering practices in each country during the whole period, with numerous musical examples, including those from Nicolaus Amerbach (1571), Diruta (1597) *The Fitzwilliam Virginal Book,*

Purcell (1696), Dandrieu (1705–10), Couperin (1717), Rameau (1731), Quantz (1752), and J. S. Bach. Many of these sources, not available in 1916 when Dolmetsch wrote the book, are now published in translation, and the reader will wish to consult them directly.

4. *The Fitzwilliam Virginal Book,* vol. I (Dover reprint, New York, 1963). Original fingerings are included in the pieces on the following pages: 19, 23 (Munday); 37, 83, 203, 214, 238 (Byrd); 42 (Morley); 335 (Philips); 196 (Farnaby); 76 (Anon.); 81 ("El. Kiderminster"); and 70, 124, and 129 (Bull).

5. Eta Harich-Schneider, *The Harpsichord* (Kassel-Basel, 1960), "Fingering," pp. 19–24. A brief, somewhat confusing, summary of baroque fingering practices, including those of the sixteenth-century Spaniards, Cabezon and Fray Tomas de Santa Maria. There are no musical examples. Her longer work *Die Kunst des Cembalospiels,* 1939, out of print and not available in translation, includes a discussion of fingering practices (pp. 34–39) as exemplified in fifteen pieces in the *Fitzwilliam Virginal Book.* I have listed them here under that title, so that you may look up the original fingerings in the Dover edition.

6. *Clement Matchett's Virginal Book* (1612), trans. and ed., Thurston Dart (London, 1957). Contains the original fingerings.

7. *My Ladye Nevells Booke of Virginal Music,* William Byrd, (1591), trans. and ed. Thurston Dart (Dover reprint, New York, 1969). Original fingerings may be found in pieces numbered 1, 2, 3, 5, 7, 36, 39, and others. Early English fingers are numbered from left to right in each hand, so that, while the right hand fingering is the customary 1 2 3 4 5 from thumb to little finger, it is the reverse in the left hand: the thumb is numbered 5, and the little finger is numbered 1.

8. Jean-Philippe Rameau, *Pièces de Clavecin,* ed. E. Jacobi (Kassel-Basel, 1958). Includes a few notes on fingering and a Minuet with original fingerings. In his preface to the *Pièces* (1724), Rameau gives instruction in the five-finger position, getting away from the old differentiation between "good" and "bad" fingers.

9. Alessandro Scarlatti, *Seven Toccatas,* ed. Rio Nardi (Kassel-Basel, 1964). The first toccata includes Scarlatti's fingerings.

APPENDIX B:

Editions

Recently when one of our daughters began working on a Handel violin sonata, I gave her my good Bärenreiter edition to use. A few days later I asked her how she liked playing from such a clear, well-edited edition. She replied, "That edition is *terrible*. No fingerings, no bowings, and it doesn't even say how you're supposed to play the ornaments!" I suddenly realized that it isn't enough to have a good edition in front of you—you have to also know how to use it.

Many students have a similar reaction when they first encounter a well-edited score, having been used to the false security of the over-edited, even inaccurate editions that were considered acceptable by many musicians until a relatively few years ago. Unless a player has some sophistication in the use of a well-edited text (which includes knowledge of earlier notational practice), he is apt to play about as inaccurately from an authoritative modern critical edition as he did from one of the earlier, capriciously edited variety, although his inaccuracies will be different ones.

What is the answer to the dilemma? Although performers of early music need to be familiar with notational practice, they clearly cannot do their own editing. Yet, in order to know how to use good editions, they ought to know how editing is done.

What, then, should good editing do? And how does the performer go about using the information a good editor provides? Walter Emery answers these questions in a succinct and down-to-earth little booklet, *Editions and Musicians* (Novello, 1957), available for a little over a dollar. Anyone who wants to know the proper use of a good text should buy it.[1]

Good editing, Emery points out, is the foundation on which all other musical activities are based; without it "no performer can safely play old music, no analyst can safely analyse it, and no historian or critic can safely assess it."[2] He defines good editing as "the process of finding out what a composer meant to write, when the composer is dead and cannot be consulted" and as making educated conjectures, clearly labelled as such, about what a composer probably meant to be *played*, when solid evidence is lacking. The editor should show how he arrived at the text he prints, listing his sources and explaining his use of them, not merely noting variants, and he should make his editorial marks so clear that they won't be confused with the composer's notations.[3]

Most performers nowadays know enough to reject what Saint Saëns did to Couperin or Griepenkerl and Czerny did to Bach, but many have gone to the other extreme and joined what Emery refers to as the Cult of the Urtext. This unquestioning faith in the idea of a pristine text can be dangerous too, for, as Emery points out, "There is no such thing as an 'original text' of any piece of old music. . . . The fact is that all modern reprints of old music have been edited in some sense, whether for good or evil."[4]

Since a performer cannot be sure whether the edition he has can be trusted without learning the editor's trade and retracing his steps, he must learn how to recognize the signs of good editorship. There are many excellent editions now in print which may serve as models in this respect. Among them are the Jacobi edition of Rameau's complete harpsichord works, the Kirkpatrick edition of sixty Scarlatti Sonatas, and the volumes in the Corpus of Early Keyboard Music series. The Ralph Kirkpatrick *Scarlatti,* as well as Sylvia Marlowe's *Selected Harpsichord Music by François Couperin le Grand* (G. Schirmer, Inc., 1970), represents a kind of ultimate in editing, with recordings available by the artist-editor.

The following list of modern critical editions will, I hope, provide a reliable guide to well-edited music for solo harpsichord. Although rather long, the list is not by any means complete. I have omitted the piano-oriented editions of the late nineteenth and early twentieth centuries, for, although collections like Farrenc's *Le Tresor des Pianistes* (1861–72) and Ernst Pauer's *Alte Meister* (1868–85) are of historical interest, they are of little practical use to the reader of this book.[5] Also I have entirely omitted twentieth-century harpsichord music, because this task has been undertaken by Robert Conant and Frances Bedford of the University of Wisconsin, whose index of twentieth-century harpsichord music should be available soon. And I have made no attempt to list all the good commercially available editions of *selections* from various composers. I have listed *some* volumes in this category, such as those small, inexpensive volumes in the excellent series of English Keyboard Music published by Stainer and Bell, since a student who is starting a library of harpsichord editions might prefer to acquire a wider selection of scores than to concentrate at first on fewer and fatter volumes.

It is almost inevitable that some of the volumes listed include music from the beginning of the harpsichord period that can be played on either harpsichord or organ or music from the end of it that can be played on either harpsichord or piano. But in the main this listing can be regarded as containing music written specifically for the harpsichord alone.

Most of the volumes are commercially available, except for some which are part of an out of print historical or collected edition; and many of those are being reprinted. When a volume is not available at a reasonable price, it should be in the collection of any reasonably large university.

For those new to the harpsichord I would recommend that they begin with Howard Ferguson's two volumes from *Style and Interpretation* listed in the anthologies section and continue with his other volumes of *Early Keyboard Music*. In addition to the extremely well-edited music, his concise and informative comments on the music are invaluable as an introduction to the use of authentic editions of harpsichord music.

The reader will note that the large bulk of these editions have appeared in the last two decades, a great number of them in the past few years, and excellent editions continue to pour out in great profusion. When the player is trying to decide which of several editions of a composer's works to buy, he can usually, though not always, find the most recent edition to be the best choice because its editor has been able to avail himself of the most recent advances in scholarship in that particular area.

Abbreviations Used

CdMI	*I Classici della musica italiana*
CEKM	*Corpus of Early Keyboard Music*
CMI	*I Classici musicali italiana*
DdT	*Denkmäler deutscher Tonkunst*
DTB	*Denkmäler der Tonkunst in Bayern*
DTOe	*Denkmäler der Tonkunst in Oesterreich*
MB	*Musica Britannica*
MMA	*Mitteldeutsches Musik-Archiv*
MMB	*Monumenta Musica Belgicae*
MME	*Monumentos de la Música Española*
MMN	*Monumenta Musica Neerlandica*
NMA	*Nagels Musik Archiv*
PM	*Portugaliae Musica*
PSFM	*Publications de la société française de musicologie*
PSMS	*Penn State Music Series*
SBK	*Stainer & Bell Keyboard Series*
Torchi	Torchi, *L'arte musicale in Italia*
VNM	*Vereniging voor nederlandsche Muziekgeschiedenis*

Collections and Anthologies

Apel, Willi. *Keyboard Music of the Fourteenth and Fifteenth Centuries.* Vol. 1 of *CEKM.* Rome: American Institute of Musicology, 1963.

————. *Musik aus früher Zeit.* 2 vols. Mainz: B. Schott's Söhne, 1934.

Botstiber, Hugo. *Wiener Klavier-und Orgelwerke aus der zweiter Hälfte des 17. Jahrhunderts.* DTOe, vol. 27. Vienna: Osterreichischer Bundesverlag, 1906. Reprinted Graz, Austria: Akademische Druck-und Verlagsanstalt, 1959–.

I Classici della musica italiana [ed. d'Annunzio]. 36 vols. Milan: Società Anonima Notari La Santa, 1919–21.

I Classici musicali italiana [ed. G. Benvenuti & others]. 15 vols. Fondazione Eugenio Bravi. Milan: I Classici musicali italiana, 1941–43, 1956.

Corpus of Early Keyboard Music. Willi Apel, ed. Rome: American Institute of Musicology, 1963–.

Curtis, Alan. *Nederlandse Klaviermuziek uit de 16e en 17e eeuw.* Vol. 3 of *MMN.* Amsterdam: Nederlandse Muziekgeschiedenis, 1961.

Dawes, Frank. *Schott's Anthology of Early Keyboard Music.* 5 vols. London: Schott, 1951–.

Denkmäler deutscher Tonkunst. Folge I. 65 vols. Leipzig: Breitkopf & Härtel; Graz, Austria: Akademische Druck-und Verlagsanstalt, 1957–61.

Denkmäler der Tonkunst in Bayern [*Denkmaler deutscher Tonkunst,* Folge II]. 36 vols. Braunschweig: H. Litolff's Verlag, 1900–38; new rev. ed., 1962–.

Denkmäler der Tonkunst in Oesterreich. Vienna: Osterreichischer Bundesverlag, 1894–19–. Reprinted Graz: Akademische Druck-und Verlagsanstalt, 1959–.

Ferguson, Howard, *Early English Keyboard Music.* 2 vols. London: Oxford University Press, 1969.

————. *Early French Keyboard Music.* 2 vols. London: Oxford University Press, 1969.

————. *Early German Keyboard Music.* 2 vols. London: Oxford University Press, 1969.

————. *Early Italian Keyboard Music.* 2 vols. London: Oxford University Press, 1969.

————. *Style and Interpretation.* 2 vols. Vol. 1, *Early Keyboard Music: England and France.* Vol. 2, *Early Keyboard Music: Germany and Italy.* London: Oxford University Press, 1969.

Fischer, Hans, and Fritz Oberdörffer, eds. *Deutsche Klaviermusik des 17. und 18. Jahrhunderts.* 9 vols. Berlin: Vieweg Musikverlag, 1936. 2nd ed., 1960. English ed., *German Keyboard Music of the Seventeenth and Eighteenth Centuries.* 9 vols. Berlin, 1960. See vols. 2 and 3.

Georgii, Walter. *400 Jahre europaischer Klaviermusik.* Vol. 1 of *Das Musikwerk.* Cologne: Arno Volk, 1951. (English ed., *400 Years of European Keyboard Music.* Vol. 1, *Anthology of Music.* Cologne: 1959.

————. *Musik aus alter Zeit.* 3 vols. Cologne: Arno Volk, 1960. English ed., *Keyboard Music of the Baroque and Rococo.* 3 vols. Cologne, 1960.

Golos, Jerzy, and Adam Sutkowski. *Keyboard Music from Polish Manuscripts.* 4 vols. *CEKM,* vol. 10, part 3, Fantasias, for Harpsichord. Rome: American Institute of Musicology, 1962.

Heartz, Daniel. *Keyboard Dances from the Earlier Sixteenth Century.* *CEKM,* vol. 8. Rome: American Institute of Musicology, 1965.

Jackson, Roland. *Neopolitan Keyboard Composers, circa 1600.* *CEKM,* vol. 24. Rome: American Institute of Musicology, 1967.

Kastner, M. S. *Cravistas Portuguezes.* 2 vols. Mainz: B. Schott's Söhne, 1935.

————. *Silva Iberica.* Mainz: B. Schott's Söhne, 1954.

Keller, Hermann. *Alte Meister der Klaviermusik.* 4 vols. Leipzig, n.d.

Kipnis, Igor. *A First Harpsichord Book.* New York: Oxford University Press, 1970.

Lincoln, Harry B. *Seventeenth-Century Keyboard Music in the Chigi Manuscripts of the Vatican Library.* 3 vols. *CEKM,* vol. 32. Rome: American Institute of Musicology, 1968.

Malipiero, Gian Francesco. *Eighteenth Century Italian Keyboard Music.* Bryn Mawr: Presser, 1952.

Mitteldeutsches Musik-Archiv. Veroffentlichungen des Musikwissenschaftlichen Seminars der Friedrich-Schiller-Universität Jena. Reihe I: *Klaviermusik.* 7 vols. Leipzig: Breitkopf & Härtel, 1955–.

Monumenta Musica Belgicae. Berchem and Antwerp: Vereniging voor Muziekgeschiedenis te Antwerpen, 1932–51, 1960.

Monumentos de la Música Española. Barcelona: Consejo Superior de Investigaciones Científicas, Instituto Español de Musicología, 1941–.

Monumenta Musica Neerlandica. Amsterdam: Nederlandse Muziekgeschiedenis, 1959–.

Musica Britannica. Published for the Royal Music Association with the support of the Arts Council of Great Britain, London: Stainer & Bell, 1951–.

Nagels Musik Archiv. Nr. 1. Hannover: Adolph Nagel, 1927–.

Newman, William. *Sons of Bach.* New York: Music Press, 1947.

Organum. Reihe 5: *Klaviermusik.* Ed. H. Albrecht and Lothar Hoffmann-Erbrecht. Leipzig: F. Kisner & C. F. W. Siegel, 1950–.

Pessl, Yella. *The Art of the Suite.* New York: Marks, 1947.

Penn State Music Series. University Park: Pennsylvania State University Press, 1963–.

Portugaliae Musica. Lisbon: Fundacao Colouste Gulbenkian, 1959–.

Publications de la société française de musicologie. Paris: E. Droz, 1925–.

Seay, Alfred. *Transcriptions of Chansons for Keyboard (Pierre Attaingnant, 1531). Corpus mensurabilis musicae,* vol. 20. Rome: American Institute of Musicology, 1961.

Stainer & Bell Keyboard Series. London: Stainer & Bell, 1955–.

Torchi, Luigi. *L'arte musicale in Italia.* [ed. Luigi Torchi]. Milan, Rome: G. Ricordi & Co., 1897–1908?

Vereniging voor nederlandsche Muziekgeschiedenis. Amsterdam: G. Alsbach & Co., 1869–, 1938, 1955–.

Valentin, Erich. *The Toccata. Das Musikwerk,* vol. 17. Cologne: Arno Volk, 1951.

Individual Composers and Manuscripts

Arne, Thomas. *VIII Sonatas or Lessons for the Harpsichord.* Facs. of original (1756) ed. with introductory note by Gwilym Beechey and Thurston Dart. London: Stainer & Bell, 1969.

Bach, Carl Philipp Emanuel. *Klavierwerke: Die sechs Sammlungen von Sonaten, freien Fantasien und Rondos für Kenner und Liebhaber.* Ed. Carl Krebs. 6 vols. Leipzig: Breitkopf & Härtel, 1895. Reprint, rev. Lothar Hoffmann-Erbrecht, Leipzig: Breitkopf & Härtel, 1953.

———. *Preussische Sonaten.* Ed. Rudolf Steglich. *NMA,* vols. 6 and 15. Hannover, Nagel, 1927–28.

———. *Württembergische Sonaten.* Ed. Rudolf Steglich. *NMA,* vols. 21 and 22. Hannover: Nagel, 1928.

Bach, Johann Christian. *10 Klavier-Sonaten.* Ed. Ludwig Landshoff. Leipzig: Brietkopf & Härtel, 1925.

———. *Sechs Leichte Sonaten.* Ed. Hugo Ruf and Hans Bemmann. Mainz: B. Schott's Söhne, 1966.

Bach, Johann Sebastian. *Clavier-Büchlein vor Wilhelm Friedemann Bach.* Facs. Introduction by Ralph Kirkpatrick. New Haven: Yale University Press, 1959.

———. *Harpsichord Music.* New York: Dover, 1970. Reprints the English Suites, French Suites, Partitas, Goldberg Variations and Two- and Three-Part Inventions from the Bach-Gesellschaft Edition, 1863 and 1883.

———. *Keyboard Practice, Consisting of an Aria with Thirty Variations [The Goldberg Variations].* Ed. Ralph Kirkpatrick. New York: Schirmer, 1938.

————. *Klavierwerke.* Ed. Ludwig Landshoff, Kurt Soldan, Alfred Kreutz, and Hermann Keller. New York: Peters.

————. *Klavierwerke.* Ed. Rudolf Steglich, Otto von Irmer. Munich: G. Henle Verlag, 1956–70.

————. *Neue Ausgabe sämtliche Werke.* Herausgegeben vom Johann-Sebastian-Bach-Institut Göttingen und vom Bach-Archiv Leipzig. 8 series. 86 or 87 vols. planned. Kassel: Bärenreiter, 1954–. Ser. V. Keyboard and Flute Works. 12 vols. proposed. Vol. 3, *Inventions and Sinfonias;* ed. Georg von Dadelsen, 1970; vol. 4, *Die Klavierbüchlein für Anna Magdelena Bach (1722 & 1725),* ed. G. Dadelson, 1957; vol. 5, *Klavierbüchlein für Wilhelm Friedemann Bach,* ed. Wolfgang Plath, 1962.

————. *Two- and Three-Part Inventions.* Facs. Introduction by Georg Schünemann (in German) and Ralph Kirkpatrick. New York: Peters, n.d.

————. *Two- and Three-Part Inventions.* Facs. of autograph with reprint of the Bach-Gesellschaft Edition. Introduction by Eric Simon. New York: Dover, 1968.

————. *Werke.* Herausgegeben von der Bach-Gesellschaft. 47 vols. Leipzig: Breitkopf & Härtel, 1851–1926. Reprint, 46 vols. Ann Arbor: J. W. Edwards, 1947.

Bach, Wilhelm Friedemann. *Klaviersonaten.* Ed. Friedrich Blume. *NMA,* vols. 63, 78, and 156. Hannover, Nagel, 1930–40. New York: Bärenreiter, 1959–64.

Böhm, Georg. *Sämtliche Werke, Klavier-und Orgelwerke.* New ed. by Gesa Wolgast. Wiesbaden: Brietkopf & Härtel, 1952–.

Boismortier, Joseph Bodin de. *Quatre Suites de pièces de clavecin.* Ed. Erwin R. Jacobi. Munich: F. E. C. Leuckart, 1960.

Boutmy, Josse. *Werken voor klavecimbel.* Ed. J. Watelet. *MMB,* vol. 5. Berchem and Antwerp, 1943.

Bull, John. *Harpsichord Pieces from Dr. John Bull's Flemish Tabulatura.* Transcribed by H. F. Redrich. Wilhelmshaven: Naetzel, 1958.

————. *Keyboard Music I and II. MB,* vols. 14 and 19. Vol. 14 ed. J. Steele, F. Cameron, and T. Dart, vol. 19 ed. T. Dart. London: Stainer & Bell, 1960 and 1963.

————. *Ten Pieces.* Selected from *MB,* vol. 14. London: Stainer & Bell, 1960.

Buxtehude, Dietrich. *Klavierwerke. Dietrich Buxtehudes Werke,* vol. 14. Klechen, Ugrino: Abteilung Verlag, 1925–37, 1958.

————. *Klaver Vaerker.* Ed. Emilius Bangert. Copenhagen and Leipzig: Wilhelm Hansen, 1942. 2nd ed., 1944.

Byrd, William. *Collected Works.* Ed. Edmund H. Fellowes, 20 vols. London: Stainer & Bell, 1937–1950. Keyboard music in vols. 18, 19, and 20.

————. *Fifteen Pieces.* Transcribed and selected from *The Fitzwilliam Virginal Book* and *Parthenia. SBK,* vol. 4. London: Stainer & Bell, 1956. 2nd rev. ed., 1969.

————. *Forty-Five Pieces for Keyboard Instruments.* Ed. Stephen D. Tuttle. Paris: Oiseau-Lyre, 1939.

————. *My Ladye Nevells Booke of Virginal Music.* Ed. Hilda Andrews. New York: Dover, 1969. Reprint of the 1926 edition published by J. Curwen & Sons Ltd., London, with a new introduction by Blanche Winogron.

Cabezón, Antonio de. *Claviermusik.* Rev. and ed. M. S. Kastner. Mainz: B. Schott's Söhne, n.d.

————. *Obras de Música para tecla, Arpa y Vihuela. MME,* vols. 27–29. 1st ed. Felipe Pedrell, new ed. with corrections by Higinio Anglés. Barcelona: Instituto Español de Musicología, 1966.

Chambonnières, Jacques Champion de. *Les deux livres de clavecin.* Ed. Thurston Dart. Monaco: Oiseau-Lyre, 1969.

————. *Oeuvres Complète de Chambonnières.* Ed. Paul Brunold and André Tessier. Paris: Senart, 1925. Reissued by Broude Bros., New York, 1966.

Clement Matchett's Virginal Book (1612). Ed. Thurston Dart. *SBK,* vol. 9. London: Stainer & Bell, 1957. Rev. 1969.

Clérambault, Louis Nicolas. *Pièces de clavecin.* Ed. P. Brunold. Paris: Oiseau-Lyre, 1938.

———. *Pièces de clavecin.* Ed. Paul Brunold and Thurston Dart. Monaco: Oiseau-Lyre, 1964.

Coehlo, M. R. *Flores de musica pera o instrumento de tecla & harpa.* Ed. M. S. Kastner. *PM,* vols. 1 and 3. Lisbon: Fundacao Colouste Gulbenkian, 1959 and 1961.

Costa de Lisboa, J. da, G. dos Reis, and others. *Tenção* [selections from], ed. C. R. Fernandes. *PM,* vol. 7. Lisbon: Fundacao Colouste Gulbenkian, 1963.

Couperin, François. *L'art de toucher de clavecin. Oeuvres Complètes de François Couperin,* vol. 1. Paris: Oiseau-Lyre, 1933.

———. *Oeuvres complètes.* Ed. Maurice Cauchie and others. Paris: Oiseau Lyre, 1932–33. Vols. 2, 3, 4, and 5 contain *Pièces de clavecin.*

———. *L'Art de toucher de clavecin.* Ed. and trans. into German by A. Linde, trans. into English by M. Roberts. Wiesbaden: Brietkopf & Härtel, 1933.

———. *Pièces de clavecin.* Ed. Johannes Brahms and Friedrich Chrysander. 4 vols. London: Augener, 1888.

———. *Pièces de clavecin.* Ed. Kenneth Gilbert. "Le Pupitre." Paris: Heugel, 1969–70.

———. *Selected Harpsichord Music of François Couperin.* Ed. Sylvia Marlowe. New York: Schirmer, 1970.

Couperin, Louis. *Pièces de clavecin.* Ed. Paul Brunold and Thurston Dart. Monaco: Oiseau-Lyre, 1959.

———. *Pièces de clavecin.* Ed. Alan Curtis. "Le Pupitre." Paris: Heugel, 1971.

Dagincourt, François. *Pièces de clavecin.* Ed. Howard Ferguson. "Le Pupitre," no. 12. Paris: Heugel, 1969.

Dandrieu, François. *Music for Harpsichord.* Ed. John R. White. *PSMS,* no. 6. University Park: Pennsylvania State University Press, 1965.

D'Anglebert, Jean-Henri. *Pièces de clavecin.* Ed. Marguerite Roesgen-Champion. *PSFM,* vol. 8. Paris: Librairie E. Droz, 1934.

Dieupart, Charles. *Six suites de clavessin.* Ed. Paul Brunold. Paris: Oiseau-Lyre, 1934.

The Dublin Virginal Manuscript. Ed. John Ward. *The Wellesley Edition,* vol. 3. Wellesley: Wellesley College, 1954. 2nd rev. ed., 1964.

Dumont, Henri. *L'Oeuvre pour Clavier.* Paris: Editions musicales de la Schola Cantorum, 1956.

Duphly, J. *Pièces pour clavecin.* "Le Pupitre," no. 1. Paris: Heugel, 1971.

Durante, Francesco. *Sei Sonate (Studii) e Sei Divertimenti per Cembalo.* Ed. Bernhard Paumgartner. Kassel: Bärenreiter, 1949.

———. *Sonate, toccate e divertimenti.* Ed. I Pizzetti. *CdMI,* vol. 11. Milan: Società Anonima Notari La Santa, 1919–21.

Erbach, Christian. *Ausgewählte Werke.* Ed. E. von Werra. *DTB,* vol. 7(4.ii). Leipzig, 1903. With keyboard works of Hassler.

———. *Complete Works.* Ed. Clare Rayner. *CEKM.* Rome: American Institute of Musicology, in process.

Facoli, Marco. *Collected Works.* Ed. Willi Apel. *CEKM,* vol. 2. Rome: American Institute of Musicology, 1963.

Farnaby, Giles. *17 Pieces.* Transcribed and selected by Thurston Dart from *The Fitzwilliam Virginal Book. SBK,* vol. 11. London: Stainer & Bell, 1957. 2nd rev. ed., 1968.

Farnaby, G. and R. *Keyboard Music.* Ed. R. Marlow. *MB,* vol. 24. London: Stainer & Bell, n.d.

Fiocco, J.-H. *Werken voor clavecimbel. MMB,* vol. 3. Berchem & Antwerp: Vereniging voor Muziekgeschiedenis te Antwerpen, 1936.

Fischer, Johann Kaspar Ferdinand. *Ausgewählte Klavierwerke.* Ed. Erich Doflein. Mainz: B. Schott's Söhne, 1935.

———. *Musikalisches Blumenbuschlein: eine Auswahl aus dem Klavierwerk.* Ed. L. J. Beer. Magdeburg: Heinrichshofen's Verlag, 1943.

————. *Sämtliche Werke für Klavier & Orgel.* Ed. Erich von Werra. Leipzig: Breitkopf & Härtel, 1901. Reprinted by Broude Bros., 1965.

The Fitzwilliam Virginal Book. Ed. John Alexander Fuller-Maitland and W. Barclay Squire. 2 vols. Leipzig: Breitkopf & Härtel, 1899. Reprinted by Dover, 1963.

Forqueray, A. *Pièces de clavecin.* Ed. Colin Tilney. "Le Pupitre." Paris: Heugel, 1971. Viol pieces transcribed for harpsichord by Jean-Baptiste Forqueray.

Frescobaldi, Girolamo. *Organ and Keyboard Works.* Ed. Pierre Pidoux. 5 vols. Kassel: Bärenreiter, 1961. Vols. 3 and 4 of special interest to harpsichordists.

————. *Unpublished Keyboard Works.* Ed. W. R. Shindle. 3 vols. *CEKM,* vol. 30. Rome: American Institute of Musicology, 1968.

Froberger, Johann Jacob. *Ausgewählte Klavierwerke.* Ed. Kurt Shubert. Mainz: B. Schott's Söhne, n.d.

————. *Orgel und Klavierwerke.* Ed. Guido Adler. *DTOe,* vols. 8, 13, and 21. Vienna: Osterreichischer Bundesverlag, 1897, 1899, 1903. Reprint, Graz, 1960. Complete harpsichord works.

————. *Selected Works for Cembalo.* Ed. Helmut Schultz. Leipzig: Peters, 1935.

Fux, Johann Joseph. *Werke für Tasteninstrumente.* Ed. Erich Schenk. *DTOe,* vol. 85. Vienna: Osterreichischer Bundesverlag, 1947.

Gabrieli, Andrea. *Orgel & Klavierwerke.* Ed. Pierre Pidoux. 5 vols. Kassel: Bärenreiter, 1943–59.

Gabrieli, Giovanni. *Complete Keyboard Works.* 3 vols. Ed. Sandro dalla Libera. Milan: Ricordi, 1956–57.

————. *Werke für Tasteninstrumente.* Ed. G. S. Bedbrook. Kassel: Bärenreiter, 1957.

Galuppi, Baldassare. *Dodici sonate per il cembalo.* Ed. Giacomo Benvenuti. Bologna, 1920.

————. *Quatro Sonate per Pianoforte o Clavicembalo.* Ed. Piccioli. Milan: Edizioni Suvini Zerboni, 1952.

Gibbons, Christopher. *Keyboard Compositions.* Ed. Clare G. Rayner. *CEKM,* vol. 18. Rome: American Institute of Musicology, 1967. Organ and harpsichord works.

Gibbons, Orlando. *Eight Keyboard Pieces. SBK,* vol. 26. London: Stainer & Bell, 1960.

————. *Keyboard Music.* Ed. Gerald Hendrie. *MB,* vol. 20. London: Stainer & Bell, 1962.

————. *A Selection of Short Dances. SBK,* vol. 17. Ed. Margaret Glyn. London: Stainer & Bell, 1925. 2nd rev. ed., ed. Thurston Dart, 1960.

Graupner, Johann Christoph. *Acht Partiten. MMA.* Ed. Lothar Hoffmann-Erbrecht. Leipzig: Breitkopf & Härtel, 1954.

Grazioli, Giovanni Battista. *Dodici sonate per cembalo.* Ed. Ruggiero Gerlin. *CMI,* vol. 12. Milan: I Classici musicali italiana, 1943.

Guillet, C., G. Macque, and C. Luython. *Werken voor orgel of voor vier speetuigen. MMB,* vol. 4. Ed. R. B. Lenaerts. Berchem and Antwerp: Vereniging voor Muziekgeschiedenis te Antwerpen, 1938.

Handel, G. F. *Keyboard Works.* 5 vols. Vols. 1, 2, 3, and 5 ed. Walter Serauky. Vol. 4 ed. Friedrich Glasenapp. Leipzig: Peters, n.d.

————. *Klavierwerke. (Hallische Händel Ausgabe,* Series IV, vols. 1, 5, and 6. Ed. Rudolf Steglich, Peter Northway, and Terence Best. Kassel: Bärenreiter, 1955–70.

Hassler, H. L. and J. *Ausgewählte Werke.* Ed. Erich von Werra. *DTB,* vol. 7(4.ii). Braunschweig: H. Litolff's Verlag, 1903. With keyboard works of Erbach.

Havingha, Gerhardus. *Werken voor clavecimbel. MMB,* vol. 7. Berchem and Antwerp: Vereniging voor Muziekgeschiedenis te Antwerpen, 1951.

Helmont, Charles Joseph van. *Werken voor Orgel en/of Clavicembel.* Ed. Joseph Watelet. *MMB,* vol. 6. Berchem and Antwerp: Vereniging voor Muziekgeschiedenis te Antwerpen, 1948. Includes works of Raick.

Hurlebusch, Conrad Friedrich. *Compositioni musicali per il cembalo.* Ed. Max Sieffert. *VNM,* vol. 32. Amsterdam and Leipzig: G. Alsbach & Co., 1912.

Jacquet de la Guerre, Elizabeth. *Pièces de clavecin.* Ed. P. Brunold and Thurston Dart. Monaco: Oiseau-Lyre, 1965.

————. *Pièces de clavecin.* Ed. Paul Brunold. Paris: Oiseau-Lyre, 1938.

Johannes of Lublin. *Tablature of Keyboard Music.* Ed. J. R. White. 6 vols. *CEKM,* vol. 6. Rome: American Institute of Musicology, 1964–1967.

Kerll, Johann Kaspar von. *Ausgewählte Werke.* Ed. Adolf Sandberger. *DTB,* vol. 3/(2.ii). Braunschweig, H. Litolff's Verlag, 1901.

————. *Stücke fur Tasteninstrumente.* Ed. W. Hillemann. *NMA,* vol. 87. Hannover: Nagel, n.d.

Kirnberger, Johann Philipp. *Tanzstücke für Klavier (oder Cembalo.)* Ed. Kurt Hermann. Mainz: B. Schott's Söhne, n.d.

Krieger, J. and J. B. *Gesammelte Werke für Klavier und Orgel.* Ed. Max Seiffert. *DTB,* vol. 30(18). Braunschweig: H. Litolff's Verlag, 1917.

Kuhnau, Johann. *Ausgewählte Klavierwerke, Partiten & Sonaten.* Ed. Kurt Schubert. Mainz: B. Schott's Söhne, n.d.

————. *Klavierwerke.* Ed. Carl Päsler. *DdT,* vol. 4. Leipzig: Breitkopf & Härtel, 1901. Reprinted Graz, 1958.

————. *Six Biblical Sonatas for Keyboard (1700).* Ed. Kurt Stone. New York: Broude, 1953.

LeBègue, Nicolas. *Oeuvres de clavecin.* Ed. Norbert Dufourcq. Monaco: Oiseau-Lyre, 1956.

LeRoux, Gaspard. *Pieces for Harpsichord.* Ed. Albert Fuller. New York: Alpeg Editions, 1959.

Locke, Matthew. *Keyboard Suites.* Trans. and ed. by Thurston Dart. *SBK,* vol. 6. London: Stainer & Bell, 1959. Rev. 1964.

Loeillet, Jean Baptiste. *Werken voor Clavecimbel.* Ed. Joseph Watelet. *MMB,* vol. 1. Berchem and Antwerp: Vereniging voor Muziekgeschiedenis te Antwerpen, 1932.

Macque, Giovanni. *Werken voor orgel of voor vier spieltuigen. MMB,* vol. 4. Ed. Joseph Watelet. Berchem and Antwerp: Vereniging voor Muziekgeschiedenis te Antwerpen, 1938. Contains works of Guillet and Luython. For organ and harpsichord.

Marcello, Benedetto. *Composizioni per cembalo od organo.* Ed. G. Francesco Malipiero. *CdMI,* vol. 17. Milan: Società Anonima Notari La Santa, 1920.

————. *Sonates pour clavecin.* Ed. Lorenzo Bianconi et Luciano Sgrizzi. "Le Pupitre." Paris: Heugel, 1971.

Marchand, Louis. *Pièces de clavecin.* Ed. Thurston Dart. Monaco: Oiseau-Lyre, 1960.

Martini, Giovanni Battista. *Sechs Sonaten für Cembalo oder Klavier.* Ed. Lothar Hoffmann-Erbrecht. *MMA.* Leipzig: Breitkopf & Härtel, 1954.

————. *Sonate.* Ed. A. Lualdi. *CdMI,* vol. 28. Milan: Società Anonima Notari La Santa, 1920.

Mattheson, Johann. *Die Wohlklingende Fingersprache.* Ed. Lothar Hoffmann-Erbrecht. *MMA.* Leipzig: Breitkopf & Härtel, 1953.

Mayone, Ascanio. *Secondo libro di diversi capricci per sonare (Orgue et Liturgie).* Paris: Les Editions Musicales de la Schola Cantorum et de la Procure Générale de Musique, 192?–. Vols. 63 and 65 published 1964–65.

Mondonville, J.-J. Cassanéa de. *Pièces de clavecin en sonates.* Ed. Marc Pincherle. *PSFM,* vol. 9. Paris: E. Droz, 1935.

Morley, Thomas. *Keyboard Works.* Ed. Thurston Dart. 2 vols. *SBK,* vols. 12 and 13. London: Stainer & Bell, 1959. 2nd rev. ed., 1964.

Muffat, Gottlieb. *Componimenti musicali per il cembalo.* Ed. Guido Adler. *DTOe,* vol. 7. Vienna: Osterreichischer Bundesverlag, 1896. Reprinted Graz: Akademische Druck-und Verlagsanstalt, 1959.

————. *72 Versetlsamt und 12 Toccaten.* Ed. Walter Upmeyer. Kassel: Bärenreiter, 1952.

————. *Zwölf Toccaten und 72 Versetlsamt.* Ed. Guido Adler. *DTOe,* vol. 58. Vienna: Osterreichischer Bundesverlag, 1922. Reprinted Graz: Akademische Druck-und Verlagsanstalt, 1960.

The Mulliner Book. Ed. Denis Stevens. *MB,* vol. 1. London: Stainer & Bell, 1951. Rev. ed. 1962.

————. *The Mulliner Book: Eleven Pieces.* Ed. Denis Stevens. *SBK,* vol. 3. London: Stainer & Bell, 1951.

Murschhauser, F. X. A. *Gesammelte Werke für Klavier und Orgel.* Ed. Max Sieffert. *DTB,* vol. 30 (18). Braunschweig: H. Litolff's Verlag, 1917.

Musick's Handmaid: I. (1663). Ed. Thurston Dart. *SBK,* vol. 28. London: Stainer & Bell, 1969.

Musick's Handmaid, The Second Part of (1689). Ed. Thurston Dart. *SBK,* vol. 10. 2nd rev. ed. London: Stainer and Bell, 1962.

Müthel, Johann Gottfried. *Zwei Ariosi mit zwölf Variationen.* Ed. Lothar Hoffmann-Erbrecht. *MMA.* Leipzig: Breitkopf, 1955.

Oevering, Rynoldus Popma van. *VI Suittes voort' Clavier.* Ed. H. B. Buys. *VNM,* vol. 46. Amsterdam: G. Alsbach & Co., 1955.

Pachelbel, Johann. *Ausgewählte Klavierwerke.* Ed. Erich Doflein. Mainz: B. Schott's Söhne.

————. *94 Kompositionen Fugen über das Magnificat für Orgel oder Klavier.* Ed. H. Botstiber and Max Sieffert. *DTOe,* vol. 17. Vienna: Osterreichischer Bundesverlag, 1901. Reprinted Graz: Akademische Druck-und Verlagsanstalt, 1959.

————. *Seven Chorale Partitas. Selected Organ Works,* vol. 4. Ed. Karl Matthaei. Kassel: Bärenreiter, 1936. Also for harpsichord.

———— and Wilhelm H. Pachelbel. *Klavierwerke; Orgelkompositionen.* Ed. Max Sieffert. *DTB,* vols. 2 and 6 (2.i and 4.i). Braunschweig: H. Litolff's Verlag, 1901.

Pachelbel, Wilhelm H. *Werke für Orgel & Clavier.* Ed. Moser & Fedtke. Kassel: Bärenreiter, 1957.

Paradisi, Pietro Domenico [Paradies]. *Sonate.* Ed. G. Benvenuti and Dante Cipollini. *CdMI,* vol. 22. Milan: Società Anonima Notari La Santa, 1920.

————. *Sonate di Gravicembalo.* 2 vols. Ed. Hugo Ruf and Hans Bemmann. Mainz: B. Schott's Söhne, 1971.

Parthenia. Transcribed and ed. Thurston Dart. *SBK,* vol. 19. London: Stainer & Bell, 1960. Rev. ed. 1962.

————. Ed. Kurt Stone. New York: Broude, 1951.

Parthenia In-Violata or Mayden-Musicke. Facs. reprint. Critical notes by Thurston Dart, R. Wolfe, and Sydney Beck. New York: New York Public Library, 1961. (available from Peters)

————. Ed. Thurston Dart. New York: Peters, 1961.

Pasquini, Bernardo. *Collected Works for Keyboard.* Ed. M. B. Haynes. 7 vols. *CEKM,* vol. 5. Rome: American Institute of Musicology, 1964–68.

Pasquini, Ercole. *Collected Keyboard Works.* Ed. W. R. Shindle. *CEKM,* vol. 12. Rome, American Institute of Musicology, 1966.

Picchi, G. *Complete Keyboard Works.* Ed. Evan Kreider. *CEKM.* Rome: American Institute of Musicology, in progress.

————. *Intavolatura di Balli d'Arpicordo.* Facs. reprint. Milan: Bolletino Bibliografico Musicale, 1934.

Platti, Giovanni B. *Zwölf Sonaten für Cembalo oder Klavier.* Ed. Lothar Hoffmann-Erbrecht. *MMA,* vols. 3 and 4. Leipzig: Breitkopf & Härtel, 1953.

Podbielski, J. *Praeludium for Organ or Harpsichord.* Ed. Adolf Chybiński. *Denkmäler Altpolnischer Musik,* vol. 18. Warsaw: Polskie Wydawnictwo Muzycyne, 193?–.

Poglietti, Alessandro. *Harpsichord Music.* Ed. William Earle Nettles. *PSMS,* no. 9. University Park: Pennsylvania State University Press, 1966.

————. *Wiener Klavier-und Orgelwerke aus der zweiten Hälfte des 17. Jahrhunderts.* Ed. H. Botstiber. *DTOe,* vol. 27. Vienna: Osterreichischer Bundesverlag, 1906.

Purcell, Henry. *Eight Suites.* Ed. Howard Ferguson. 2nd, rev. ed. London: Stainer & Bell, 1964.

————. *Miscellaneous Keyboard Pieces.* Ed. Howard Ferguson. 2nd. rev. ed. London: Stainer & Bell, 1964. These 2 vols. comprise Purcell's complete works for harpsichord.

Radino, Giovanni Maria. *Il primo libro d'intavolatura di balli d'arpicordo.* Ed. R. E. M. Harding. Facs. reproduction and transcription. Cambridge: W. Heffer & Sons, Ltd. and New York: Broude Bros., 1949. Ed. Susan Ellingworth. *CEKM.* Rome: American Institute of Musicology, 1968.

Raick, Dieudonné. *Werken voor orgel en-of voor clavecimbel. MMB,* vol. 6. Berchem and Antwerp: Vereniging voor Muziekgeschiedenis te Antwerpen, 1948. With works of C.-J. Helmont.

Rameau, Jean-Philippe. *Pièces de clavecin.* Ed. Erwin Jacobi. Kassel: Bärenreiter, 1958. 2nd ed. 1960.

Reinken, Adam. *Collected Keyboard Works.* Ed. Willi Apel. *CEKM,* vol. 16. Rome: American Institute of Musicology, 1967.

Reinken, J. A. *Partite diverse sopra l'aria: Schweiget mir von Weiber nehmen. VNM,* vol. 14. Amsterdam: G. Alsbach & Co., n.d.

Ritter, J. C. *Drei Sonaten.* Ed. Erwin Jacobi. Leipzig: Deutscher Verlag für Musik, 1968.

Roseingrave, Thomas. *Compositions for Organ & Harpsichord.* Ed. Denis Stevens. *PSMS,* no. 2. University Park: Penn State University Press, 1964.

Rossi, Michelangelo. *Composizioni per organo e cimbalo.* Ed. A. Toni. *CdMI,* vol. 26. Milan: Società Anonima Notari La Santa, 1920. See also Torchi, vol. 3.

———. *Works for Keyboard.* Ed. John Reeves White. *CEKM,* vol. 15. Rome: American Institute of Musicology, 1966.

Rutini, Giovanni Maria. *Sonate per cimbalo.* Ed. F. Pratella. *CdMI,* vol. 27. Milan: Società Anonima Notari La Santa, 1921.

Salvatore, Giovanni. *Collected Keyboard Works.* Ed. Barton Hudson. *CEKM,* vol. 3. Rome: American Institute of Musicology, 1964.

Sandoni, P. G. and G. Serini. *Sonate per cimbalo.* Ed. B. Pratella. *CdMI,* vol. 29. Milan: Società Anonima Notari La Santa, 1921.

Scarlatti, Alessandro. *Primo e secondo libro di toccate.* Ed. Ruggiero Gerlin. *CMI,* vol. 13. Milan: I Classici musicali italiana, 1943.

———. *Seven Toccatas.* Ed. Rio Nardi. Kassel: Bärenreiter, 1964.

Scarlatti, Domenico. *Complete Keyboard Works.* Ed. in facs. by Ralph Kirkpatrick. 18 vols. New York: Johnson Reprint Corp., 1972.

———. *Sixty Sonatas.* Ed. Ralph Kirkpatrick. New York: Schirmer, 1953.

———. *Sonatas.* Ed. Kenneth Gilbert. 9 vols. "Le Pupitre." Paris: Heugel, 1970–.

———. *[150] Sonaten nach der Quellen.* Ed. Hermann Keller and W. Weissmann. 3 vols. Leipzig: Peters, 1957.

Scheidt, Samuel. *Ausgewählte Werke für Orgel und Klavier.* Ed. Hermann Keller. New York: Peters, 1939.

———. *Liedvariationen für Klavier.* Ed. Wolfgang Auler. Mainz: B. Schott's Söhne, n.d.

———. *Werke.* Ed. G. Harms and Christhard Mahrenholz. 8 vols. Hamburg, 1923–34.

Seixas, C. *80 Sonatas para instrumentos de tecla.* Ed. M. S. Kastner. *PM,* vol. 10. Lisbon: Fundacao Colouste Gulbenkian, 1965.

Soler, Antonio. *Conciertos para dos instrumentos de tecla.* Ed. M. S. Kastner. 6 vols. Barcelona: Musica Hispana, 1952–62.

———. *Sonatas.* Ed. Frederick Marvin. 3 vols. London: Mills Music, Inc., 1953–59.

———. *Sonatas.* Ed. P. Samuel Rubio. 6 vols. Madrid: Union Musical Española, 1957–62.

Storace, B. *Selva di varie compositioni d'intavolatura per cimbalo ed organo.* Ed. Barton Hudson. *CEKM,* vol. 7. Rome: American Institute of Musicology, 1965.

Strozzi, Gregorio. *Caprici da sonare cembali et organi.* Ed. Barton Hudson. *CEKM,* vol. 11. Rome: American Institute of Musicology, 1967.

Sweelinck, Jan Pieterzoon. *Ausgewählte Werke für Orgel & Klavier.* Ed. D. Hellmann. 2 vols. New York: Peters, 1957.

———. *Liedvariationen für Klavier.* Ed. Erich Doflein. Mainz: B. Schott's Söhne, n.d.

————. *Opera Omnia.* Vol. 1, *The Instrumental Works,* parts 1–3, Ed. Gustav Leonhardt, Alfons Annegarn and Frits Noske, 3 vols. *VNM.* Amsterdam: G. Alsbach & Co., 1968.

————. *Werken voor Orgel en Clavicimbal.* Ed. Max Seiffert. Leipzig: Breitkopf & Härtel, 1894. Reprinted Amsterdam: G. Alsbach & Co., 1943.

Tallis, Thomas. *Complete Keyboard Works.* Ed. Denis Stevens. London and Frankfurt: Peters Edition and Hinrichsen Edition, 1953.

Techelmann, F. M. *Suiten für Tasteninstrumente.* Ed. H. Knaus, *DTOe,* vol. 115. Vienna: Osterreichischer Bundesverlag. Reprinted Graz: Akademische Druck-und Verlagsanstalt, 1966.

Telemann, Georg Philipp. *Kleine Fantasien für Klavier.* Ed. Erich Doflein. Mainz: B. Schott's Söhne, 1961.

————. *Sechs Ouvertüren für Cembalo.* Ed. Hugo Ruf. Mainz: B. Schott's Söhne, 1966.

————. *Three Dozen Clavier Fantasias.* Ed. Max Seiffert. Kassel: Bärenreiter, 1964. Reprint of 1923 edition.

Tisdale's Virginal Book. Ed. Alan Brown. *SBK,* vol. 24. London: Stainer & Bell, 1966.

Tisdall, William. *Complete Keyboard Works.* Transcribed and edited from *The Fitzwilliam Virginal Book* and the *John Bull Virginal Book* by Howard Ferguson. *SBK,* vol. 14. London: Stainer & Bell, 1958.

Tomkins, Thomas. *Fifteen Dances.* Ed. Stephen D. Tuttle. *SBK,* vol. 2. London: Stainer & Bell, 1965.

————. *Keyboard Music.* Ed. Stephen D. Tuttle. *MB,* vol. 5. London: Stainer & Bell, 1955. 2nd rev. ed., 1964.

Trabaci, Giovanni Maria. *Composizioni per organo e cembalo.* Ed. Oscar Mischiati. *Monumenti di Musica Italiana,* vols. 3 and 4. Kassel: Bärenreiter, 1964.

Turrini, Ferdinando. *Sonate per cembalo.* Ed. C. Pedron. *CdMI,* vol. 33. Milan: Società Anonima Notari La Santa, 1919.

Venegas de Henestrosa, Luis. *Libro de cifra nueva para tecla, harpa y vihuela.* Ed. by Higinio Anglés. In *La música en la corte de Carlos V. MME,* vol. 2. Barcelona: Instituto Español de Musicología, 1944. Rev. ed. in progress.

Wagenseil, George Christoph. *Divertimenti per cimbalo.* Ed. Friedrich Blume. *NMA.* Hannover: Nagel, 1929.

Zipoli, Domenico. *Composizioni.* Ed. A. Toni. *CdMI,* vol. 26. Milan: Società Anonima Notari La Santa, 1919. See also Torchi, vol. 3.

————. *Orgel und Cembalowerke.* Ed. L. F. Tagliavini. 2 vols. Heidelberg: Willy Mueller, Süddeutsche Musikverlag, 1959.

APPENDIX C:

Additional Information on Tuning

MEAN AND EQUAL TEMPERAMENT

The main difficulty in tuning any keyboard instrument arises from the fact that a keyboard cannot practically divide the octave into more than twelve divisions, although other divisions have been tried. And if there are only twelve divisions, intervals in the scale cannot be pure, if one is going to modulate freely in playing. The keyboard instrument must be ready to play in any key, and it cannot adjust its intervals to pure ones as a string quartet can because its tuning is fixed. All intervals in the scale of twelve semitones must therefore be altered slightly, or tempered, from what they would be as pure intervals. And enharmonic tones ($G^{\#}$ and $A^{\flat}$ and so on), that are theoretically different, have to be made the same. It would be desirable—and consistent with music theory—if one could go around the circle of fifths (A-E, E-B, B-$F^{\#}$, and so on) in pure fifths and land back exactly on the octave, but this simply doesn't work out: going around the circle of fifths brings one to a point that is 531441/524288 beyond the octave. The octave is simply too small to contain what, from the point of view of Western music, should be its natural parts.

The attempts to deal with this pesky but serious problem have produced dozens of different systems of tempered tunings, chief among which are mean-tone temperament (in a wide variety of forms most of which are of more interest mathematically than musically) and equal temperament, the system that is all but universally used today. Mean-tone temperament in its pure form, based on a division of the pure third, favors the intervals in some keys at the expense of others, producing the "mean-tone wolf fifth," which sounds as vicious as its name, in keys remote from the tonic. Some modifications of mean-tone tuning tame the wolf a good bit and by so doing approach equal temperament. Equal temperament simply divides the octave into twelve equal intervals (by a ratio for a semitone of $\sqrt[12]{2}$ and so makes intervals in all keys the same. The purity of the intervals is compromised in favor of uniformity, so that while no interval is really good, in the sense that a good interval is pure or very close to it, no interval is really bad either, and one can modulate with complete freedom.

Mean-tone tuning has at least theoretical interest to a harpsichordist because it was used, in one form or other, well into the eighteenth century. But the difference between equal temperament and the modification of mean-tone tuning probably used by J. S. Bach, for instance, in his celebrated 48 preludes and fugues and equal temperament is sure to be very slight.[1] Bach, who took a practical point of view toward tuning, had his own system and was impatient with the theoretical obsessions of some of his contemporaries.

SCIENTIFIC TUNING

Tuning by ear is an art, not a science, and individual tuners will almost always make slight modifications of any temperament, often inadvertently. The only scientific method of tuning is that which uses an electronic instrument, like the Strobotuner (or its more elaborate relative, the Strobo-conn). This stroboscopic machine has a small wheel with a pattern on it rotating at a controlled rate past a small window. When the acoustical vibrations of the string, transformed into flashes of light, correspond with the correct rate for that pitch, the whirling pattern in the window seems to stop. Using the Strobotuner, one simply tunes each string without bothering to think about temperament because equal temperament is taken care of by the pattern on the wheel. The Strobotuner also makes possible modifications from equal temperament, one of the systems of mean tone tuning for instance, by an adjustment in "cents," 1/100 of a semitone. The Strobotuner is available from C. G. Conn, Ltd., 1101 East Beardsly, Elkhart, Indiana 46514.

Another electronic device is an accoustical tone generator like the Peterson Chromatic Tuner (available from Peterson Electro-Musical Products, Dept. 27, Worth, Ill. 60482). It is a very compact device (and much less expensive than the Strobotuner) that produces audible tones for all steps of the scale. I have not tried one, but its accuracy is said to be good. Peterson also produces a stroboscopic tuner.

You can also buy a whole chromatic set of tuning forks for about thirty dollars. They are available from supply houses catering to piano technicians, and a friendly tuner might pass some of his discount to you. Usually, forks in a set could be expected to be quite well in tune with each other, but you should know that forks can vary in pitch from what they are marked to be.

BEATS

Tuning by ear requires hearing "beats," a word I put in quotation marks because it is surrounded by confusion. Beats used in tuning are slow undulating amplifications of the sound. Most reference books, including books on musical acoustics, explain beats only for the simple case of the unison. What they are talking about is a beat frequency; they mean the difference between two frequencies close together, like A = 440 and A = 435, that gives a beat frequency of 5 Hz (formerly called cycles per second but now given a unit name after the scientist Herz). Actually, we are interested in the beat frequencies of unisons and octaves only because their presence tells us we are out of tune; we want to get rid of them as quickly as possible. But tones farther apart, like fifths, have difference frequencies, too, and in these the situation becomes much more complicated because there are both difference frequencies and "beats." There are also sum frequencies, although these are not heard very well.

Let us take the common intervals of the fifth and third as examples, because we will use them in practical tuning. When the pure fifth of A = 440 and E = 660 is sounded, we hear fairly clearly (if we listen hard) a ghostly third tone at a pitch of 220; this pitch is the difference tone between 440 and 660 and is A an octave below the A of the fifth we played. Tartini, the famous violinist, discovered this in music and called it "terza suono" or third tone. Present in the sound of the pure fifth is also the sum tone of 1100, which probably contributes something to the characteristic sound of the pure fifth but is impossible to hear on the harpsichord with its light, quickly decaying sound. Likewise, the pure third, with its integral ratio of 5/4, generates a third tone that corresponds to the lower member of the interval. In A = 440 and C#=550, we get a difference tone of 110, which is A two octaves below, and again with careful listening we can hear it.

These difference frequencies are used in tuning pure intervals, and they sound steadily and sonorously because the pure intervals are formed on integral arithmetical relationships. Their distinctive characteristic is that, although they generate beat frequencies that are the sums and differences of the frequencies they are formed by, they generate no "beats." We get beats in these intervals only when we *un*tune them from their integral relationships by altering their ratios in tuning to a tempered scale. The pure fifth has a ratio of 3:2, or 1.5.

But in equal temperament there is no pure fifth. The fifth is compromised a bit in forming all semitones of equal size,[2] so that it has a ratio of 1.4983. In the octave of A = 440, it has a frequency of 659.24 + instead of 660. So in the tempered fifth, we no longer hear the lower octave exactly right, because the difference tone between 440 and 659.44 is not half of 440 but 219.24+, and no note corresponds to this frequency in a scale based on A = 440. We come close enough to the natural interval to accept it as a fifth, but because it is out of tune, there will be a beat against a unison in an upper partial. The rate of the beat varies with the interval, because the unison appears at different partials for different intervals. So that if the fifth is untuned by one vibration, it will beat twice per second; if the fourth is likewise untuned, it will beat at three times per second; and the third will beat at four times per second. In the fifth above A = 440, tempering produces an interval that is about .75 cycles flat, and this will beat at 1.5 times per second.[3]

It is this beat resulting from the deviation of the fifth from the pure fifth that we want to hear, because we must try to measure its rate in tuning the fifths of equal temperament "out" by the right amount to divide the octave in twelve equal parts. The same goes for thirds except that their beats are four times the difference between the pure and tempered pitch.

We have to compute the frequencies of the equally tempered scale to several decimal places, but of course nobody's ear can hear the resulting beats accurately enough to justify such accuracy. The history of tuning is full of mathematical speculation which cannot be put into actual practice if only because an instrument, especially a harpsichord, won't stay in tune long enough. But the figures are worth having for reference, and they are given in the following table.

For practical application, I have included a tuning guide (Fig. 6) that shows the actual beats in graph form. The graph shows an important fact about beats: they rise exponentially up the scale, doubling in rate every octave. This exponential rise cannot be ignored, even though the best one can do in practice is to approximate it. Frequencies and therefore beat rates are based on A = 440, which has been standard since 1939 although tuning books based on A = 435 are still sold.

THE EARL OF STANHOPE'S SYSTEM OF TUNING

An irregular temperament of some interest is that by Charles, Third Earl of Stanhope, reported in the *Philosophical Magazine* for 1806. Stanhope didn't like equal temperament for the very reason that it has gained ascendency, namely that all keys sound alike in it. His temperament was

Frequencies in Herz (cycles per second) for Equal Temperament

A = 440

Note	Frequency
C	130.81
C#	138.59
D	146.83
D#	155.56
E	164.81
F	174.61
F#	185.00
G	196.00
G#	207.65
A′	220.00
A′#	233.08
B′	246.94
C′	261.63
C′#	277.18
D′	293.66
D′#	311.13
E′	329.63
F′	349.23
F′#	369.99
G′	392.00
G′#	415.30
A″	440.00

intended to differentiate the keys and hence heighten the effect of modulation. The interest of this temperament for the present discussion lies in the great ease with which tuning may be accomplished, for there are only five tempered intervals to be tuned and these can be tuned by adjusting only three notes. All other intervals are pure. Stanhope calls the intervals to be adjusted "bi-equal" thirds and "tri-equal" fifths. He says the two thirds should have the same number of beats and so should the three fifths, but the upper intervals could have a more rapid beat rate. Here is the way the temperament is tuned, shown in notation. The notes proceed in the order in which they should be tuned—except that from Step 2 on, the notes already tuned are shown filled in. Only one fork, pitched at C, is needed.

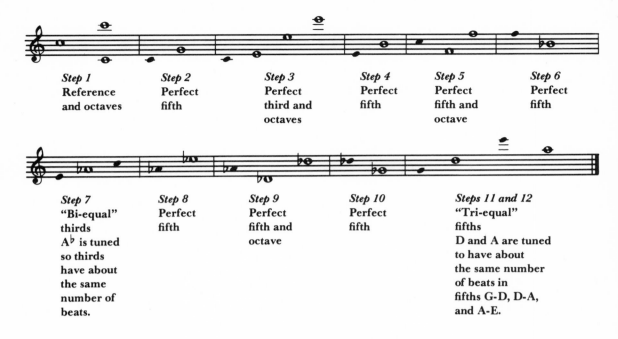

Step 1
Reference
and octaves

Step 2
Perfect
fifth

Step 3
Perfect
third and
octaves

Step 4
Perfect
fifth

Step 5
Perfect
fifth and
octave

Step 6
Perfect
fifth

Step 7
"Bi-equal"
thirds
A♭ is tuned
so thirds
have about
the same
number of
beats.

Step 8
Perfect
fifth

Step 9
Perfect
fifth and
octave

Step 10
Perfect
fifth

Steps 11 and 12
"Tri-equal"
fifths
D and A are tuned
to have about
the same number
of beats in
fifths G-D, D-A,
and A-E.

Obviously, this is not an authentic temperament for the harpsichord, since it came after the harpsichord had been eclipsed by the piano. But it is very easy to do, and the pure intervals in the common keys give a very interesting sound, like a version of mean-tone tuning, and, while some keys are favored, no key sounds really bad. The vigorous controversy surrounding this and other tunings and temperaments in the pages of the *Philosophical Magazine* and elsewhere suggests how much in flux the tuning of keyboard instruments still was. Experimentation in tuning for the authentic performance of older music is warranted, although absolute authenticity is hard to achieve, since some composers like Rameau changed their minds about temperaments. The temperament used by J. S. Bach for his celebrated preludes and fugues is probably impossible to get just right. Equal temperament, especially on the harpsichord with its short duration of tone, is a pretty good compromise, and, as Barbour suggests, it probably existed in practice or was very closely approached much earlier than is commonly supposed.

Notes

1. For an account of Challis's philosophy of building instruments, see an interview with him in *Harpsichord* 2 (1969), 14–23.

2. Frank Hubbard, *Three Centuries of Harpsichord Making* (Cambridge, Mass., 1965), p. vi.

3. See Raymond Russell, *The Harpsichord and Clavichord: An Introductory Study* (London, 1959), pp. 107–8, and Hubbard, pp. 331–33.

4. See Hubbard, pp. 355, 357.

5. The information on pedals is gleaned from Hubbard, passim.

6. Hubbard, pp. 126, 326.

7. Additional kit makers are Carl Fudge, Eric Herz, and William Post Ross, whose addresses are all listed in Zuckermann's book. Kits are also now available from Ancient Instruments, P.O. Box 552, Forestville, California 95436.

8. No such list, however, can remain up to date since new makers are so frequently established. The flowering of the New England makers known as the Boston School is a case in point. Seven of these makers are in or near Boston and they all make historically-oriented harpsichords. I have not been able to try instruments from the newer makers among them, but Frank Hubbard's word that there isn't much difference between his instruments and those of others working in the same style is good enough for me. Makers launched too recently to be listed in Zuckermann's book include Hendrik Brockman, Richard B. Earle, Monadnock Harpsichord, Inc. (Anthony Anable, Jr.), John Nargesian, George Stilphen, Joel van Lennep, and Edward Winslow. For an account of the work of the Boston School, see Anthony Anable, Jr., "For Love Nor Money," *Yankee,* November 1972, pp. 135–37ff. and Thomas Dotton, "Making Harpsichords," *Boston Globe,* December 10, 1972, pp. 30–40ff.

CHAPTER 2

1. Arthur H. Benade, *Horns, Strings and Harmony* (New York, 1960), p. 119.

2. Otto Ortmann, *The Physiological Mechanics of Piano Technique* (New York, 1962), p. 231.

3. François Couperin, *L'art de toucher le clavecin* (1717), trans. Anna Linde (Weisbaden, 1933), pp. 10–11.

4. Jean-Philippe Rameau, "On the Technique of the Fingers on the Harpsichord," in *Pièces de clavecin,* ed. Erwin R. Jacobi (Kassel-Basel, 1958), p. 17.

5. Ortmann, p. 31.

6. *Harvard Dictionary of Music,* 2nd ed. (Cambridge, Mass., 1969), p. 676.

7. Ortmann, p. 337. In speaking of the production of different "tone qualities" on the piano, Ortmann states that: "It is now definitely known through both theory and experiment that all qualitative differences, excepting the variations in the noise-element, are quantitative differences. Tetzel, the leader in Germany in the defence of this principle, has pointed out the intensity determinant a number of years ago, and sums it up in a law of dynamic or intensity relativity, as a result of which variations in or the relationship among the intensities of the tones is the fundamental determinant. This is true, if we add variations in the noise-element."

8. Domenico Scarlatti, *Sixty Sonatas,* ed. Ralph Kirkpatrick (New York, 1953), 1: xi.

9. Ralph Kirkpatrick, *Domenico Scarlatti* (Princeton, 1953), pp. 367–71.

CHAPTER 3

1. Quoted in Eta Harich-Schneider, *The Harpsichord* (Kassel-Basel, 1960), p. 21.

2. Carl Philipp Emanuel Bach, *Essay on the True Art of Playing Keyboard Instruments* (1753), trans. William J. Mitchell (New York, 1949), p. 42.

3. It is interesting that the English chose the thumb, middle finger, and little finger as the "best," while the Germans and Italians preferred the second and fourth fingers. See Arnold Dolmetsch, *The Interpretation of the Music of the XVII and XVIII Centuries,* 2nd ed. (London, 1946), p. 365.

4. Quoted in Dolmetsch, p. 376.

5. C. P. E. Bach, pp. 46–47.

6. Otto Ortmann, *The Physiological Mechanics of Piano Technique* (New York, 1962), p. 37. Ortmann works out the motion in great detail, describing the muscles and joints involved.

7. C. P. E. Bach, pp. 74–75.

8. Fray Tomas de Santa Maria, *Libro llamado arte de tañer fantasia,* 1565. Quoted in Eta Harich-Schneider, p. 21.

9. François Couperin, *L'art de toucher le clavecin* (1717) trans. Anna Linde (Wiesbaden, 1933), p. 16.

10. Mary Mapes Dodge, *Hans Brinker and the Silver Skates* (Cleveland, 1946).

CHAPTER 4

1. Carl Philipp Emanuel Bach, *Essay on the True Art of Playing Keyboard Instruments,* trans. William J. Mitchell (New York, 1949), p. 79.

2. Putnam Aldrich, "Ornamentation," *Harvard Dictionary of Music,* 2nd ed. (Cambridge, Mass., 1969), p. 629.

3. Robert Donington, "A Problem of Inequality," *Musical Quarterly* 63 (1967): 503–4.

4. Thurston Dart, *The Interpretation of Music* (New York, 1963), p. 102.

5. Arnold Dolmetsch, *The Interpretation of the Music of the XVII and XVIII Centuries,* 2nd ed. (London, 1946), p. 89.

6. Putnam Aldrich, "The Principal *agréments* of the Seventeenth and Eighteenth Centuries: A Study in Musical Ornamentation," (Ph.D. diss., Harvard, 1942); Robert Donington, *The Interpretation of Early Music* (London, 1963).

7. *Clement Matchett's Virginal Book* (1612), trans. & ed. Thurston Dart (London, 1957), p. 17. Dart also suggests that these signs were a kind of stage direction to the performer: "Ornament-signs often seem to be used in virginal music for no other purpose than to draw attention to an accented note—to point an unusual harmony or to bring out some of the many cross-rhythms that add such a sparkle to the music—and in performance they are sometimes best omitted altogether."

8. Howard Ferguson, *Style and Interpretation: An Anthology of Keyboard Music* (London, 1963), 1: 14.

9. Frederick Neumann, "Misconceptions About the French Trill in the 17th and 18th Centuries," *Musical Quarterly* 10 (1964): 188–206, differs with the accepted opinion that the upper auxiliary invariably began the trill.

10. Wilfrid Mellers, *François Couperin and the French Classical Tradition* (New York, 1968), p. 307.

11. Robert Donington, *The Interpretation of Early Music* (London, 1963), p. 130.

12. Ibid., pp. 130–31.

13. Ibid., pp. 131–32.

14. Dolmetsch, pp. 159–60.

15. C. P. E. Bach, p. 87.

16. Dolmetsch, p. 93.

17. Quoted in Donington, *Interpretation,* p. 142.

18. C. P. E. Bach, p. 87.

19. C. P. E. Bach, p. 88.

20. Robert Donington, "Ornaments," *Grove's Dictionary of Music and Musicians,* ed. Eric Blom, 5th ed. (New York, 1955), 6: 365.

21. C. P. E. Bach, pp. 87–88.

22. Donington, *Interpretation,* p. 137.

23. C. P. E. Bach, pp. 94–95.

24. Donington, *Interpretations,* p. 142.

25. J. F. Agricola, *Anleitung zur Singkunst, Aus dem Italiänischen des Herrn Peter Franz Tosi, . . . mit Erläuterungen und Zusätzen von Johann Friedrich Agricola* (Berlin, 1757), quoted in Ralph Kirkpatrick, *Domenico Scarlatti* (Princeton, 1953), pp. 369–70.

26. C. P. E. Bach, p. 87.

27. C. P. E. Bach, p. 88.

28. C. P. E. Bach, p. 91.

29. C. P. E. Bach, pp. 91–92.

30. C. P. E. Bach, pp. 92–93.

31. Johann Joachim Quantz, *On Playing the Flute,* trans. Edward R. Reilly (New York, 1966), p. 93.

32. C. P. E. Bach, p. 98. Quantz speaks of the passing appoggiatura in terms of approval (p. 94), but Bach has an entirely different reaction.

33. Quantz, p. 97.

34. Putnam Aldrich, "Appoggiatura," *Harvard Dictionary of Music,* 2nd ed., p. 45.

35. A style, popular during the rococo (1725–75), characterized by elegance and lightness, exemplified in the works of Telemann, François Couperin, J. K. F. Fischer, and others.

36. C. P. E. Bach, p. 132.

37. Donington, *Interpretations,* p. 152.

38. Francesco Gasparini, *The Practical Harmonist at the Harpsichord,* trans. Frank S. Stillings, ed. David L. Burrows (New Haven, 1963).

39. Gasparini, p. 79.

40. Gasparini, p. 80.

41. Gasparini, p. 81.

42. Francesco Geminiani, *A Treatise of Good Taste in the Art of Musick* (London, 1749), quoted in Dolmetsch, p. 289.

43. C. P. E. Bach, pp. 159–60.

44. C. P. E. Bach, p. 127.

45. Kirkpatrick, *Domenico Scarlatti,* p. 396. See also Chapter 10, pp. 207–50, "Scarlatti's Harmony," for additional background on Scarlatti's use of acciaccaturas. The performer should consult this book on any baffling points on ornamentation in Scarlatti, for its copious background information and analysis and its numerous illuminating insights.

46. Kirkpatrick, pp. 396–97.

47. François Couperin, *L'art de toucher le clavecin,* trans. Anna Linde (Wiesbaden, 1933), p. 39.

48. C. P. E. Bach, p. 128.

49. Dart, p. 120.

50. Quantz, p. 101.

51. In the eighteenth century C. P. E. Bach talked about the four trills that he considered necessary for every harpsichordist: the "normal" trill, the ascending trill, the descending trill, and the half or short trill. Marpurg's table shows the plain trill (the same as J. S. Bach's Trillo) and longer trills which have prefixes or suffixes. Couperin's table of ornaments in his *L'art de toucher le clavecin* shows six different trills, for which the terminology is most illogical and confusing. These six trills are all longer trills and differ from each other in the manner of their beginning and ending. Three are prepared in the baroque sense, with long appoggiaturas, and three are unprepared; two have turned suffixes, two have the stopping point on the main note, one has the note of anticipation as the termination, and one has no termination indicated. Couperin also speaks of the accelerated trill, although he makes no attempt to notate it in his table. J. S. Bach's table, which he made for the use of the young Wilhelm Friedemann in 1720, is also concerned with (1) the difference between the short trill and the long trill and (2) the inclusion of prefix or suffix or both in the long trill. Quantz makes the rather inclusive statement that in the case of trills of any length whatsoever every shake begins with an appoggiatura, whether prolonged or not, and ends with a turn.

52. C. P. E. Bach, p. 110.

53. See C. P. E. Bach, note on "Der Schneller," p. 142.

54. Bach's table is reproduced in Walter Emery, *Bach's Ornaments* (London, 1953), p. 13.

55. In ibid.

56. See Putnam Aldrich's invaluable article, "On the Interpretation of Bach's Trills," *Musical Quarterly* 49 (1963), 289–310, for an explanation of trills of longer duration as used by French eighteenth-century composers. He demonstrates the importance to the French of variety in playing ornaments by listing and describing the various types of trills (fourteen to be exact) that result from varying the three components of the longer trill. His description of the components (from Bacilly, F. Couperin, and Monteclair) is: "1) the *appuy,* or *preparation,* a dwelling on the upper accessory, 2) the *battements,* repercussions of the two notes, and 3) the *point d'arrêt,* stopping point on the main note, *or the liaison,* a connection with the next note. This *liaison* may take the form of an anticipation of the following note . . . or of a turn around the main note produced by substituting the lower neighbor note for the last appearance of the upper accessory . . ." (p. 291). Various writers have used other terms, but there is no complete agreement among them; I have merely tried to use terms which are descriptive and self-explanatory.

57. Couperin, p. 17.

58. Quantz, pp. 101–2.

59. Quantz, p. 103.

60. Donington, *Interpretation,* p. 171.

61. Putnam Aldrich, "The Turn," *Harvard Dictionary of Music,* 2nd ed., pp. 878–79.

62. C. P. E. Bach, p. 114.

63. C. P. E. Bach, p. 115.

64. Aldrich, "The Turn," p. 879.

65. C. P. E. Bach, p. 119.

66. C. P. E. Bach, p. 114.

67. Aldrich, "The Turn," p. 878–79.

68. C. P. E. Bach, p. 121.

69. Dolmetsch, pp. 209–10.

70. Walter Emery, pp. 146–47, has shown that these *are* mordents and not the trills that most editors have indicated. His evidence is that the trills in the first half of the piece become the mordents of the second half because Bach has carried the "inversion of the thematic material down to the details of the ornamentation."

71. C. P. E. Bach, p. 127.

72. Dart, p. 120.

73. Ibid.

74. Gioseffo Zarlino, *The Art of Counterpoint,* trans. Guy A. Marco and Claude V. Palisca (New Haven, 1968), p. 110.

75. Eta Harich-Schneider, *The Harpsichord,* 2nd ed. (Kassel-Basel, 1960).

76. Christopher Simpson, *The Division Violist: or, an Introduction to the Playing upon a Ground* (London, 1659); 2nd ed. published as *Chelys, minuritionum artificio exornata . . . The Division-Viol.* (London, 1665); facs. of 2nd ed., ed. N. Dolmetsch (London, 1955).

CHAPTER 5

1. Reproduced in Howard Ferguson, *Style and Interpretation,* (London, 1969), 1: 9.

2. See Curt Sachs, *Rhythm and Tempo* (New York, 1953), p. 311. Sachs has reorganized Saint-Lambert's table to make it more accessible.

3. Ibid., pp. 312–14.

4. Ibid., p. 316. The four sources are Louis-Léon Pajot, Count of Ons-en-Bray (1732), Jacques-Alexandre La Chapelle (1737), Henri-Louis Choquel (1759), and Michel L'Affillard (1697).

5. Ferguson, p. 4.

6. Quoted in Sachs, p. 280.

7. Hans T. David and Arthur Mendel, *The Bach Reader* (New York, 1966), p. 312.

8. Sachs, p. 316.

9. Eugène Borrel, "Les notes inégales dans l'ancienne musique française," *Revue Française de Musicologie* 12 (November 1931), pp. 278–89. Wilfrid Mellers summarizes Borrel's conclusions in *François Couperin and the French Classical Tradition* (New York, 1968), p. 298–300.

10. Ibid.

11. G. F. Handel, *Sechs Sonaten für Violine und Bezifferten Bass,* ed. J. P. Hinnenthal (Kassel, 1955), p. 26.

12. J.-P. Rameau, *Pièces de clavecin,* ed. E. Jacobi (Kassel, 1958), pp. 40–41.

13. Ibid., pp. 1–2.

14. There are two recent editions of Louis Couperin's works, both listed in Appendix B. Two other sources for practical suggestions on playing unmeasured preludes are: 1) *Revue Musicale,* 1920–21, Supplément Musical of November 1, 1920 (realization by Paul Brunold); and 2) *Encyclopaedia of Music* by Lavignac & Laurencie, part I, vol. 3, p. 1242 (realization by Henry Quittard).

CHAPTER 6

1. See Frank Hubbard, *Three Centuries of Harpsichord Making* (Cambridge, Mass., 1965), p. 252. From "The Harpsichord," in *Encyclopédie méthodique* volumes entitled *Arts et metiers* (1785), (pp. 241–55 in Hubbard). This contemporary account of this innovation describes the soft leather as "caressing" the string rather than plucking it.

2. The scale is long for extra volume. The plucking point for all registers is closer to the same percentage of string length and hence the tonal differentiation between the registers is considerably less than that of the historical instrument.

3. *Harvard Dictionary,* 2nd ed., pp. 327–28.

4. Ralph Kirkpatrick, *Domenico Scarlatti* (Princeton, 1953), p. 180.

5. Ibid., p. 181.

CHAPTER 7

1. Francesco Bianciari's little treatise entitled "Breve regola per imparar a sonare sopra il Basso con ogni sorte d'Instrumento" ("A short guide for learning to play on a Bass with every kind of instrument"), published in 1607, is a guide to the early style of continuo playing. It is a set of rules for playing from an *unfigured* bass, with a single exception; this exception, as F. T. Arnold remarks, "clearly indicates that he recognized that, in certain cases at least, they [figures] were indispensable to a correct performance." The English translation of this work appears in Arnold's *The Art of Accompaniment from a Thorough-Bass,* (London, 1931 and New York, 1965), 1: 74–80.

2. Thurston Dart, *The Interpretation of Early Music,* (New York, 1963), p. 143.

3. Ibid., pp. 140–41.

4. Perhaps the great profusion of harpsichords available in the eighteenth-century made easy what would be a nuisance today, if one considers the difficulties of finding, hauling, and tuning a harpsichord "section." On the other hand, it seems to me that an altogether practical way of obtaining the same proportion of harpsichord sound would be the electrical amplification of the lone harpsichord which accompanies a large chorus and orchestra production of such works as Handel's *Messiah.*

5. Eta Harich-Schneider, *The Harpsichord,* (Kassel-Basel, 1960), p. 61. Harich-Schneider differentiates between two main types of accompanying, which she calls the "organ style" and the "finer accompaniment."

6. Ibid.

7. "Thoroughbass," *Harvard Dictionary of Music* 2nd ed. (Cambridge, Mass.: 1969), article on p. 850.

8. Mellers bases his remarks largely on what are perhaps the two most important eighteenth-century works on the interpretation of figured bass in French baroque music, the *Traité de l'accompagnement* of Saint-Lambert (1707) and that of Boyvin (1715). He quotes profusely from the French sources; I have taken the liberty of translating, rearranging, and condensing them. His complete discussion can be seen on pp. 311–16 of *François Couperin and the French Classical Tradition* (New York, 1968).

9. Robert Donington, *The Interpretation of Early Music,* (London, 1963).

CHAPTER 8

1. See Frank Hubbard, *Three Centuries of Harpsichord Making* (Cambridge, Mass., 1965), plate 25.

2. The subject of pitch and tuning of instruments continues to interest scholars and performers. According to his own notes on the record jacket, Albert Fuller recorded J.-P. Rameau's *Pièces de clavecin* (Nonesuch H-71278) in 1973 with a harpsichord tuned to A′ = 415.3 Hz, a pitch which corresponds to our modern G$^\#$ on the basis of evidence that mid-eighteenth-century French harpsichords seem to have varied between 409 and 422 Hz for A′. (Pascal Taskin, the eminent eighteenth-century French builder, owned a 409 fork.)

3. See Robert Donington, *The Interpretation of Early Music* (London, 1963), p. 444 for a concise summary of the evidence for historical pitches.

Appendix B

1. Walter Emery, *Editions & Musicians* (London, 1957). Emery illustrates his points in specific and fascinating detail with first-hand information about Bach editing. The reader should also own *Editing Early Music* by Thurston Dart, Walter Emery, and Christopher Morris (London, 1963), a pamphlet that begins where *Editions and Musicians* ends. It is concerned with how the text is presented in the printer's copy.

2. Ibid., p. 14.

3. Ibid., pp. 7, 45.

4. Ibid., p. 9.

5. A list that does include these earlier editions, as well as editions of organ and piano music, may be found in F. E. Kirby, *A Short History of Keyboard Music* (New York, 1966). See also John Gillespie, *Five Centuries of Keyboard Music: An Historical Survey of Music for Harpsichord and Piano* (Belmont, California, 1965).

Appendix C

1. J. M. Barbour, *Tuning and Temperament: A Historical Survey* (East Lansing, Mich., 1951).

2. The degrees of the scale in equal temperament are formed by dividing the octave into twelve equal ratios. Since the octave is itself merely a ratio, it must be divided into ratios. This is done by taking the twelfth root of 2 (which equals 1.0594). The twelfth root of 2, of course, is that number which multiplied by itself twelve times equals 2. Each degree of the scale is obtained by raising the powers of the twelfth root of 2. Starting at A = 440, for instance, the bottom note has a ratio of $\sqrt[12]{2}\,^0$ or 1, so the note has a frequency of 1 x 440. B$^\flat$ has a ratio of $\sqrt[12]{2}\,^1$ or 1.0594, which multiplied by 440 gives a frequency of 466.16. B is $\sqrt[12]{2}\,^2$ and has a ratio of 1.1225 or a frequency of 493.88, and so on. The octave is $\sqrt[12]{12}\,2\,^{12}$, which of course equals 2.

3. An easily located and authoritative discussion of this interesting phenomenon is found in *Grove's Dictionary of Music and Musicians* (London, 1954), 1: 38–40. The great work in this area is Hermann Helmholtz, *On the Sensations of Tone* (English translation, London, 1885, reprinted by Dover Publications, New York, 1954), to which all subsequent discussions are indebted. See especially chapters 10 and 11. The appendices by the translator Alexander Ellis contain a great deal of practical and historical information on tuning.

Bibliography

I have limited the bibliography to readily available books in English that would be good for anyone to buy if he is seriously interested in the harpsichord. Fuller bibliographies are to be found in the works by Robert Donington, Manfred F. Bukofzer, Frank Hubbard, and others.

Apel, Willi. *History of Keyboard Music To 1700,* trans. Hans Tischler. Bloomington: Indiana University Press, 1972. (*Geschichte der Orgel und Klaviermusik bis 1700.* Kassel: Bärenreiter, 1967.)

Arnold, Frank T. *The Art of Accompaniment from a Thorough-Bass as Practiced in the XVIIth and XVIIIth Centuries.* London: Oxford, 1931; rpt. with introduction by Denis Stevens, 2 vols., New York: Dover, 1965.

Bach, Carl Philipp Emanuel. *Essay on the True Art of Playing Keyboard Instruments,* trans. William J. Mitchell. New York: W. W. Norton, 1949. (*Versuch über die wahre Art das Clavier zu spielen.* Berlin, 1753; part 2, Berlin, 1762.)

Barbour, J. Murray. *Tuning and Temperament: A Historical Survey.* East Lansing: Michigan State University Press, 1951.

Bodky, Erwin. *The Interpretation of Bach's Keyboard Works.* Cambridge: Harvard University Press, 1950.

Bukofzer, Manfred F. *Music in the Baroque Era.* New York: W. W. Norton, 1947.

Caldwell, John. *English Keyboard Music Before the Nineteenth Century.* Oxford: Basil Blackwell, 1973.

Couperin, François. *The Art of Playing the Harpsichord,* trans. Mevanwy Roberts; *Die Kunst das Clavecin zu Spielen,* trans. Anna Linde; *L'art de toucher le clavecin,* Paris, 1716; [Enl. ed.] Paris, 1717. Wiesbaden: Breitkopf & Härtel, 1933.

Dart, Thurston. *The Interpretation of Music.* London: Hutchinson & Co., 1954; New York & Evanston: Harper & Row, 1963.

Dart, Thurston, Walter Emery, and Christopher Morris. *Editing Early Music.* London: Novello & Co., Oxford University Press, and Stainer & Bell, 1963.

David, Hans T. and Arthur Mendel. *The Bach Reader.* New York: W. W. Norton, 1945; rev. with suppl. 1966.

Dolmetsch, Arnold. *The Interpretation of the Music of the XVII & XVIII Centuries.* London: Novello & Co., 1916; 2nd ed. 1946.

Donington, Robert. *The Interpretation of Early Music.* London: Faber & Faber, 1963.

———. *A Performer's Guide to Baroque Music.* London: Faber & Faber, 1973.

Emery, Walter. *Bach's Ornaments.* London: Novello & Co., 1953.

———. *Editions & Musicians.* London: Novello & Co., 1957.

Geiringer, Karl, in collaboration with Geiringer, Irene. *Johann Sebastian Bach: The Culmination of an Era.* New York: Oxford University Press, 1966.

Girdlestone, Cuthbert. *Jean-Philippe Rameau: His Life & Work.* London: Cassell & Co. Ltd., 1957; rev. ed. New York: Dover, 1969.

Harich-Schneider, Eta. *The Harpsichord: An Introduction to Technique, Style and the Historical Sources.* Kassel & St. Louis, 1954; 2nd ed. Kassel: Bärenreiter, 1960.

Hubbard, Frank. *Harpsichord Regulating & Repairing.* Boston: Tuner's Supply Co., 1963.

———. *Three Centuries of Harpsichord Making.* Cambridge: Harvard University Press, 1965.

Keller, Hermann. *Phrasing & Articulation,* trans. Leigh Gerdine. New York: W. W. Norton, 1965; London: Barrie & Rockliff, 1966.

———. *Thoroughbass Method,* trans. and ed. Carl Parrish. New York: W. W. Norton, 1965.

Kirby, F. E. *A Short History of Keyboard Music.* New York: The Free Press, 1966.

Kirkpatrick, Ralph. *Domenico Scarlatti.* Princeton: Princeton University Press, 1953.

Landowska, Wanda. *Landowska on Music,* trans. & ed. Denise Restout, assisted by Robert Hawkins. New York: Stein & Day, 1964.

Lang, Paul Henry. *George Frideric Handel.* New York: W. W. Norton, 1966.

Matthews, Denis, ed. *Keyboard Music.* Harmondsworth, Middlesex, England: Penguin Books Ltd., 1972.

Mellers, Wilfrid H. *François Couperin and the French Classical Tradition.* London: Denis Dobson Ltd., 1950; New York: Dover, 1968.

Newman, William S. *The Sonata in the Baroque Era.* Chapel Hill, N.C.: University of North Carolina Press, 1959.

Palisca, Claude V. *Baroque Music.* Englewood Cliffs: Prentice-Hall, 1968.

Quantz, J. J. *On Playing the Flute,* trans. with introduction and notes by Edward R. Reilly. New York: The Free Press, 1966. *(Versuch einer Anweisung die Flöte traversiere zu spielen.)*

Russell, Raymond. *The Harpsichord and Clavichord: An Introductory Study.* London: Faber & Faber, 1959.

Sachs, Curt. *Rhythm and Tempo.* New York: W. W. Norton, 1953.

Schott, Howard. *Playing the Harpsichord.* London: Faber & Faber, 1971.

Strunk, Oliver. *Source Readings in Music History.* New York: W. W. Norton, 1950.

Terry, Charles Sanford. *The Music of Bach.* New York: Oxford University Press, 1933; New York: Dover, 1963.

Zuckermann, Wolfgang Joachim. *The Modern Harpsichord: Twentieth-Century Instruments and Their Makers.* New York: October House, 1969.

Index

Ortiz, Diego: on divisions, 155
Ortmann, Otto: on touch, 16, 18, 81, 236n7

Parrish, Carl, 189
Peau de buffle, 168, 240n1
Pedal point, 62
Pedals, 5, 6, 9, 166, 168
Perpetuo moto figures, 61
Petite Reprise, 74
Pincé (mordent), 153
Plectra: altering of, 207; damping action of, 21; leather, 9, 168, 207, 210; maintenance of, 207–10; relation to touch, 208; replacing of, 209; thinning of, 209; mentioned, 203, 210, 213. *See also* Delrin
Pleyel harpsichord, 1, 2
Plucking point, 205, 240n2
Pointer (Piquer), 161
Port de voix (appoggiatura), 82, 130
Portamento (appoggiatura), 114
Pralltriller. *See* Trill: half-trill
Production harpsichord, 11–12
Proportions, 158
Purcell, Henry: fingering of, 216; tempi of, 157
Purchasing a harpsichord, 9–12

Quantz, Johann Joachim: on continuo instruments, 180; fingering of, 216; on passing appoggiatura, 122–23; on speed of trills, 143–45; on tempo measurements, 157–58; on trills, 130; mentioned, 189
Quill action: description of, 208
Quills. *See* Plectra

Rameau, Jean-Philippe: fingering of, 216; "Gavotte et Doubles," 58, 82, 168, 171; "Les Cyclopes," 168; "Les Niais de Sologne," triplet rhythm in, 164; "Le Tambourin," 73–75; mordent of, 153; unmeasured prelude, 164; mentioned, 17, 18, 114, 180, 218, 234
Recorder, 187
Register (stop), 4, 168, 203, 213
Registration: in accompanying, 188; of J. S. Bach's French Suite no. 6, 172; of J. S. Bach's Inventions, 175–76; in binary form, 171–72; coloristic, 169–70; of echo effects, 178; harpsichord and organ compared, 170; on one manual, 165, 167, 170; of polyphony, 174–76; potentials of, 165–70; purpose of, 169; of repeats, 172; of rondeau form, 174; for structural clarification, 170, 178; in ternary form, 173; in terrace dynamics, 177–78; on two manuals, 167; uses of, 178; in variation form, 170–71
Relaxation: in playing ornaments, 103–4
Releases, 42, 44, 46, 48, 50, 73
Repairs, 212–13
Repeated notes: playing of, 24
Repeats: registration of, 172
Resonator: for tuning, 192–93, 196

Rhythm: triplets, 162–64; two against three, 164; unmeasured preludes, 164
Rondeau form, 68–69, 73, 174
Russell, Raymond, 3

Sachs, Curt: on baroque tempos, 158–59
Saint-Lambert, Michel de: on fingering, 78, 105; on tempos, 157
Santa Maria, Fray Tomás de: on divisions, 155–56; on fingering, 80, 82; mentioned, 216
Sargent, George, 200
Scales, 62, 76, 240n2
Scarlatti, Alessandro: fingering of, 80, 216
Scarlatti, Domenico: acciaccatura in, 129; fingering in, 82; registration in, 172–73; Sonata in D major, K. 492, 75–76; Sonata in D minor, K. 141, 24; mentioned, 7, 15
Schneller, 133
Seating position, at harpsichord: Couperin and Rameau on, 17–18
Shake. *See* Trill
Simpson, Christopher, 156
Six Little Preludes (J. S. Bach), 44–56, Prelude no. 1, 44–45; Prelude no. 2, 46–47, 61; Prelude no. 3, 48–49; Prelude no. 4, 50–52; Prelude no. 5, 52–54; Prelude no. 6, 54–56
Sixteen-foot register, 2, 3, 4, 12, 165, 168, 169, 170
Sixths: playing of, 40
Slide, 124–25, 130, 154
Slur, 73, 76
Soft stop: half-hitches used as, 9
Sonata for Flute and Harpsichord in B minor (J. S. Bach), 184
Speerhake harpsichords, 168, 169
Spinet: description, 10
Staccato: comparison of harpsichord and piano, 17
String: breaking of, 214; displacement of, 207–8; replacement of, 211–12; wire for, 211
Strobotuner, 192, 200, 230
Substitution, 68, 69, 82–83
Supply houses for harpsichord products, 192–93
Suspensions, 57
Sweelinck, Jan Pieterzoon, 155, 171

Tartini, Giuseppe, 231
Taskin, Pascal, 168, 241n2
Temperament: explained, 229–30; setting of, 197–98
Tempo: and articulation and fingering, 84–85, 159; J. S. Bach's, 158; baroque, 158; notation of, 157
Ternary form: registration of, 173
Terrace dynamics, 177–78
Terza suono, 197, 231
Theorbo effect, 170
Thirds: playing of, 40; tuning of, 233
Thorough bass. *See* Basso continuo
Tied notes: treated as rests, 57, 61, 76
Time signatures, 157
Toccata and Fugue in C minor (J. S. Bach), 175

Touch, 29–30; comparison of harpsichord and piano, 16, 19–20; Otto Ortmann, on piano touch, 236n7; percussive and nonpercussive, 16; and quilling, 208–9. *See also* Détaché; Legatissimo; Legato

Trill, 134–41; acceleration of, 141; accent in, 145–47; Putnam Aldrich on, 238n56; analysis of, 130–47; and appoggiatura, 141; C. P. E. Bach on, 238n51; J. S. Bach's, 134, 142–43, 238n51; François Couperin on, 238n51; Walter Emery on, 239n70; fingering of, 78, 103, 104; half-trill (Pralltriller), 132–33; long half-trill (Trillo), 133–34; F. W. Marpurg on, 238n51; Frederick Neumann on, 237n9; notation of, 131–32; note of anticipation in, 132, 138, 139; preparation of, 135–37; J. J. Quantz on, 238n51; rhythm of, 141–43; Schneller, 133; speed of, 143–47; structure of, 135–41; and tempo, 73, 75; termination of, 137–38; in virginalists, 154; mentioned, 51, 109

Trillo. *See* Trill: long half-trill

Triplet rhythm, 162–64

Tuners, 192, 230

Tuning: for accompanying, 187; J. M. Barbour on, 234; comparison of harpsichord and piano, 190–91; Albert Fuller's in recording Rameau's *Pièces de clavecin,* 241n2; mean-tone system of, 200; by thirds, 200; three-fork method, 191–92, 194–99; traditional method, 191

Tuning forks, 191, 230–31

Tuning hammers, 192–93

Tuning pin (wrestpin), 211, 212

Turn: accented, 147–48; C. P. E. Bach on, 147–48, 149; J. S. Bach's, 149; François Couperin's, 149; described, 147–50; Robert Donington on, 147; inverted, 147–48; with trill, 138, 139, 140, 141; unaccented, 148

Twentieth-century harpsichord music, index of, 218

Two-manual harpsichord (double), 167–68

Unmeasured prelude, 164

Variations: registration of, 170–71

Venetian swell, 6

Virginalists: fingering of, 66, 82, 215–16; ornaments of, 154–55

Virginals, 11

Voicing, 203–4

Vorhalt (appoggiatura), 114

Vorschlag (appoggiatura), 114

Well-Tempered Clavier, Book I (J. S. Bach), 163, 176; Fugue no. 4, registration, 176; Prelude no. 1, 61; Prelude no. 4, 61; Prelude no. 7, 61; Prelude no. 8, 61; Prelude no. 15, 61; Prelude no. 21, 62

Well-Tempered Clavier, Book II (J. S. Bach): Prelude no. 5, 163

"Wolf" sounds, 196

Wrestplank, 211

Zarlino, Gioseffo: on improvisation, 155

Zuckermann, Wallace: kits of, 7, 8; mentioned, 11, 12